MASTERING
THE *Digital*
World

THIS IS A CARLTON BOOK

Text and design copyright © 2005 Carlton Books Limited

This edition published by Carlton Books Limited 2005
20 Mortimer Street
London
W1T 3JW

A CIP catalogue for this book is available from the British Library.

ISBN 1 84442 461 8

Executive editor: Stella Caldwell
Editor: Jonathan Hilton
Art editor: Emma Wicks
Designer: Jim Lockwood
Production: Lisa Moore

Printed and bound in Dubai

MASTERING
THE *Digital*
World

**A GUIDE TO UNDERSTANDING,
USING AND EXPLOITING
DIGITAL MEDIA**

PETER COPE

CONTENTS

INTRODUCTION

TWO HUNDRED YEARS AGO THE WORLD TOOK ITS FIRST STEPS INTO THE INDUSTRIAL AGE. FOR OUR FOREBEARS, WHO HAD ALWAYS LIVED IN AN AGRARIAN ECONOMY, THE CHANGES THAT SWEPT AROUND THEM CERTAINLY DEMANDED THE TERM "REVOLUTION". AS MEADOWS GAVE WAY TO FOUNDRIES AND WHEAT FIELDS TO MILLS, WHOLE WAYS OF LIFE WERE CHANGING – OFTEN FOR THE BETTER, BUT SOMETIMES FOR THE WORSE. INDUSTRIALIZATION OFFERED THE PROMISE OF A NEW GOLDEN AGE, A PATH TO A UTOPIA IN WHICH, ULTIMATELY, MACHINES WOULD TAKE ON THE DRUDGERY OF DAY-TO-DAY LIFE AND PEOPLE WOULD BE LIBERATED TO EXPRESS THEMSELVES THROUGH ART AND LEISURE.

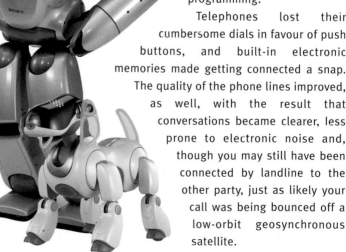

"In the future robots will do all the work we hate." Perhaps, one day. Meantime Sony's vision is much more entertaining.

Concepts such as these may have been the motivational vision for the factory owners, but few – very few – of those who stoked boilers or fed looms saw any of the benefits. But, the revolution continued to gather speed, ensuring that the world would never be the same again.

It's probably hard for most of us to appreciate how tumultuous those years were, yet today we are in the middle of another revolution that, ultimately, is just as profound and promises to realize many of those dreams and visions. This digital revolution may appear lower key when compared with the industrial revolution that changed the face of the world, yet it is impacting on almost every aspect of our lives.

Think back barely a generation to when the silicon chip, which underpins this revolution, first appeared in consumer devices. Take just two of these devices – the television and telephone – and we can see the impact the technology has had. Televisions before this time were expensive, unreliable and limited in their operation. Valve technology made sets large, slow to respond and, to the bane of the television trade, uncomfortably heavy. Turning to the telephone, communications were largely limited to fixed landlines with handsets equipped only with the ubiquitous dial – instruments which today children believe come out of a museum.

A few years on, however, and things had changed. The appearance of the microchip meant that television sets became more reliable, more effective and could offer more features. Parallel technologies at the studio provided viewers with better-produced, better-quality, more-entertaining programming.

Telephones lost their cumbersome dials in favour of push buttons, and built-in electronic memories made getting connected a snap. The quality of the phone lines improved, as well, with the result that conversations became clearer, less prone to electronic noise and, though you may still have been connected by landline to the other party, just as likely your call was being bounced off a low-orbit geosynchronous satellite.

Advances were not limited to just these two technologies; almost every

Digital photography has breathed new life into a medium that even its fans might admit was becoming a little staid. The immediacy of results offered by digital cameras has done much to introduce photography to new and demanding markets.

sphere of our daily lives became transformed. But in technology terms the best was yet to come. This first minor technological revolution, profound though its impact might have seemed to those experiencing it, was essentially more along the lines of an evolution. One technology – that based on valves, relays and mechanical switches – was being replaced by another, based this time on integrated circuits but still substantially trading the old technology for a solid-state equivalent.

Now we are in the middle of the true digital revolution. Building on these solid foundations, technology is empowering us as never before. But what exactly do we mean by a digital world?

A considerable mythology has built up around the term "digital". In popular culture the term is used almost too freely to describe things that are

Digital techniques make it possible to combine many technologies in a single solution. The latest DVD recorders feature hard discs and allow us to compress stacks of traditional video tapes, camcorder tapes and photo albums into a few compact DVDs.

cutting edge or just "modern". In the loosest sense, virtually every electronic device could be described as being digital, but for our purposes that definition needs to be more sharply focused.

The dictionary definition is: "Technique for recording, processing and transmitting information through the use of electronic or optical pulses that represent binary digits or bits (0 and 1)." At the crux of the definition is the conversion of data to binary digits. This data could be images, in the case of photographs, video, music or even the spoken word.

Once the data has been interpreted as a numerical sequence, we have great power over what we do with it. We can, for example, copy the data almost without limit with no loss or corruption of the detail of the original. For a start, this means we can make copies of photographs, movies or our favourite music without losing quality. Without digital technology, copies from originals were always inferior. And copies of copies ... well, they were often not worth considering.

Second, we can manipulate this data mathematically. Then, when we decode the data back into its original form (whether it be a movie, music or whatever), it can be altered, improved or converted.

The result of this is that we could, for example, manipulate our digital images, combine them with movie footage, and add our favourite (or even a specially composed) soundtrack to produce a professional-looking multimedia adventure.

We can create movies on our mobile phones, edit them and send them to family and friends in an instant; put our entire music collection – towers of CDs in a tiny pocketable player; turn holiday movies into DVDs; even recreate movie theatres in our own home. And that is just the beginning. Through this book we'll explore just some of the many opportunities digital technologies offer. Best of all, we'll cut through the hype and jargon and see how you can exploit those technologies.

Is the iPod the archetypal digital device? Arguably so. It has succeeded because it uses technology in a way that makes it not only desirable but also well-nigh essential for many of us.

But this is not just a technical journey. It's a cultural one, too. Perhaps this is no better typified than in the way the Internet in a timespan that is even shorter than that of the microchip's emergence and maturity has now carved itself a pivotal role in our lives – in many aspects of our lives.

The Internet has superseded many a shelf of library books as a repository for knowledge and a source of reference, and it has given us the opportunity to share our work and experiences instantly. But, most significantly for our purposes here at least, it has given new ideas the opportunities to flourish and given us the chance to enrich our lives. We'll discover just some

of these as we go on our digital adventure.

Perhaps best of all, we'll discover that this adventure is for all of us. It's not just for the technophiles and geeks. And it's an adventure that becomes more exciting every time we experience it!

Throughout this book we will be examining a number of technologies and the devices associated with them. The nature of these discussions is such that branded products are mentioned and, in some cases, used as the basis of demonstrations and tutorials. In these cases, we've tried to be as even-handed as possible: including a particular product does not necessarily represent our endorsement of that product. We feel our choice best illustrates, for the purpose of this book, the technology. Sadly, nobody has provided us with any free equipment, tools or software in consideration for being included in this title! We've provided a list of resources at the end that gives, as far as is practicable, alternatives to many of the mentioned products.

Some products of the digital revolution are unexpected. The Segway personal transport relies on advanced digital technology to deliver its unique form of motion. True to the digital ethic, it's a liberating device in an unusually literal sense.

BRAVE NEW WORLD

"I THINK THERE IS A WORLD MARKET FOR MAYBE FIVE COMPUTERS."
THOMAS J WATSON, CHAIRMAN IBM

"COMPUTERS IN THE FUTURE WILL WEIGH NO MORE THAN ONE AND A HALF TONS." *POPULAR MECHANICS* 1950

"THERE IS NO REASON WHY ANYONE WOULD WANT A COMPUTER IN THEIR HOME." KEN OLSEN, CHAIRMAN AND FOUNDER DEC COMPUTERS

"WE'LL HAVE TO THINK UP BIGGER PROBLEMS IF WE ARE TO KEEP THEM BUSY." HOWARD AIKEN, CO-DESIGNER OF HARVARD UNIVERSITY'S MARK I COMPUTER, 1944

Half a century ago pundits were already making predictions about the future of digital technology. Now, with the benefit of hindsight, we can raise a wry smile as we read their informed but off-beam comments.

Our modern homes contain numerous computers, all weighing somewhat less than *Popular Mechanics* predicted. Some of these computers are obvious – the box that sits on our desk giving us access to the Internet; others are less so, living out their days embedded in the electronic equipment that we take for granted. Cameras, televisions, children's toys, even kitchen appliances owe their ability to function, if not their existence, to the microchip. To some, this second industrial revolution, built on silicon rather than iron, has been pernicious, giving rise to an insidious overdependence on technology.

For the rest of us, the outlook is optimistic. Not only has the microchip empowered us – just think how much smarter electronics are today – it has opened up new opportunities. The key to all of this is that often overused term "digital".

Fig 1 – Communications are crucial for our private and business lives. Mobile communication devices, such as Blackberry, provide all the benefits of a mobile (cell) phone with email no matter where you may be.

Fig 2 – *Digital technology can create new business opportunities no matter how incongruous they may seem. Thanks to Parkmobile, you can pay parking fees simply by using your mobile phone.*

There is nothing mystical about digital technology. Whether it's applied to television, telephones or cameras digital simply means that the essential data – the programming, voice and photos, respectively – is stored as a series of numbers (actually 1s and 0s) that a computer chip can deal with.

This gives us some key advantages. First, the data is easily transmitted and received – for example, in the case of television – without degradation. You don't lose pictures because of environmental factors. Second, you can also copy the digital code without any degradation. Make copy after copy of a digital movie, say, and the last is as good as the first. Try that with conventional videotape and you'll soon see the limitations.

Third, and most significantly, this digital code is understood by computers. Throw a computer into the equation and suddenly the opportunities multiply many-fold. With the data in your computer you can copy it, change it, manipulate it and share it. In practice this means we can take a photograph and improve it, take a movie and edit it, even create fantastic musical compositions from scratch. We can then go on and combine these disparate technologies – combine our photos and movies on a DVD and add a soundtrack, for example. We can take the movies from our camcorder and share them with friends via their telephone handsets. Take music from our old vinyl collection, from digital radio, or even our CD collection and carry it everywhere with us on an MP3 player. The possibilities are endless.

Fig 3 – *The days of the wired computer are long gone. Just as laptops freed us from the need for mains cables, so wireless communications give us Internet access without the need to connect directly to a telephone line.*

THE DIGITAL HUB

Here is an easy way to picture the ways different devices link together. It's called the digital hub and although there is no definitive configuration, this is as potent as any. The core is the computer (though, as we will see later, this is not necessarily an essential component for anyone wanting to join the digital revolution). Arranged around it are the key digital technologies, linked by the ability, either directly or via a computer, to exchange digital code.

THE DIGITAL HUB IN YOUR HOME

Many consumer electronics companies have a slightly different vision of the digital hub. Theirs is built around the television – although that term might be a bit superficial for the interpretation they offer. In their world, the television links to digital television sources and DVD (as we would expect, and as already happens in an increasing number of homes), but further connections enable us to use the not-so-humble television to view digital photographs, surf the Internet and video-call friends and family on their mobile telephones. You can also program your household appliances, heating and lighting through the same television.

DIGITAL VIDEO

DVD

GAMING

Fig 4

MOBILE COMMUNICATIONS

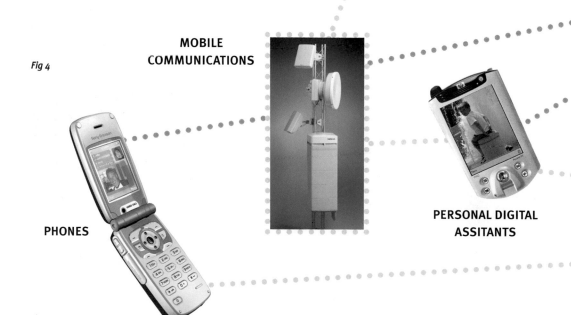

PHONES

PERSONAL DIGITAL ASSITANTS

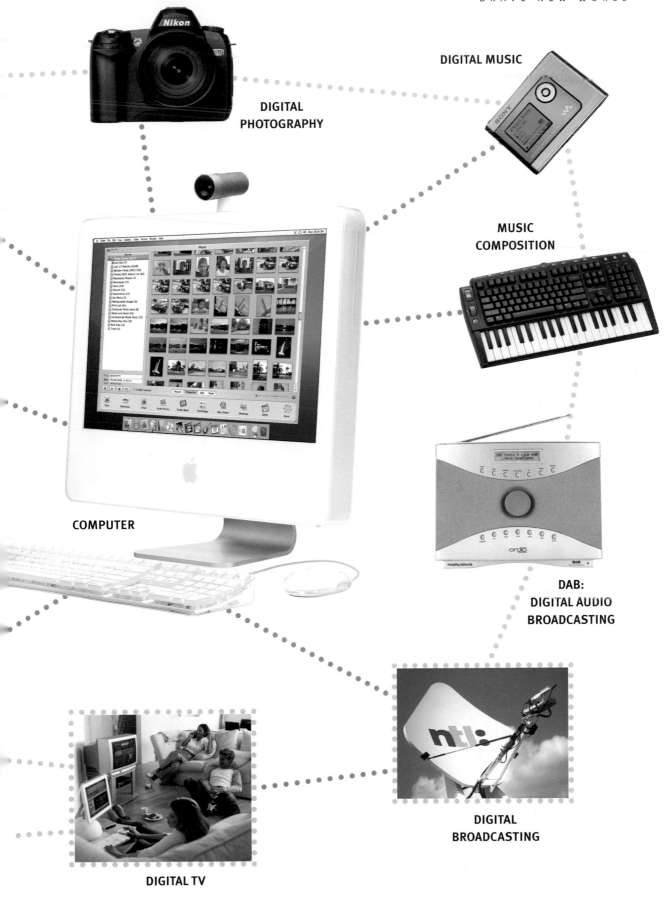

DIGITAL
PHOTOGRAPHY

DIGITAL MUSIC

MUSIC
COMPOSITION

COMPUTER

DAB:
DIGITAL AUDIO
BROADCASTING

DIGITAL
BROADCASTING

DIGITAL TV

Fig 5 – Digital television is probably the most obvious manifestation of digtial technology in the home.

THE DIGITAL LIFESTYLE AT HOME

The second half of the twentieth century saw something of a revolution in our homes. General affluence was rising and our increased disposable income was looking for new outlets. These were provided by countless companies producing just about everything we needed, or thought we needed, to live a comfortable life. Not least, electronics companies capitalizing on the post-war technology boom were aiming to fill our homes with the latest in consumer innovations. The pace of innovation accelerated as the century drew to a close and our homes were filling up with a wide range of essentials, luxuries and gadgets.

The trouble was, all these exciting innovations tended to live a little in isolation. True, some home entertainment systems managed to cross traditional demarcation lines and offer you the opportunity to play television sound through your hi-fi set-up or perhaps, for those at the cutting edge, the chance to distribute music right around the home.

It would take the exponential developments in computer technology to bring everything really together. Suddenly, cameras, camcorders, music systems and even televisions could talk to the computer and, ultimately, each other.

So what of today's homes? What has digital technology delivered? Perhaps most obviously, it's the television. Unrestrained by broadcasting restrictions, satellite and cable channels have always offered viewers greater choice. Once they "went digital", however, the capacities multiplied. Hundreds of new channels and stations have appeared, riding on the wave of cheaper transmission costs and – again thanks to digital technology – cheaper cameras and studio equipment. In addition, there is a growing market of viewers to be satisfied.

In a very few years DVD has usurped the VCR as an alternate delivery method. And since it is a digital medium, DVD content is as equally at home on your computer as it is on your television. High quality, low cost and loads of extras.

We could go on. But as many people are discovering, digital technology allows us to be creative. Activities such as movie-making and photography have been reinvigorated. No more looking at clichéd (and dull) home movies or albums of badly composed, poorly exposed photos. Just a modest embracing of digital technology gives each of us the chance to produce multimedia showpieces that other people may actually want to see.

THE DIGITAL LIFESTYLE ON THE MOVE

There is no need to keep your digital lifestyle at home. You can now carry it with you wherever you go. The mobile phone, for example, was the "must-have" item of the 1980s and 1990s. Today, it has become even more indispensable. Reinvented as the Smartphone, the mobile now lets us exchange photos as a matter of course and make video calls from (almost) anywhere in the world.

In the car the same phone can even help you get quickly and easily to your destination. Navigation systems for your phone or PDA (personal digital assistant) are now commonplace, so there's no longer any excuse for being late for a date!

For a long time music fans have been well catered for on the move. The Walkman from Sony revolutionized music listening on the go and the name Walkman has entered our everyday language. Its spiritual descendant, the MP3 player, has taken that concept a stage further and lets us take our whole musical world with us wherever we go.

Apple, with its ubiquitous iPod, has turned the MP3 player into a fashion and design icon. A triumph of marketing over design? Not a bit. The success of the iPod is due to clever and intelligent design combined with first-rate ergonomics. But iPod has never rested on its laurels – through a process of continual reinvention it has stayed at the forefront of the market. With iPod Photo, Apple took the concept a stage further: not only can you carry your music with you but you can also take your photo album, too.

Want to add to that photo collection? The digital camera is another of those "must-have" digital technologies that show the true impact of digital technology. After mimicking conventional cameras, they have now moved on into areas undreamed of just a few years ago.

The movie-maker is even better served. Digital camcorders make the compact camcorders of yesterday appear positively monolithic. Stick one in

your pocket and you'll never miss that once-in-a-lifetime event. And once you have recorded it, why not email it to friends or family straight away? Just a couple of clicks and your movie is on its way.

Of course, now that you can take your life with you, you won't be at home all that much. But don't worry, you can program your DVD or hard-disc recorder to record your favourite programmes from wherever you are in the world; or you can let your personal video recorder predict what you would like to watch.

Fig 6 – By adding simple-to-use photo album capabilities to the iconic iPod, it has become the ideal tool for people on the move.

DIGITAL CONVERGENCY

Those working in the digital media and commentators on digital technologies have long had the vision – not dissimilar to Einstein's elusive Unified Field Theory, known affectionately as the Theory of Everything – of a Holy Grail that will unify all digital resources. For some, this is perceived in the form of a third industrial revolution in which all traditional media will be consigned to museums and a new digital order will take effect. Back in the real world, many predict that with the differences between the key pillars of the digital hub – the computer and the television – becoming smaller and smaller, sometime soon we will see both replaced. In their place we will have media centres that, at least in the domestic environment, will cater for all our entertainment and work needs. One centre that will provide us with television programming, music (whether originally from CD, DVD or online), video resources, photos and even books.

This convergent media centre (which, in evolutionary terms, is some years away from the devices now described as such) would also control our home environment, from ensuring the lighting was set to our preferred levels at different times, controlling air-conditioning and central heating to even monitoring websites to ensure that information we may want is there at the touch of a button.

Fig 7 – OK, so no amount of digital technology will prepare the breakfast rolls for you, but the Beyond™ Coffee Maker is just one kitchen appliance that can communicate with the Home Hub. It is a fine example of how digital technology helps make life easier and more enjoyable.

Pie in the sky? Convergency will work only if the solutions it offers are those that genuinely make our lives simpler and better. Let's face it, even today's computers with their slick graphical interfaces that are a cinch to use are not ideal for everyone. True convergency will depend on an even slicker system that, for general use, at least, breaks free of the keyboard.

It's possible that full convergence is unlikely, but further and tighter integration of many digital devices is just about on us already. And through the course of this book we will look at many of them.

Fig 8 – Convergency on a modest scale: The Beyond™ Home Hub looks like a bedside clock/radio. As well as playing your favourite radio stations it will wake you to important financial quotes, news reports and even crucial family reminders. It will even tell you if the coffee in the kitchen is ready before you get up.

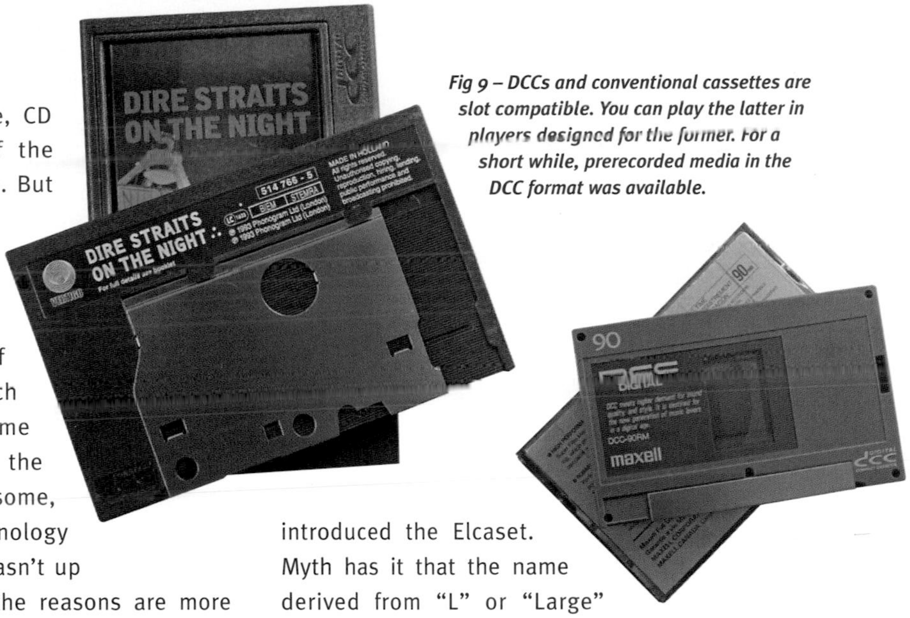

WHAT MIGHT HAVE BEEN

Think of the VHS video tape, CD and DVD and you think of the standards in video and audio. But the path to these universal standards is littered with those that didn't make it. Some lit up the consumer electronics world for a brief time, others kept a dim torch burning for years. And some never found their way into the electronics stores at all. For some, this was down to the technology they incorporated – it just wasn't up to the job. But for others, the reasons are more complex and due, largely, to the fickle nature of the marketplace. Here's a selection of those formats that could have been universal but are instead teetering on the brink of obscurity.

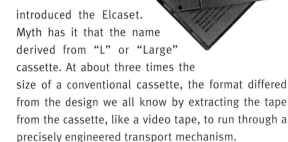

Fig 9 – DCCs and conventional cassettes are slot compatible. You can play the latter in players designed for the former. For a short while, prerecorded media in the DCC format was available.

Audio

ELCASET, Sony 1976

In the mid-1970s, before new tape formulations and precise engineering enabled the compact cassette to rival reel-to-reel formats, Sony thought that the only way forward was a bigger, better cassette. So it introduced the Elcaset. Myth has it that the name derived from "L" or "Large" cassette. At about three times the size of a conventional cassette, the format differed from the design we all know by extracting the tape from the cassette, like a video tape, to run through a precisely engineered transport mechanism.

Technically superb, it was virtually ignored by the consumer marketplace (the key to any format's success), but adored by audiophiles. It was abandoned by Sony in 1980.

DIGITAL COMPACT CASSETTE (DCC), Philips early 1990s

The DCC was Philips's attempt to produce a recordable digital format that would improve on the original cassette while maintaining compatibility. DCC players could play conventional tapes but record only on DCC tapes. Quality was better than an analogue cassette, but did not match that of a CD (compact disc). Its timing was also unfortunate as it came up against the better-quality (in audio terms) DAT (digital audio tape) tape and MiniDisc.

Philips dropped the format in 1996 when, after disappointing sales, it was clear that alternate formats would give better results in the marketplace.

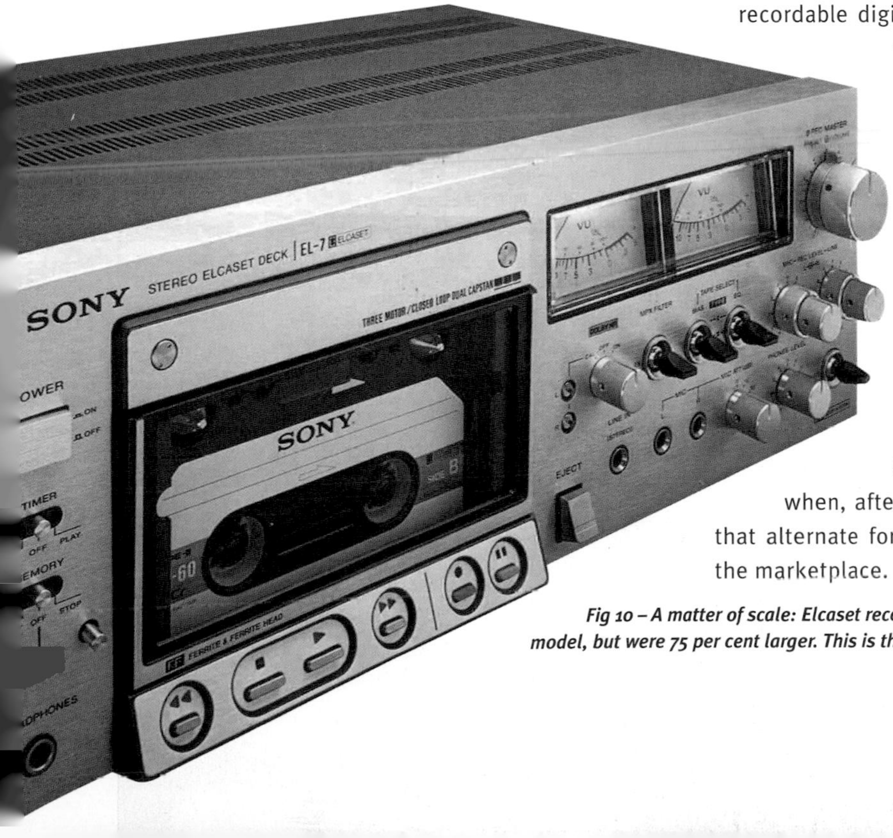

Fig 10 – A matter of scale: Elcaset recorders looked just like a compact cassette model, but were 75 per cent larger. This is the cover of a Sony catalogue of the time.

Video

LONGITUDINAL VIDEO RECORDER (LVR), BASF late 1970s

Before VHS had assumed its dominant position in the video tape recorder market, there were several alternate designs. Tape giant BASF proposed and developed LVR. Rather than a slow-moving tape and spinning tape head producing the long recording tracks for video recording, LVR passed the tape at high speed over a static tape head. At the end of the tape the direction would reverse and another track would be described along the tape.

LVR was mechanically simple and cheap to produce, but it demanded a robust tape format. It never made it into full commercial production even though prototypes were demonstrated by companies new to video, such as the cine camera manufacturer Eumig.

N1500, N1700, Philips early 1970s, SVR, Grundig

Distinguished as the first commercially available home video cassette format (in 1973), early adoption of the original N1500 format was slow. Prices were high and tapes had a maximum recording time of 70 minutes. Units were bulky and almost entirely mechanical. Ongoing development resulted in a long-play version of the format, which was dubbed the N1700. Tapes eventually played for three hours, but this was made possible only by using a very thin tape base that was liable to damage.

Philips's notional partner company, Grundig, further refined the format to produce its SVR, which allowed recordings of up to four hours, essentially by reducing the tape speed. Although Philips licensed the N1500 and N1700 formats to other companies, SVR remained unique to Grundig.

VIDEO 2000, Philips early 1980s

With no more mileage in the N1700 format, Philips created a new competitor to the successful Betamax and VHS – Video 2000. This format offered a recording time of up to eight hours on a flip-over cassette. Special tracking circuitry gave it an edge

Fig 11 – Less idiosyncratic than its predecessors, the V2000 format video recorders missed the tide of popular acceptance.

in terms of picture quality over its competition. Despite modest market penetration, it always lagged in third place. Those who know describe this as the success of marketing (of VHS, particularly) over technical prowess.

Video discs

LASERVISION, LASERDISC and CD-VIDEO, Philips early 1970s

With dual-sided discs measuring 7 or 12 inches in diameter, LaserVision discs were capable of giving up to one hour of broadcast-quality colour television per side. Using the same technology that would later lead to the development of the CD, users could skip through a disc in a similar way to DVD or CD tracks and, on certain discs, even pause, fast forward or play in slow motion with perfect picture quality. The entire format – sound and vision – was analogue. Longevity of the media means many are still in circulation and playable on the LaserDisc format.

LaserDisc, which appeared in the early 1980s, used digital audio from the compact-disc format to deliver better sound. CD-Video discs were CD-compatible audio discs with additional video content that could be played on a LaserDisc player. These formats remain in circulation, mainly supported by loyal fans who rate the quality above that of many DVDs.

CED VIDEODISC, RCA early 1980s

With LaserVision and LaserDisc very much both premium products, RCA launched the CED VideoDisc as a cheaper alternative. Offering only VHS quality, it scored an immediate hit with its keenly priced machines and discs. CED stands for Capacitance Electronic Disc, the method used to encode video

Fig 12 – LaserVision discs were silver and carried analogue video and audio signals. LaserDiscs (also known as CD-Video) were gold coloured in many countries and carried digital audio and analogue video.

data. Using a grooved disc, a stylus reads variations in capacitance in the groove and decodes this into video and audio signals. Being just a replay system, it didn't do well in a marketplace keen on time-shifted recording. That, and its so-so picture quality, led to its demise.

VHD VIDEO DISC, JVC 1980s

Aiming to do for the video disc format what it did for the video cassette recorder, JVC planned the format to be technically extremely advanced (for the day), offering a very high specification. Discs were 10 inches in diameter and created in vinyl on standard "LP" presses. Despite setting about building up a commendable catalogue of launch titles, JVC found that the format never really made an impression on the buying public.

Fig 13 – CDs with video were novel when Philips and Sony introduced the CDi format with VideoCD playback.

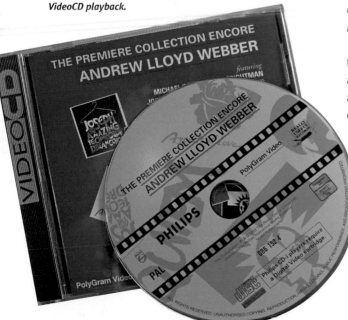

COMPACT DISC INTERACTIVE (CDi), Philips and Sony mid 1980s

The CDi is a still-image, video and interactive format designed around media that is the same size and type as the CD. Interactive games titles were also available. The basic player was a stripped-down computer with CPU (central processing unit), memory and operating system. For video, an additional processor unit had to be purchased and installed. Video quality was similar to VHS, though digital, and encoded in the MPEG1 format. Cost and lowly specified machines hampered take-up, but the format did serve to prepare the market for the superior DVD format that would appear within a few years.

COMPUTERS AND THE DIGITAL HUB

IN THIS CHAPTER WE WILL:

- Look at how computers have evolved from industry workhorses to essential personal tools.
- Examine the key elements of the technology.
- Look at what we need to enhance our experiences of computers.
- Gain an understanding of the key communications that computers, and other digital devices, use.

THE COMPUTER IS PERHAPS THE FUNDAMENTAL DIGITAL DEVICE. ALTHOUGH WE NOW KNOW IT BEST AS A TOOL FOR STORING AND LISTENING TO MUSIC, MAKING VIDEOS OR SENDING TREASURED PHOTOS AROUND THE WORLD, AT ITS CORE IS A COMPLEX PROCESSOR THAT HANDLES JUST DIGITAL DATA. WHETHER WE CHOOSE MUSIC, VIDEO OR ANY OTHER MEDIUM, BEFORE WE CAN USE IT WITH OUR COMPUTER THE SIGNAL MUST BE CONVERTED TO A DIGITAL FORM. THANKFULLY, THE PROCESSES INVOLVED IN DOING THIS ARE BEYOND THE SCOPE OF THIS BOOK AND OF NO CONSEQUENCE FROM THE USER'S POINT OF VIEW. WHAT WE ARE INTERESTED IN ARE THE RESULTS! IN THIS CHAPTER WE'LL TAKE A LOOK AT HOW THE COMPUTER HAS GRADUATED FROM SCIENTIFIC AIDE TO THE ALL-PERVASIVE BUSINESS AND RECREATIONAL ESSENTIAL.

In the last chapter we recalled some famous – though now infamous – predictions in the form of quotes from some of the key movers and shakers in the computer business just a generation or two ago. We can point to a number of milestones that have taken us from that time to the here and now:

- The first IBC PC, ancestor of today's Windows PCs.
- The first Macintosh: a revolutionary step-change in the thinking about computer functionality and ease of use.
- WYSIWYG (What you see is what you get): early personal computers tended to be text based – WYSIWYG applications let you see exactly what your finished documents would look like.
- Adobe's Photoshop. A professional-grade application that lets photographers and graphic designers perform "magic" on photographs.
- Windows 95. Brought much of the ease of use of the Macintosh to the humble PC.
- Consumer digital media application programs. Suddenly, applications that professional users had enjoyed for years spawned siblings that made digital music, video and even DVD production available to the rest of us.

Of course, if you ask a range of people to produce their own list of milestones, they will all come up with slightly – or dramatically – different selections. But the message that comes through is that the computer today is now an accessible device for us all. Prices in real terms have never been lower, while the power and capabilities of the machine have never been greater. If you already own one, this comes as read; if not, then your choice has never been greater. And the good news is that virtually all computers today can sit at the centre of your digital world and become the core of your own digital hub.

MAC, WINDOWS ... OR LINUX?

When choosing a computer, the choice has been simple. A Macintosh or Windows PC. Windows PCs are very widely available, are produced by countless manufacturers and command the lion's share of the market. Windows PCs also tend to be more keenly priced and boast a considerable advantage when it comes to the total number of software applications that are available.

So why do some people continue to support the Macintosh? Ask an enthusiast, and he or she will

Fig 1 – Less than a generation ago, our computer hardware and software were somewhat less developed than they are today.

have a hundred and one (at least) reasons. Those of us who must be impartial will cite the Macintosh being simpler to use, better able to support graphical applications (such as photo-editing software) and boasting more efficient processors. Software may not be as common (nor as cheap), but you will find that all the key applications are compatible and that many of the most popular lifestyle applications (like iTunes, iMovie and iPhoto) are designed for the Mac – even if iTunes has now migrated to Windows. It's often the case that Windows users shy away from Macs, but once they have realized how simple they are to use they never look back. There is a comment that is not attributed but probably sums up the difference in more tangible terms: "I always use a PC at work, but at home, when I have to spend my own money, it's always a Mac."

There is also the question of design. Although most people don't choose a computer on the basis of its looks, Macs have always been pleasant to live with. They don't have that industrial look that makes them incongruous in most of our homes. Don't think of this as a fatuous comment. As hi-fi manufacturers have already discovered, we consumers no longer want to spend our hard-earned cash on anonymous, and often ugly, black boxes; quality performance – wherever we seek it – also needs to be stylishly packaged.

While most people opt for Windows PCs and the others for Macs, another operating system, which can sit on computers designed for Windows or the

Fig 2 – Linux may be the outsider, but the resources and programs available are growing in both number and complexity. This image editor, GIMP, is a good match for the industry-leading application, Photoshop.

Macintosh operating system, has been quietly gaining ground. Linux is an evolution of the UNIX operating system used by industrial and scientific computers. It scores in being an "open source" operating system. Applications developed for the platform are generally made available free of charge or for nominal cost. Spiritual cousins of the mega-program applications found on Windows or Macs appear in Linux for a fraction of the price. If you can't afford the sometimes absurd prices of conventional software, Linux could be a solution. Drawbacks? Limited market share and sometimes unstable. Support, too, tends not to be the 24-hour support lines provided by the big software houses; instead it is often restricted to news groups and forums on the Internet.

This has not stopped Linux becoming the operating system of choice for many embedded computing systems – such as digital television receiving boxes and Internet file servers (fig 2).

MAKING A GOOD THING BETTER

If you have a computer – or you are shopping for one – what do you also need to make your digital hub complete? In the following chapters we will look at all those essential – and some not-so-essential –

lifestyle accessories, but what about your computer? What can you add to make your experiences even better?

Memory

Adding memory to your computer is arguably the simplest and most effective way to boost performance. Even those computers a couple of years old (veterans in IT terms) can show astonishing gains in performance by boosting their memory.

Increasing the RAM – Random Access Memory – gives your computer more headroom to work on large calculations and large files. Video and photo applications, particularly, need loads of memory to flourish. Digital cameras, for example, deliver ever-increasing image resolutions. This in turn gives better image quality but also larger image files. Increasing the RAM available lets you manipulate your images more effectively with less time spent watching the hourglass or stopwatch icon as your instructions are processed. Guidelines? Boost the 256MB of memory that most computers now come with to at least twice that amount. If you can install more, do so.

Incidentally, more and more computers make it

simple to add new or additional memory chips, but if you don't want to do it yourself then the computer store that supplied the memory can usually arrange to do it for you, either for free or a nominal charge.

Hard drives

Once, our computers played host only to the most modest of files: documents and spreadsheets. We could comfortably accommodate most of these on a small hard disc and exchange them using a floppy disc. Today, the picture is very different. Photos, movies and music collections are likely to comprise the bulk of what we store, and these files can be very large indeed. For those routine portfolios of photos and our collection of MP3 music, the enormous hard discs now standard on computers are usually just sufficient. But start editing your photos and the free space shrinks almost as you watch. Start compiling and editing digital video, and any residual space will be gone in a blink.

With a big desktop computer you will probably find you have the space to add a second hard disc inside the enclosure. Adding one is not difficult (though opening the case – as in the case of adding memory – can be unnerving). Don't want to risk it? Then do what those with laptop or non-expandable computers (such as the iMac) do: add an external hard drive.

External drives connect via your USB, USB2 or

Fig 3 – Truly pocketable, the USB drive is the modern equivalent of the floppy disc, but it is eminently more portable, much smaller and more robust.

Fig 4 – Pocket drives let you store large amounts of digital video, huge music collections and albums of photos and take them with you.

Firewire connection and let you expand your disc space by tens or hundreds of gigabytes. You will have the choice not only of connection type (it's best to ignore USB as it's too slow for digital video or large file copying), but also a desktop or portable drive. Desktop drives – as you might have guessed – are designed to sit on your desktop, whereas portable drives – sometimes called pocket drives (fig 4) – are smaller and more robust. You can use portable drives for carrying around not only your essential documents, but also your photo album and movies.

Stick drives, or USB drives (fig 3), are rarely drives at all, but rather solid-state memory (like you would find in a memory card). They offer similar memory storage to memory cards, much less than a pocket drive, but they are tiny and can even be used on your keyring. They are ideal for carrying those essential or important documents that you need all the time or as a way of easily copying resources – where it's legal to do so – from friends' computers.

Printers

Long gone are the days when printers were used simply to print out our correspondence and school projects. Now, one device can print out all those letters one minute and produce photo quality prints the next. The good news is that photo-grade printers are affordable and reliable. The bad news is that they can cost an arm and a leg to run: inks and dyes suitable for long-lived prints don't come cheap.

It makes sense to buy a good-quality printer if you intend to print a great number of photos, but if you want lots of prints for albums and sharing, then dedicated photo printers can be a better bet. These produce high-quality prints from the computer or even directly from a camera.

Hubs

Not high in the glamour stakes, hubs help you manage all your peripheral devices (fig 6). New computers score high on connectivity – you can

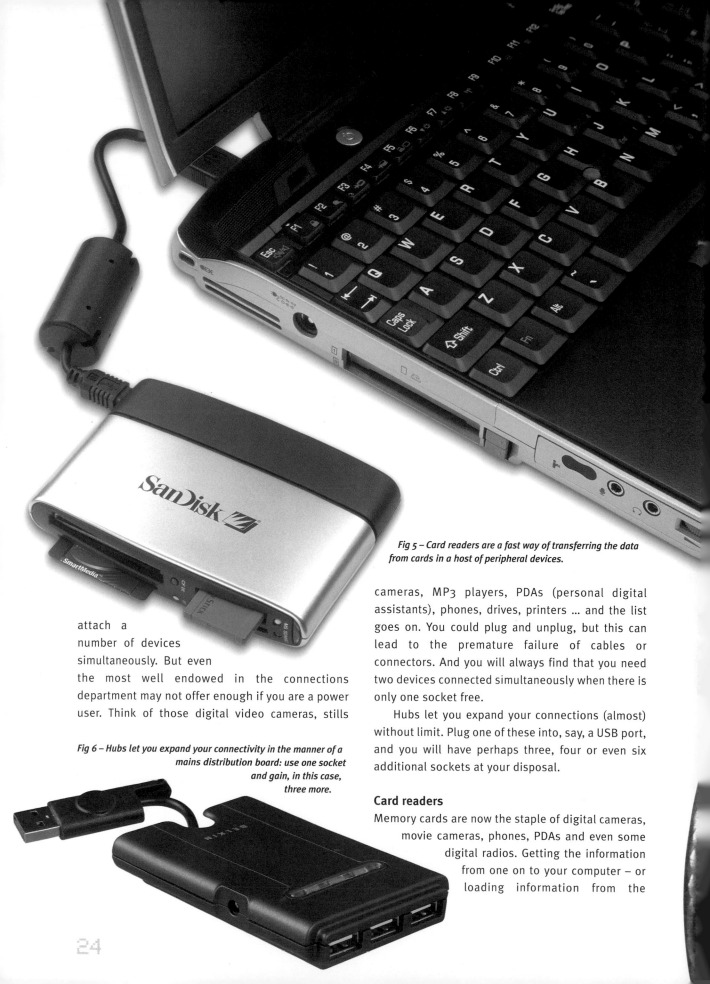

Fig 5 – Card readers are a fast way of transferring the data from cards in a host of peripheral devices.

attach a number of devices simultaneously. But even the most well endowed in the connections department may not offer enough if you are a power user. Think of those digital video cameras, stills

Fig 6 – Hubs let you expand your connectivity in the manner of a mains distribution board: use one socket and gain, in this case, three more.

cameras, MP3 players, PDAs (personal digital assistants), phones, drives, printers … and the list goes on. You could plug and unplug, but this can lead to the premature failure of cables or connectors. And you will always find that you need two devices connected simultaneously when there is only one socket free.

Hubs let you expand your connections (almost) without limit. Plug one of these into, say, a USB port, and you will have perhaps three, four or even six additional sockets at your disposal.

Card readers

Memory cards are now the staple of digital cameras, movie cameras, phones, PDAs and even some digital radios. Getting the information from one on to your computer – or loading information from the computer – can involve connecting the device directly. A more elegant solution is to fit a card reader (Fig 5). Often accepting up to eight different card formats in a single unit (see pages 52–3 for more about memory cards), they save the wear and tear on your cameras and other devices and can simplify the number of connections necessary to your computer. There are even in-built options for some desktop computers.

CONNECTORS

Look around the back of any computer (or along the side of some laptops) and you will see all the connectors (fig 7). Sometimes they are colour coded to make connection simple but often you will have to know them by their shape and by what they are used for. Fortunately, the last few years has seen something of a shakedown in connectors, with the old guard of relatively slow connections making way for a more limited but standardized collection. The table here provides a summary of those you are likely to find around the back of your computer – and what you will probably attach to them.

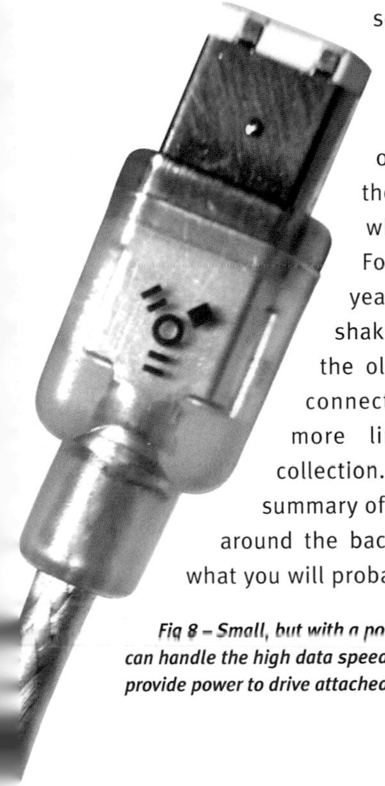

Fig 8 – Small, but with a powerful punch. The Firewire cable can handle the high data speeds required for digital video and provide power to drive attached devices.

Fig 7 – The illustration here shows what the sockets look like. Fortunately, each type of connector is unique and, where relevant, backwardly compatible. Hence you can plug a USB2 cable into a USB socket, but the attached device will then operate only at the slower USB speeds.

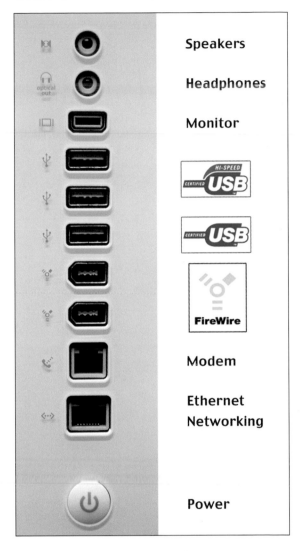

Connector type	Mostly used for	Also used for
USB	Keyboard, mouse, printer	Hard drive, camera, scanner
USB 2.0	Hard drive	Camera, scanner
Firewire	Video camera	iPod, hard disc, card reader
Firewire 800	Video camera, hard disc	
Wireless	Networking	Printing
Bluetooth	Printer, phone	
Modem	Internet connection	
Ethernet	Local networking	Broadband internet
Line	Audio input/output	Speaker system

HOME NETWORKING

If you have more than one computer at home – perhaps you have bought a new model and reckon there is still some mileage in the old one, or you have one in the study and the children have one in their bedroom – why not connect them? Once your computers start talking to each other, you can share resources and create a digital powerhouse. Here's just some of the things you can do:

- Share a single, fast broadband Internet connection.
- Share printers. Send your documents to the fast laser printer in the study and print out your photos on the photo-printer in the lounge.
- Access all your resources and, where relevant, programs.
- Use common hardware – such as hard discs and scanners – even if they are attached to another computer.

There are lots of ways you can network your home. The traditional method – if traditional is a term you can apply to such a new technology – is to use dedicated wiring. A special cable is laid around your home, much in the manner of telephone cabling. You can then connect computers to ports – like phone sockets – at selected points around your home.

This is the most expensive and, if your home is already built, the most disruptive system to install. Many new homes are now prewired with network cabling, which makes installation painless. However, the limitation of this system is the need to connect via a port, and you will need to ensure you have enough ports and that they are in the right places.

So, for most domestic installations, less costly and simpler systems need to be considered. These are power line networking, phone line networking and wireless networking (fig 9).

Fig 9 – Networking computers – and wireless networking in particular – can add tremendous versatility to your digital world, whether for pleasure or business. Courtesy SES Astra.

Fig 10 – This Powerline adaptor allows you to connect computers over your home electrical wiring without any additional hardware.

Phone line and power line networking take advantage of those networks of cabling already built into our homes (fig 10)– that for the phone system and electrical power, respectively. The systems are similar, though the power line solution is the most effective since it allows you to connect a computer wherever there is an electrical socket. In most, if not all, homes there will be more of these than there will be phone sockets.

Using special adaptors that plug into the electrical outlets, computer data can be sent into the home's ring main electrical supply. Any computer (or appropriate peripheral device) can be addressed by this data signal and, using a similar adaptor, filter out the data. It's convenient and requires no new cabling. Adaptors themselves are comparatively cheap and can be built into mains plugs.

The drawback is the speed of the network, which tends to be slower than that of a dedicated wiring system or that of a wireless network. With many systems there is also a chance of signal leakage – signals escaping to the wiring in the street and neighbouring homes. But on a more positive note, power line systems can score over others where it is impossible to install hard wiring or where walls are too thick for successful wireless networking.

Going wireless

Many users now see wired systems as inelegant and inefficient. After investing in a laptop computer that can operate without connection to a mains power supply, it seems something of a compromise to then reinstate a connection, albeit only for networking. You don't have to connect through a wire now. Wireless networks are being increasingly built into computers, especially laptops. Wireless networks give you the ultimate in portability, not restricting you to specific locations in your home. You can wander freely – even into neighbours' homes – and still maintain your network. We'll take a look at the mechanics of networking wirelessly over the next few pages and see that the opportunities on offer are extensive.

WARCHALKING

At the turn of the century, as wireless networking made its first tentative steps into the commercial world, a new phenomenon began: warchalking. In the streets of cities around the globe, strange hieroglyphs were appearing. Although restricted to a shadowy underworld at first, these symbols indicated locations where those who owned wireless-enabled computers could find wireless networks. If you knew how to interpret the signs, you could identify the type of network and whether it was open or closed to outsiders.

Needless to say, this was quickly identified as a security risk by many organizations, who then realized how vulnerable they were to hacking from outside (even though most warchalkers' intentions were merely to gain Internet access). Passwords and encryption, features that lie dormant on the wireless networks, were invoked and the networks closed down.

If you wander around now with a laptop, or even a PDA, you will be able to identify many wireless networks not just in cities, but in neighbourhoods, too. Most of them are secure ...

WIFI AND THE WIRE-FREE HOME

Computer networks are common in the workplace and increasingly so in the home. But while we find it acceptable to tear up floors, ceilings and walls in the office to accommodate networking cables, we are less disposed to do this to our homes. So, unless you are involved in a new-build home project, you need to use an alternative.

That alternative is a wireless connection using a system dubbed WiFi. It's simple to install and simple to use. And once installed on your computer, it not only helps you create a home network, you can then connect to other WiFi networks in the neighbourhood, at the office or even at your favourite coffee shop.

In fact, many computers, particularly laptops, already come with the essential WiFi card built in. But even if yours does not, it is easy enough to fit one afterwards. If you have a laptop with a PC card slot, you can fit a WiFi PC card and be up and running in moments (figs 13, 14). If you have a Macintosh, if it is not already fitted, add an AirPort card. Again, fitting it is simple – straight under the keyboard in the case of iBooks and Powerbooks (fig 11).

Fig 11 – Installing a WiFi card is simple if you have the nerve to delve inside your computer. This AirPort card simply slips into a vacant slot in this iMac G5.

Hotspots

With your computer empowered, you next need to add a WiFi base station or, as they are usually known, hotspots. This is a box that connects to the Internet through a hard-wired connection and to the WiFi-equipped computers and peripherals wirelessly. In the case of Macs, the usual base

station is the AirPort itself (fig 12). But since WiFi works independently of the computer platform, those PC users who fancy an AirPort base station are in luck. In fact, your choice of components will be governed by the speed you want your network to run at, always bearing in mind any limitations imposed by your hardware.

Fig 12 – AirPort is a simple WiFi networking scheme that works on Mac and PC systems with appropriate cards.

Whatever you choose, a hotspot will transmit over a range of about 30 m (100 ft) in the open or about 20 m (65 ft) indoors, allowing for walls and furniture. If you have a particularly large house, you can get booster units to extend this range.

Configuring

Unless some parochial security has been installed, most computers will identify a network and link to it automatically. This applies to most recent Windows

FAST OR FASTER?

When you go shopping for WiFi components, you will have a choice between fast wireless, which has been given the name 802.11b, or very fast, 802.11g. Apple has been more inventive in its naming strategy, and call 802.11b AirPort, and 802.11g AirPort Extreme. Normally your network will only be as fast as the slowest component, so go for the faster option every time, unless you are limited by your computer. 802.11g is around five times faster, so it's worth the modest extra expense.

home using this frequency, you may experience interference. Only one way, however. WiFi will give bursts of noise on your television but television transmissions won't affect WiFi. But if you make extensive use of a microwave, you will probably be used to video sender interference.

Fig 14 – Want to connect to your network (or any other) using your PDA? Use an SD-based WiFi card.

Fig 13 – Your laptop does not have WiFi? No problem. If it has a PC card slot, you can add a CompactFlash-based card such as this. And it still adds 256MB of flash memory.

PCs and most Macs built since 2000. Older PCs will need to be manually configured to connect. Here is how to do it:

1. Identify and select the WiFi software. In Windows XP you will see it in the System Tray at the bottom right of the screen.
2. Click on the Search button to display a list of all the available networks.
3. Click on your network to select it.

Whether you have manually or automatically connected, you do need to be mindful of WiFi security. The fact that you managed to connect without hassle means that, theoretically, any of your neighbours could connect to your network, too, and use your Internet bandwidth or even scan your computers. This is of no consequence to many users, but if security is an issue, you can still secure your network so that only people in your household can access it. Create a WEP (Wired Equivalent Privacy) key – the WiFi software talks you through the process – and your system will be virtually impregnable.

Interference

WiFi uses the 2.4GHz frequency band. In the UK, at least, this is also the frequency used by video senders. If you are distributing video around the

---

FINDING A WIFI NETWORK

When you are out and about, how do you know if there is a network point near by? Once, you could seek out warchalk markings – chalk marks on the road or pavement where you could link into a network. Now, you can equip yourself with one of these WiFi Locators. The keyring device from Intego will immediately identify a WiFi network.

BLUETOOTH

Bluetooth is a radio frequency wireless system but is principally designed as a low-cost communications system that can operate between portable devices. Devised originally by the Scandinavian mobile technology company Ericsson in 1994, it is often described as a cable-replacement technology as it is often used to cut down on cabling between devices. Because it requires very low power to operate, it can be built not only into laptops and desktop computers, but also mobile phones, PDAs (see pages 162–7) and headsets (fig 15).

The key differentiator between other wireless systems and Bluetooth is that Bluetooth is designed to be a very low-power solution, with a commensurate low range. This makes it ideal for communicating between, say, a phone and a headset or a computer and cordless keyboard, but limits power consumption and potential interference.

Bluetooth classes

When you examine Bluetooth devices, you will see them grouped into one of three classes:

Class 1 is high power (in Bluetooth terms) and has an operation range of around 100 m (350 ft). Computer dongles, which act as receivers for Bluetooth peripherals, are most commonly Class 1 devices. Also, the USB adaptors that enable the creation of Bluetooth networks are usually Class 1 (fig 17).

Class 2 is mid-powered and has a maximum range of around 50 m (170 ft). Class 2 devices are similar to Class 1, except in terms of their range.

Class 3, with the lowest power, has a modest range of only 10 m (35 ft). Phones, PDAs, headsets and computer peripherals tend to be Class 3.

As with all wireless communications, these distances can be affected by environmental factors, such as furniture, walls and buildings.

With regard to speed, a Bluetooth connection is mid-way between the faster infrared connections and slower ISDN phone lines. For most purposes, it can be considered similar in data-transfer speed to a modest residential broadband internet connection.

Fig 15 – Safety, security and convenience have seen sales of Bluetooth headsets for mobile phones take off and become, arguably, the most popular of Bluetooth accessories.

For many applications – such as a wireless keyboard and mouse – there is little need for high speed, but Bluetooth can also be used to communicate with printers, for which this higher speed is important.

Security

There is the inevitable worry when we discuss any form of wireless communications that people can – accidentally or otherwise – eavesdrop on other Bluetooth devices. Or they can make use of

HOW BLUETOOTH AVOIDS INTERFERENCE

OK, so you won't have many Bluetooth devices at home. But when you move around or go to a crowded office, how do you avoid devices interfering with each other?

Bluetooth works at very low power. A typical device will radiate around 1 milliwatt. Compare this with mobile phones that can radiate 3,000 times as much power. It is this low power that also places the practical limit on the range of the Bluetooth devices.

Devices also use a technique called spread-spectrum frequency hopping. A device can use any one of 79 frequency channels to broadcast on and will rapidly – up to 1,600 times a second – change. This, too, ensures continuity of connection, and even if there is interference on one channel, it will last only momentarily.

Fig 16 – Not all Bluetooth devices are serious or business focused. This toy car can be controlled by a mobile phone using Bluetooth to send commands from the phone keypad to the wheels.

Bluetooth resources to which they should not have access. In fact, this is rarely possible because Bluetooth devices need to be paired: that is, each device needs to acknowledge the presence of the other and want to be linked to it.

There are also different Bluetooth profiles. These profiles determine how different devices can communicate and what data they can exchange. A computer, for example, needs the same profile as a keyboard or mouse in order to be able to communicate with it. That computer will also need another profile in order to share data with a PDA or phone. Likewise, a phone will need to possess a particular profile in order to

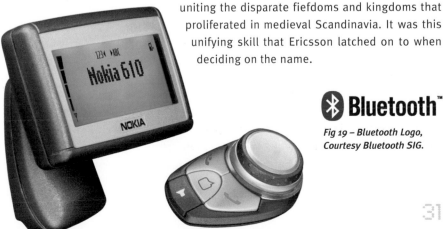

Fig 17 – A Class 1 USB adapter enables communication between a computer and selected devices within a 100 m (350 ft) range.

Fig 18 – Bluetooth makes the fitting of car kits for mobile phones much simpler, as each component connects wirelessly.

communicate with a wireless headset (for more about Bluetooth communications, see page 152).

What about the name?

There is something of an urban myth (that stands up to close inspection) that says the name derives from the nickname of King Harald Blatand, who was ruler of a substantial part of Scandinavia in the tenth century. He had a reputation for an insatiable appetite for wild blueberries, but also for uniting the disparate fiefdoms and kingdoms that proliferated in medieval Scandinavia. It was this unifying skill that Ericsson latched on to when deciding on the name.

Fig 19 – Bluetooth Logo, Courtesy Bluetooth SIG.

AIRPORT AND AIRPORT EXPRESS

Whether you have a PC or a Macintosh, Apple's Airport lets you exploit wireless networking for your home office – and your music.

Apple introduced the AirPort (fig 20)as a Mac-based solution for home and business networking in 1999. Using a small base station and a WiFi card that could easily be installed in any Mac, computers – laptop or desktop – became free of the cabling that had so often restricted home office and business layouts. Four years later, AirPort Extreme (fig 22) appeared and increased the speed of the wireless communications (between computers and to the Internet) by a factor of nearly five times, using the fast, 802.11g WiFi standard.

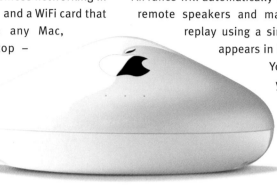

Fig 20 – When AirPort arrived, it was a revelation – people could use their computers untethered and still maintain functionality. It quickly became a "must have" on technical and aesthetic grounds.

Fig 21 – No larger than a power adaptor, AirPort Express makes enjoying your digital music around the home simple.

Barely a year later, AirPort became a family of products thanks to the release of a sibling product, AirPort Express (fig 21). This pocketable newcomer offers all computer users the option of affordable, easy-to-configure networking, and audio and printer sharing.

For many of us, building up our collections of MP3 music, downloaded from the Internet, it's been the musical capabilities that have attracted most attention. AirPort Express includes AirTunes, a cross-platform application that lets you use the ubiquitous iTunes music application across a network – and straight into your hi-fi (or to powered speakers). None of the components needs to be in the same room; AirTunes and AirPort Express ensure that the audio is delivered from your computer to your chosen device.

In the same way that a WiFi-enabled computer can automatically detect new computers and devices that connect on to a wireless network, AirTunes will automatically detect the connection of remote speakers and make them available for replay using a simple pop-up menu that appears in iTunes.

You can choose to replay your music library, use existing playlists, or create new ones to replay through your hi-fi. And if you want around-the-house hi-fi from your computer, you can invest in multiple AirPort Expresses.

When you are playing music, neither the host computer nor any other computer on the network is compromised; they can still communicate with each other and the internet. Better still, AirPort Express has some other tricks up its sleeve. If you live in a large house, or you live in a house that has thick, radio-wave-absorbing walls, or you like to work at the bottom of the garden, AirPort Express can extend the range of your network. Place the AirPort Express at some convenient intermediate position and you will have effectively made yourself a network repeater.

Printing, too, can be made more flexible. You may have more than one computer in your home but you don't need to have a printer attached to each machine.

AirPort Express includes a USB link that can be used to connect to a printer. In fact, with this link you don't need any computer to be connected to a printer – saving even more cabling problems and logistics.

For even more capabilities, you could invest in a dedicated network music player, such as Soundbridge from Roku (fig 23). Connect this unit to your hi-fi or powered speakers and you can not only hear the music but see details on the Soundbridge's display.

A large multifunction remote control ensures that you can access precise tracks and collections. For those of you who enjoy Internet radio, Soundbridge also includes an Internet radio station player to feed your favourite stations through your chosen speaker set-up. WiFi connectivity is included in most models and is available as a Compactflash slot compatible card to upgrade those without.

Fig 22 – Upping the ante, AirPort Extreme made communications significantly faster, by a factor of five, by adopting the newer 54MB/ 802.11g protocol.

Fig 23 – Roku Lab's Soundbridge offers networked digital music (MP3 and a range of other similar formats) along with the option to select tracks – and even view the music on a visualizer.

DIGITAL CAMERAS AND PHOTOGRAPHY

IN THIS CHAPTER WE:
• Examine the evolution of photography, from conventional to digital.
• Learn how digital cameras work and how they can help you take great photos.
• Discuss how to make good photos even better.
• Look at the opportunities digital photography gives us to use and share our images.

PERHAPS MORE THAN ANY OTHER DIGITAL ACCESSORY, THE DIGITAL CAMERA HAS BEEN ADOPTED AND ACCEPTED BY A HUGE PERCENTAGE OF THE POPULATION. THROUGHOUT MUCH OF THE 1990s – WHEN THE TECHNOLOGY BECAME VIABLE – DIGITAL CAMERAS WERE BEING USED BY A LOYAL BUT MODEST SELECTION OF PHOTOGRAPHERS. BUT WITH THE TURN OF THE CENTURY, COST, QUALITY AND CONVENIENCE CONSPIRED TOGETHER TO MAKE THE DIGITAL CAMERA ONE OF THOSE "MUST-HAVE" ACCESSORIES. WHETHER YOU ARE INTERESTED IN SIMPLY RECORDING EVENTS (PARTIES, WEDDINGS OR WHATEVER), OR YOU ARE MORE OF AN ENTHUSIAST OR PROFESSIONAL USER, THERE IS AT LEAST ONE DIGITAL CAMERA IDEAL FOR YOU.

AND YOU DON'T EVEN NEED TO HAVE A DEDICATED CAMERA. MULTIFUNCTION DEVICES – SUCH AS PDAs, DIGITAL VIDEO CAMERAS AND EVEN MOBILE PHONES – NOW INCLUDE STILL IMAGE CAMERAS IN THEIR SPECIFICATION. SO THERE REALLY IS NO EXCUSE NOT TO HAVE A CAMERA WITH YOU AT ALL TIMES.

THE DIGITAL CAMERA – THE STORY SO FAR

The history of photography is long and convoluted. The birth is variously ascribed to Niépce in France, Fox Talbot in England and others in the first half of the nineteenth century. Others point even further back to, for example, the Wedgwood family in the previous century, who experimented with photosensitive materials to produce patterning for their pottery business.

Digital photography, on the other hand, is a much more recent invention, though it, too, has a complex heritage. To find the antecedents of today's digital cameras we need to go back to the middle of the twentieth century, when the first practical video tape recorders were produced. For the first time, live images could be captured and stored as electrical impulses on a magnetic tape or disc. Of course, at that time the source television images, the signal recorded and the output later were all analogue. But the methodology would prove the foundation for all subsequent developments.

Space – the new frontier

The next milestone was – like so many of the technological breakthroughs of the 1960s – a result of the space programme. With computers increasing in number and growing in ability, NASA scientists used an analogue-to-digital conversion process when sending signals from space probes back to Earth. This process also allowed for elementary image manipulation, cleaning and sharpening the images, to remove noise and interference.

More covertly, the same technology was being used in spy satellites to enable photographs to be delivered from a satellite to a receiver on the ground. As part of this process, Texas Instruments issued the first patent for a camera that used no film in 1972. This was an electronic camera, rather than a digital camera. This distinction, though pedantic, was actually rather important, as electronic cameras were essentially still based on video technology – delivering still video images – rather than purely digital ones.

Fig 1 – A Viking 2 image of the Martian landscape. Note the colour patches on the lander that were (belatedly) used to calibrate the images to produce correct colour. Courtesy NASA © NASA.

Shortly afterwards we saw digital images – true digital images this time – delivered from the surface of Mars by the two Viking probes (fig 1). Slowly but surely, using an array of photocells arranged vertically, the cameras scanned the landscape and built up remarkably detailed pictures of the planet's surface.

Interestingly, the first shots showed a landscape of browns and tans under a pale blue sky. Later this was changed to stronger russet colours beneath a salmon pink sky. Colour calibration – an essential feature of the modern digital camera – was first employed to correct an obvious mistake.

The solid state

Back on Earth, solid state video cameras – which use a transistor array known as a charge-coupled device (or CCD) – appeared in the early part of the 1970s and were adopted throughout broadcast television within a very few years. By 1981 the Sony Corporation had used CCDs to produce the first embryonic digital camera, the Magnetic Video Camera, or Mavica. It is a name that Sony still uses today for many of its digital cameras.

Canon also entered the frame with its own still video camera concept – the iON (Image Online Network) (fig 2). Also known as the Xapshot in North America, this was a compact camera that essentially captured still video images at a resolution that matched that of VHS (which is OK, but no more) or SuperVHS (better, but still poor in photographic terms).

Fig 2 – Canon's iON (or Xapshot) electronic camera seeded the market for digital cameras a whole decade before consumer models appeared on the dealers' shelves.

Images from iON cameras could be downloaded to a computer in the manner of normal digital images, but they were still analogue at this point – analogue-to-digital conversion took place when the images were transferred. This format flourished, with a number of cameras being released and finding widespread use among early users of desktop publishing. When Apple introduced the Macintosh it became viable to produce cheaply polished newsletters, internal communications and even commercial documentation on your desktop. The iON camera made it simple to introduce images, too.

Good though the iON may have been, it was still not a true digital solution. In 1992 Kodak gave a preview of the capabilities of a true digital camera when it released a camera based on the Nikon F3 conventional SLR (single lens reflex). Adding a 1.5 megapixel CCD, a hard drive to store images and a battery pack to drive the electronics added substantially to the bulk of an already weighty camera, but it proved a hit with the press. Sadly, a prohibitively high price tag kept it in that professional arena.

QuickTake and the digital revolution begins

As you might imagine, technology moves fast, and within a couple of years Apple gave us the first

Fig 3 – As resolution improved over the years, so did the digital camera's ability to produce accurate colour and tone, as this simulation shows of typical cameras from 1995, 2000 and 2005.

mass-market digital camera: the QuickTake 100. On its debut in 1994 this camera, which could take pictures up to the resolution of most computer screens at that time (a modest 640 x 480 pixels), had the capacity to record only eight images at this resolution before needing to download those images from its fixed, onboard memory.

From that point models proliferated. Prices and performance still precluded the adoption of the medium by mainstream photographers (who were quick to dismiss all digital technology as irrelevant), but things would soon change. Cameras with 1 megapixel capacity (with CCDs that could record 1 million points in an image) gave way to 2 megapixel models. Digital backs appeared for professional medium format cameras, offering resolutions similar to film (fig 3).

In parallel, computing power mushroomed, enabling the storage and manipulation of digital images. Software for doing so – such as Adobe's ubiquitous Photoshop – flourished and spawned simpler derivatives designed to appeal more to the enthusiast amateur than to the seasoned professional.

Now we have digital cameras that fill just about every niche in the market, including some that the technology itself has created. Think about it. We have digital compact cameras and digital SLR cameras with interchangeable lenses and extensive accessories. Digital backs – replacing film-based ones – have breathed new life into the medium and large format cameras that are the essential tool of many professional photographers.

At the other extreme, miniature digital cameras are fitted to many phones and PDAs and can even be found on keyrings. It has never been easier to capture an image. But now it's time to learn what we can do with the image once it's in the camera. How do we get it to the computer and then how do we make it better? And having got this far, what else can we do with it? Let's discover all these things... and more.

PICTURES ON CD

We take the CD – and more recently the DVD – rather for granted as storage media for files of all sorts, but they are particularly effective for the storage of images. In fact, back in 1992 Kodak introduced the PhotoCD, a special computer CD-ROM that stored images at multiple resolutions. The rationale was set by the low resolution of contemporary digital cameras. When these were offering resolutions of only 1 or 2 megapixels, PhotoCDs could offer scans of conventional images that yielded files as large as 18 megapixels.

The idea behind the PhotoCD was that photographers would take their pictures to their normal laboratory for processing. As well as receiving negatives, slides or prints, their film would also be scanned to disc. It was the best of both worlds. Better still, PhotoCDs stored each image at multiple resolutions and could replay these images on dedicated CD players (sold as PhotoCD players by Kodak and others) and on the then-new CD-I CD players.

Despite a few years of modest success, the rapid rise in digital camera capabilities and the somewhat restricted capabilities of PhotoCDs, the format was relaunched for a professional market, where it could be used for more specialist applications of image storage.

Fig 4 – The PhotoCD – digital and high quality – was launched years before cameras could offer the same.

CHOOSING A DIGITAL CAMERA

Which digital camera is right for you? The choice can be baffling, but if you determine your principal needs, that choice can become simpler. Take a look at the options in the table here and see how the options stack up.

Type of photographs	Best choice	Good choice
Take snapshots anywhere, anytime	Phone-type camera	Ultra compact
Take hassle-free, good photos	Compact	Ultra compact
Take great photos, but without the need to carry a large, heavy camera	Power compact	Ultra compact
Take great photos in a wide range of conditions	SLR	Power compact
Take professional-quality photos anywhere, anytime	SLR	Top-of-the-range power compact
Take professional-quality pictures, as well as commercial and advertising photos	Digital camera back	SLR

Fig 5 – Phone cameras can take surprisingly good photos – like the LCD panel on the back of a digital camera, the resolution and quality of the image displayed is lower than that recorded.

Phone and PDA cameras

The cameras that were first added to phones were pretty rudimentary in quality and performance. Now they have shrugged off their low-quality "gimmick" mantle and can deliver commendable performance. Would you seriously buy a phone with a built-in camera if your primary intention was to take photographs? Unlikely. But a phone that ensures that you are always equipped to take a quick photo – well, maybe (fig 5). If you take photos regularly but don't need or want to take high-resolution shots, then you need carry only your phone with you. Better still, if you want to share those photos, you can send them to friends and family instantly, bypassing the usual image-sharing routes.

Don't forget that some PDAs (personal digital assistants) also offer camera facilities. The

Fig 6 – Camera elements are small and discretely positioned on many phones – making them ideal for candid photography.

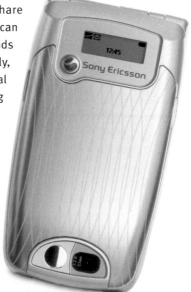

large display of these devices is also a great way to view your shots. And if you want to cut down on what you carry around, go for a model that includes a phone, too. You really can carry all your digital tools in one package (fig 6).

Ultra compact

Take the camera electronics and lens from a mobile phone and put them in a more conventional casing and you have the makings of an ultra compact camera. More so than even a phone camera, you can slip one of these into any pocket or purse. In fact, with most of these cameras the bulk of the device is made up of the batteries – unfortunately, battery technology has not kept up when it comes to miniaturization. Even so, size is a plus point with these cameras, some of which are so small that they are sold on keyrings. On the downside, you generally need to connect them to a computer to access and download your images, and image quality will be no more than OK (fig 7).

Fig 7 – This Sony ultra compact bucks the trend by offering very good picture quality in a tiny camera. It's waterproof, too.

Fig 8 – No need to be square. Some compacts (such as this Fuji model) are more curvy. And the neckstrap encourages you to wear the camera like a fashion accessory.

Compact

The compact is the biggest-selling class in both digital and conventional cameras. It's easy to see why. Compact cameras are relatively small, still just about pocket-sized, and offer good image quality (fig 8).

Digital compacts tend to use much larger CCD imaging chips than phone cameras and ultra compacts, with resulting increases in terms of image resolution (see page 46) and quality. Features unlikely to be found in smaller cameras – such as an LCD preview panel on the back and memory cards for image storage – are also standard.

Depending on the model (and how much you are prepared to spend) you will find either a fixed lens or a zoom (fig 9). Zoom lenses are preferred because, for the sake of a little more bulk, you get the opportunity to frame pictures better by cropping in on details and ensuring that superfluous elements are excluded. Most zoom lenses have a zoom ratio (that is, the amount they will magnify a scene) of around 3x, but some models offer 10x – though you

Fig 9 – Traditional styling characterizes many cameras in the compact class, yet they still boast a good optical zoom and multi-megapixel performance.

will have to pay a premium for this, both in financial terms and in terms of bulk.

THE DIGITAL ZOOM

The usefulness of a zoom lens is undoubted, but some cameras seem to offer prodigious zoom ratios, often at suspiciously low prices. Closer inspection of the camera's specifications shows that the zoom ratio is actually made up of two components. One is the conventional, optical ratio. This is the zoom achieved by optical means, adjusting the lens configuration to enlarge the image. The remainder, and often the larger amount, is attributed to a digital zoom.

The digital zoom merely takes the data from the central pixels of an image and enlarges them to the full size of the image. The result is a low-resolution image blown up to high-resolution dimensions. Frankly, avoid these. You end up with low-resolution images and large file sizes. You can achieve precisely the same result by enlarging part of an image using your computer's image-manipulation software.

Power compacts

At the top end of the compact range come the power compacts. These are the same compact size (or at least, nearly so), but with lots more features. Whereas a simple compact may have fully automatic exposure and focusing, these more serious machines will give you the opportunity to exercise at least some creative control. You can override the automatic

Fig 10 – More features and more controls give cameras such as this the opportunity to be used in a wider range of conditions without sacrificing portability and pocketability.

controls to compensate for unusual lighting situations or vary shutter speeds and aperture to suit the type of photographs you are taking. Some models will feature preprogrammed "scenes" that configure the controls to meet the needs of, say, sports, portrait, night or landscape photography.

The power compact (fig 10) is a great choice if you want to take good photographs but don't need the extra functionality (interchangeable lenses and flash modes for example) of the SLR.

SLRs and SLR-style cameras

The SLR is the stereotypical camera for professional photographers and the camera of choice for many enthusiasts (fig 11). For those who have not come across the term before, it stands for single lens reflex – harking back to a time when there were also twin lens reflex cameras in widespread use. In essence, the optical path through the camera means that the view you see though the viewfinder comes – via prisms and mirrors – through the lens of the camera itself. This makes it possible to compose and shoot a scene exactly as you see it in the viewfinder. In most – but not all – SLRs the lens can be detached and exchanged for others – perhaps a telephoto for enlarging distant views or a wide-angle for shooting in restricted spaces.

By virtue of the design and target market, these cameras tend to have the highest resolutions and offer the optimum in image

Fig 11 – Digital SLRs look much like their conventional counterparts until you take a look around the back. The LCD panel betrays their digital nature.

STILLS vs MOVIE

Not sure whether you want a stills camera or movie camera? There is no need to despair – many digital cameras will also record movie clips – often at a pretty high resolution that makes them only slightly inferior to digital video recorded on a digital camcorder.

And camcorders are increasingly able to offer a snapshot mode that takes multi-megapixel stills images and saves them to a memory card. You can then download the images from the card in the same way as you would those from a standard digital camera.

quality. They will also allow more rapid shooting than most other cameras, in the manner of their conventional motor-driven stablemates.

Because these cameras are produced in comparatively small numbers and are destined to be used by professionals and serious amateur photographers, they are expensive. This has created a market niche that sits between SLRs and the compact. Offering an electronic viewfinder rather than an optical one, and generally featuring a fixed zoom lens rather than detachable, interchangeable lenses, these compromises are reflected in the keener pricing.

Digital camera backs

In the rarefied atmosphere in which the professional photographer works, quality is paramount. This left photographers in something of a quandary. On the one hand, they needed the ultimate in quality; on the other, tight deadlines demanded fast results. For quality, film-based photography was required; for speed, it was digital.

The solution lay in digital backs for medium format cameras (fig 12). Medium format cameras – such as the Swedish icon, Hasselblad – use, as you might guess, a larger film format than 35mm compact and SLR cameras, and typically produce negatives measuring

Fig 12 – A digital back attached to a Hasselblad H1. If you have to ask the price, you can't afford it.

6 cm x 6 cm. By replacing the camera back (the interchangeable part of the camera in which the film is housed) with a large CCD sensor, the opportunity was created to produce large, high-resolution digital images.

The catch is the price. This really is a solution for the professional – for whom someone else is often paying the bill. But for several years, and probably many more to come, these systems offer the ultimate in quality. As a nod to the evolution in camera technology, Hasselblad's latest camera, the H1, has been designed from the ground up to accept either a digital or conventional camera back,

DIGITAL CAMRERA FEATURES

Except for the most basic, digital cameras appear festooned with buttons and switches. What do they all do and what do the icons mean? Here you can see a "typical" camera. It may not look exactly like yours, but don't worry about that. Once you have discovered which button does what, everything becomes much clearer.

POP-UP ELECTRONIC FLASH
(beneath cover)

OPTICAL VIEWFINDER

SHUTTER RELEASE BUTTON

SPEAKER

HANDGRIP

ZOOM LENS

Fig 13

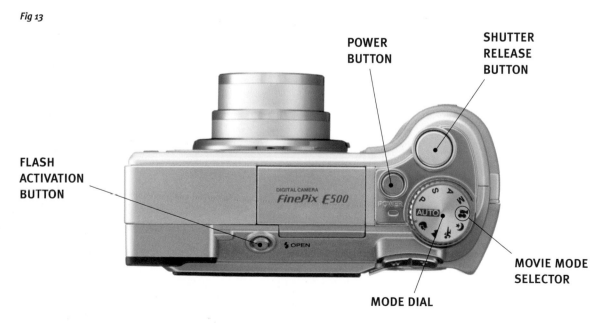

POWER BUTTON

SHUTTER RELEASE BUTTON

FLASH ACTIVATION BUTTON

MOVIE MODE SELECTOR

MODE DIAL

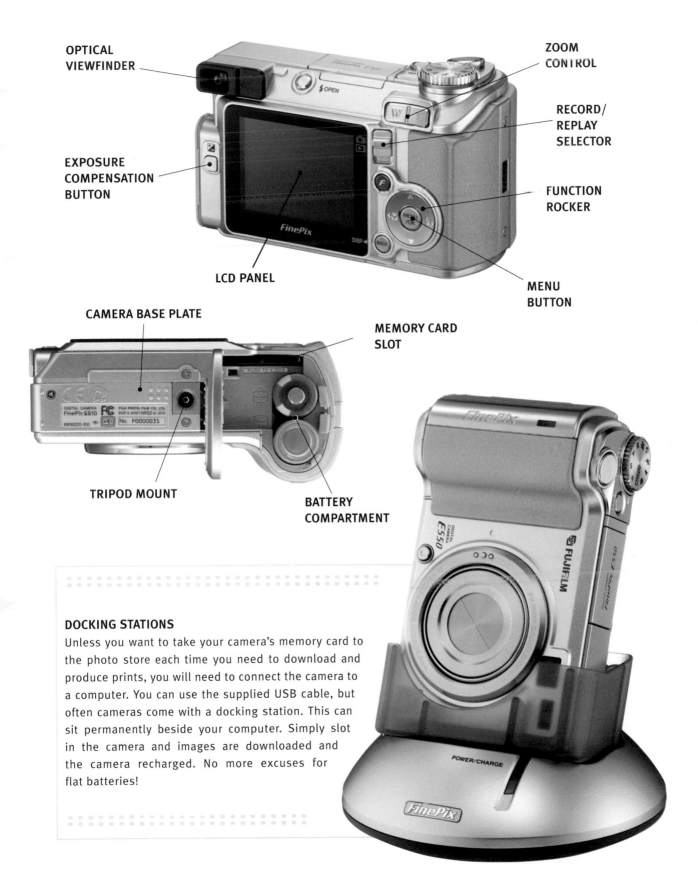

OPTICAL
VIEWFINDER

ZOOM
CONTROL

RECORD/
REPLAY
SELECTOR

EXPOSURE
COMPENSATION
BUTTON

FUNCTION
ROCKER

LCD PANEL

MENU
BUTTON

CAMERA BASE PLATE

MEMORY CARD
SLOT

TRIPOD MOUNT

BATTERY
COMPARTMENT

DOCKING STATIONS

Unless you want to take your camera's memory card to the photo store each time you need to download and produce prints, you will need to connect the camera to a computer. You can use the supplied USB cable, but often cameras come with a docking station. This can sit permanently beside your computer. Simply slot in the camera and images are downloaded and the camera recharged. No more excuses for flat batteries!

MASTERING YOUR DIGITAL CAMERA

If you are adept at using a conventional camera, you will find the switch to digital pretty painless. In fact, some of the features – such as the LCD panel for previewing and reviewing shots – makes creative use simpler. This instant feedback makes it easier to interpret the controls and functions and use them to your advantage.

For all the similarities, you will find that some controls differ, but even these are easy to master. And if you have never used any kind of camera with serious intent, this is the place to start. Here are some of the key features of a digital camera – and how to get the best from them.

LCD panel

This panel is the obvious distinguishing feature of a digital camera (fig 14). Although rarely more than a few square centimetres, this is a powerful compositional tool that allows you to preview shots instantly before committing them to the camera's memory. For most users, this is a more effective way of composing than using the viewfinder, which, on all but the professional cameras, tends to be rather small and difficult to use.

When coming to understand the creative tools and controls of the camera, seeing how these are interpreted on screen is an incredible help. Moreover, it gives you the reassurance that you have been successful in capturing images the way you intended, not merely the way the camera interpreted your vision.

White balance

Although most light sources do not produce pure white illumination, our eye/brain combination is so remarkably adept at making corrections we hardly ever notice. Conventional tungsten light bulbs, for example, produce a distinctly amber light, while overcast skies can produce a cold, bluish cast. And fluorescent lighting can deliver casts that are green through to purple-magenta (fig 15).

The auto white balance feature on a digital camera will attempt to correct any colour cast by analysing the colours in a scene and adjusting them to conform to a "neutral" standard. For most of the time this feature work wells and delivers accurate colour results. But it can be too effective. Sunsets, for example, where we want to retain the strongly saturated pinks, reds and purples, can look washed out as the auto colour balance determines the colour as an unwanted cast.

In these situations, take the colour balance off automatic and set the control manually to one that is appropriate to the scene. In the example of the sunset, you might set the balance to Daylight. Setting the balance manually can also give better overall results in mixed lighting conditions, but it's a good idea to reset it to Auto once you have finished, to avoid taking a lot of pictures with the wrong colour balance.

Sensitivity

When we load a conventional camera with film, that film has a particular sensitivity to light. This is described in terms of a standard scale – the ISO scale. An ISO200 film has twice the sensitivity of an ISO100 film, and an ISO400 film twice the sensitivity of an ISO200 film. The higher the sensitivity, the shorter the exposure needs to be. This makes it possible, for example, to select a fast shutter speed and so hand-hold shots in low light rather than having to use a tripod. It also means you can take shots in darker conditions than would be feasible with slower films (fig 16).

Why, then, don't we always use ISO400

Fig 14 – The rear LCD panel (a feature of virtually every digital camera) makes it simple to check that your photo was spot on.

Fig 15 – White balance: a correctly balanced image (Auto balance) compared with the same image shot with Tungsten Lighting and Fluorescent balances.

or even ISO800 films at all times? The trouble is that the faster films have a sting in their tail: the higher their sensitivity, the more grainy their images. If you want the sharpest results you need to use a slower (less sensitive) film. Shoot with film rated at ISO100, or even ISO50, and grain is virtually invisible. Assuming you have a first-rate camera and lens, this film produces images that can be enlarged significantly before grain becomes apparent.

So what has this to do with a digital camera, that

Fig 16 – Increasing the sensitivity from ISO200 to ISO1600 has revealed more subject detail, but the "noise" (and the contrast in the image) has become noticeably worse.

uses no film? In many respects, beyond the obvious, the CCD or CMOS chip of the camera behaves very like a film emulsion. In fact, we can change chip sensitivity: some cameras offer an effective range of ISO100 to ISO400, while other professional models offer a ISO50 to ISO1600 range. Like film, though, when we operate at a higher ISO rating, image quality deteriorates through the digital equivalent of grain – "noise".

Noise occurs in all electronic circuits, but normally the signals are much larger, so the noise has a negligible effect. But when working at very low signal levels (representing low light levels), this noise becomes obvious and manifests as spurious colours and general image degradation.

Such degradation comes into effect only at extreme ISO ratings, however, so when you use ISO100, ISO200 and even ISO400 with most cameras you can be sure of technically good results.

Resolution

The key selling point promoted by many manufacturers of digital cameras is the resolution (fig 17). This describes how detailed your image will be and how much detail can (theoretically at least) be recorded. It is usually expressed in terms of megapixels – millions of pixels (or picture elements). The camera CCD will record the brightness and colour at each of these points, so clearly the more points, the better the resolution and the better the image detail.

Digital camera experts might take exception here and point out that each pixel measures only one colour – red, green or blue – and the actual colour of a pixel is determined by averaging adjacent pixels. But for our purposes, it is acceptable to consider each pixel as recording the appropriate colour for that part of the image.

The more pixels that comprise the picture, the larger it can be printed before the pixel nature of the image becomes obvious. So if you want to produce a full-page photograph, a high-resolution camera is essential; if you want snapshots for your website, high resolution is not so crucial.

High-resolution cameras offer modes for recording images at lower resolutions, but why would you want to do this? If you were gathering

Fig 17 – Increasing resolution allows more detail to be recorded, as these enlargements of part of an image illustrate.

images for web use, for example, then the extra quality might be superfluous, and by opting to save images at small file sizes you will be able to fit considerably more on a memory card.

Shutter lag and recycling time

Here is an area where some digital cameras fall behind their conventional stablemates in performance terms. When you press the shutter release on a normal camera, the shutter opens momentarily afterwards. If it is in fully auto mode, the camera will determine exposure, set the focus, close the lens down to the correct aperture and open the shutter. In a digital camera the CCD needs also to be primed, which adds to the delay, making the lag before the picture is taken slightly, but perceptibly, longer. Although this time is still short, it can be enough for you to miss that crucial moment for your photograph.

The solution is partly to press the shutter so that focus and exposure are set and the CCD readied prior to the shot. Then, when you press the shutter release further, the shutter is activated almost instantaneously.

The recycling time is the time taken for the camera to download an image from the CCD and prepare it for the next shot. Many cameras now use memory buffers that store the image data before writing that image to the memory card, which gives a short effective recycling time. But even these cameras will fill their buffers if you shoot several shots in rapid succession. If action photography is your speciality – where fast, consecutive shots are most likely to be used – it pays to check the shooting speed and recycling time for your intended purchase.

Sharpness

Some digital controls can actually improve the images you shoot. The white balance control is one of these. Sharpness control is another, but it is a more controversial option (fig 18). It adds to the perceived sharpness of the image by, essentially, sharpening the edges in an image. It is an artificial sharpening and does not make up for not getting an image sharp in the first place.

Most photographers turn this camera control off. You can add sharpness in a more controlled fashion

Fig 18 – Sharpness: sharpening in the camera (lower image) can give an overly sharpened effect, one that makes the image look artificial, with the edges of subject details, particularly, looking too prominent.

later using image-manipulation software, but you can't remove the artificial sharpening from an image once it is shot.

RAW images

If you want to avoid the camera making any corrections or manipulations on your behalf, you need to set the camera to record RAW mode files. Not all cameras will do this; it tends to be middle-market through to the top-end models that offer this feature. When you store an image as a RAW file, you have the data that has been recorded by the CCD without any processing.

Professional photographers often use RAW as a matter of course, because mostly – though not always – it gives the best results. But RAW files are larger and cannot be directly imported into many image applications. You will need to resort to a serious image editor, such as Photoshop, to process your images first. Large files also mean that fewer images will be stored on the memory card.

PRINTING YOUR PHOTOS

Printers today – even budget models – can offer astonishing quality, which, in most regards, is equivalent to conventional photos. But what if you want something different? A large, poster print? Or a specially bound photo album? Or even a personalized T-shirt?

You won't be surprised to know that all these great (and quite a few not so great) photo products on offer to conventional photographers are also available to digital photographers. And you can create and order online.

Here's how simple it is to create an album digitally. Not just any album – this is a fully bound and professionally printed one. To create this, iPhoto has been used, but other applications are available that enable you to make similar products.

1. Collect your images together. You will need to put them in a new electronic album folder. Make sure that they are in the right order. It will make your job easier if you drag the image that you want to use on the cover to the front of the list. Double check that all images are OK. Any that are below

Fig 19

Fig 20

Fig 21

Fig 22

Fig 23

Fig 24

Fig 25

Fig26

par will need to be either replaced or manipulated to improve them. When you are happy, click the Order Book button (fig 19).

2. Wait. iPhoto will now automatically compile your album. It makes a best guess at the layout, mixing styles and layouts to produce an album that will be interesting to look at (fig 20).

3. When the process is complete, begin by adding a title for the book. This will be printed on the cover and needs to be clear and concise (fig 21).

4. You can now start manipulating the content. Click on a page if you want to change the layout, and then click on the Page Design pull-down menu. You can now alter (either up or down) the number of images on the selected page. When you add images, those on subsequent pages are included; when you reduce the number, the last images on the page are pushed over to the next (fig 22).

5. In this case, the number of images on the page has been reduced to two. The two images that remain on the page are rescaled to make best use of the page (fig 23).

6. You can also drag images around manually to alter the look and layout (fig 24).

7. When you have finished, review the results to make sure that your changes to the layout have not produced any gaffes. Then hit Order. Your album is emailed to the photolab and, a few days later, your book will be delivered! (fig 25).

8. High-quality printing via an archival printer will ensure that you have an album you can enjoy for years to come (fig 26).

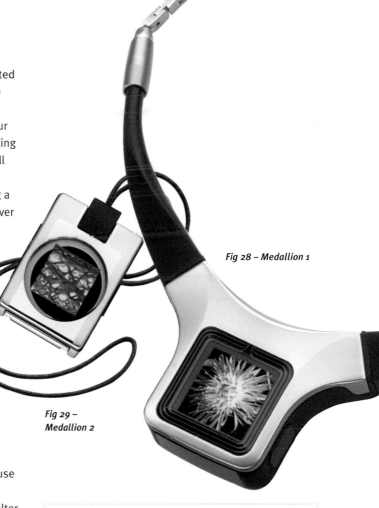

Fig 28 – Medallion 1

Fig 29 – Medallion 2

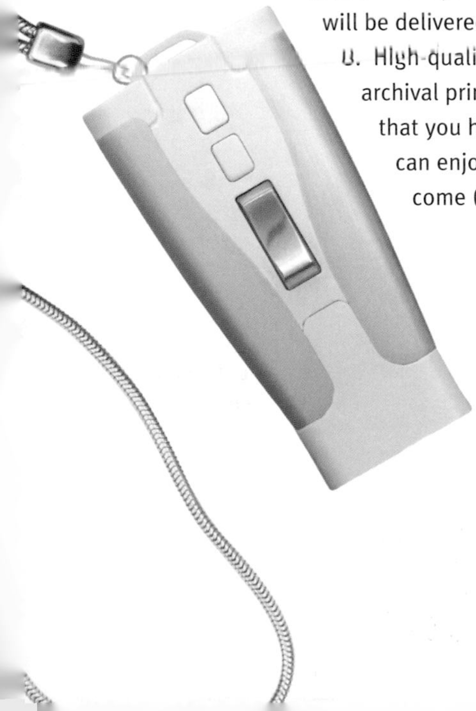

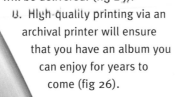

Fig 27 – Kaleidoscope 1

NOKIA IMAGEWEAR

Can any use of an image be as wacky as these from the mobile phone giant Nokia? Imagewear lets you take images (presumably with your camera phone) and turn them into head-turning jewellery pieces.

Medallion I (fig 28) is a choker-style necklace with a small square image panel on to which you can beam your selected image. You can also change the image at will – the medallion can store eight images and display them on the modest 96 x 96 pixel screen. Medallion II (fig 29) offers a similar display on a more conventional necklace.

Kaleidoscope I (fig 27) is for those who are a little more discreet. Up to 24 images can be stored in this compact unit, even more using an optional Multimedia Card. You can examine individual images or watch a picture show through the eyepiece.

MOBILE PHOTO SERVICES

When camera phones first arrived they were scoffed at – their low resolution, small lenses and awkwardness to use rendered them irrelevant in the eyes of photography commentators. But improved quality, performance and operation have brought wider acceptance. Now they offer – by virtue of their connectivity – services that cameras alone cannot.

LIFEBLOGGING – MOBILE PHOTOGRAPHY FROM NOKIA

If you learn one lesson when you begin digital photography, it's how many more pictures you take compared with conventional photography. The same applies to those of us who use camera phones. Very quickly your phone's memory limit is reached. So what do you do with the photos then? Nokia – one of the leading producers of camera phones – has the answer. It's called Lifeblog (Figs 30–32).

Lifeblog is a set of software applications, for both your camera and PC, that means you can use your photo collection as part of a multimedia diary. The great feature of Lifeblog is that it will automatically organize not only your photos, but also, if your camera supports it, video, multimedia messages and even text messages. By placing them all in chronological order, they become easy to track. Synchronizing computer and phone in this way means that you always have the most relevant photos and information on your phone. Anything that you don't designate as a favourite is removed but safely archived on your phone.

Because all your media is stored on your computer it becomes easier to sift through important and less-important material. And to make it more relevant, when downloaded to the computer you can add notes to the images and video.

Lifeblog is totally automatic – you don't need to have the software running on your phone. Once installed, it will begin building your diary, adding new images and video to the record. The next time you connect with your computer, all this new content will download and free up space on the phone for your next round of photography.

Of course, in your image collection there will be those images that you want to keep on the phone – photos of family or, perhaps, videos of some recent events that you want to share. By placing these in the Favourites section, you can ensure they are synchronized between PC and camera. You can use a version of the Timeline program, similar to that used on the computer, to find and navigate your media.

Fig 30 – Downloaded digital assets – photos, messages and video – are displayed in a pseudo-diary format that makes them easy to browse by date. You can also add notes to supplement your memories or explain the content that has been downloaded from your camera.

Fig 31 – The timeline on your computer can also be displayed on your phone's display. This makes it easy to review your Lifeblog and share its contents, either by using your phone handset or by sending selected items to someone else with a compatible camera phone.

Fig 32 – No matter how prolific your photography, you can track down all the photos and video you have recorded by simply using the Timeline view.

MOBILE PHOTOGRAPHY FROM KODAK

Launched towards the end of 2003 in the United States and about six months later in Europe, Kodak's Mobile Photography service (fig 33) is a resource offering camera phone users access to both digital photos and digital video. It's a very comprehensive service that allows users to manage, print and share photos and do much the same (with the exception of printing) with their video content. In particular, registered users can:

1. Store all the images and video from their phone (or phones) in one central location.
2. Have prints produced and delivered from their phone or via the Kodak Mobile website.
3. Share all the resources on their phone or those stored at the Kodak Mobile central servers.
4. Organize, manage and view all their images and video from the website or remotely via their phone.

The good thing about this service (and similar ones) is that the operators don't demand that you have the latest generation of phone. As long as you have a camera phone and it is capable of supporting the WAP 2.0 protocol (as virtually all camera phones can) you can set up and use an account.

Fig 34 – You can also print images from your phone yourself using Kodak Print Kiosks. In this case, you can even perform simple edits on images or choose alternate sizes. However, images from camera phones with small megapixel counts should not be printed too large – results will look better when printed smaller.

Fig 33 – The Kodak Mobile imaging service is available from your phone handset or computer. If you take a great photo and you want prints made from it straight away, you can order them with just a few clicks on your handset.

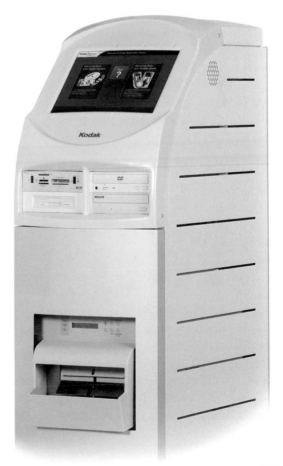

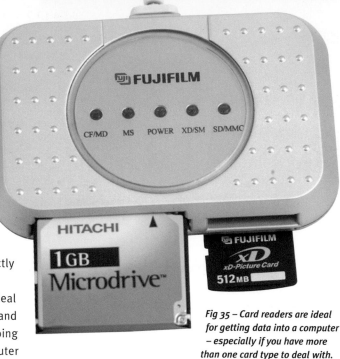

ALL ABOUT MEMORY CARDS

Memory cards have rapidly become a popular way of storing and exchanging digital data. We are familiar with them for storing digital images, MP3 music and personal data on our PDAs, but memory card slots are also finding their way into mobile phones, digital radios, camcorders and even televisions. Printers, too, will now accept memory cards from cameras and print images directly from them.

With capacities of up to 8GB, they are ideal for storing large amounts of information and provide a surprisingly robust method of doing so. At their core is a special type of computer memory known as flash memory. This is a non-volatile memory that retains information when the cards are removed from a host device. Later, that information can be deleted and new data stored. The name, incidentally, is attributed to Toshiba, which found that the cards could be erased "in a flash".

Memory cards come in a variety of shapes, sizes and capacities. Some are compatible only with a single device; those used in games consoles are a good example. Others conform to a standard that makes them usable across a range of devices. Today, your digital devices are likely to be one of the following main types:

Fig 35 – Card readers are ideal for getting data into a computer – especially if you have more than one card type to deal with.

- CompactFlash
- SmartMedia
- Secure Digital
- MultiMedia Card
- xD Picture Card
- Memory Stick

Fig 36 – CompactFlash is the big daddy of cards – in capacity as well as physical size.

Since you are likely to come across one or more of these, let's look at each a little more closely.

CompactFlash (CF)

The most bulky of the cards, CompactFlash (fig 36) is the staple of many digital cameras because its size offers a degree of ruggedness and space for high-performance memory. Dating back to 1994, the first cards had modest capacities of only a few megabytes, but this has multiplied and 1, 2 and 4GB cards are now commonplace.

Significantly, they feature a controller chip that handles onboard memory management. This makes it possible to store large quantities of data – such as from a fast-shooting digital camera – quickly.

A variation of the CompactFlash is the MicroDrive. Originally produced by IBM, this is nothing less than a tiny hard drive. Originally they had the advantage of substantially higher capacity than solid state cards, but this advantage has been lost as solid state cards offer increasingly higher memory.

SmartMedia (SM)

Diminutive and wafer thin, SmartMedia cards (fig 37) are characterized by a gold chip on the front, similar to those found on credit cards. The size of the card means there is insufficient space for a controller to be incorporated: this needs to be built into the host equipment – the camera or PDA. Although small, SmartMedia cards are still larger than some alternatives, but they have topped out at capacities of 128MB, meaning they are now used

Fig 37 – Commonly compromised by limited capacity, the SmartMedia card is distinguished by the gold "chip".

only in those digital cameras with modest performance.

Secure Digital (SD) and MultiMedia Cards (MMC)

We can discuss these two types together as they share the same shape (or "footprint") and some devices can use either card interchangeably. Smaller than SmartMedia cards, they are available in a range of sizes up to 1GB, though larger capacities will be introduced. The key difference between the two is that SD cards can be used to store copyrighted material and prevent unauthorized copying – important for ensuring that the copying of MP3 music and copyright images is properly managed. They are most commonly found in MP3 players, phones and PDAs.

xD Picture Card

A comparatively recent introduction, xD Picture Cards were designed by Fuji and Olympus partly so as to overcome the capacity limitations of SmartMedia and partly to produce a small-sized card that could be freely used in their cameras. The discussion at the launch included the ability to produce smaller cameras. The cards – about the size of a thumbnail and of similar shape – are offered in capacities similar to those of SD cards and they remain – at the moment – confined to Fuji and Olympus cameras.

Memory Stick

Sony, never shy about launching a new format, introduced the Memory Stick (fig 38) as a portable storage medium for camcorders,

FAST CARDS

Some memory cards attract a premium price because they have a higher rated "speed", often described at "20X", "40X" or more. What does this mean and are they worth the money?

The speed describes a card's ability to have data written to or read from it. In approximate terms, a 20X card transfers data at 3MB/second, 40X at 6 MB/second. This is particularly important, as has already been noted, for digital cameras, where image data can come thick and fast. If you plan to use your camera for fast shooting (such as sports photography), a fast card can give you the potential of better performance and more shots before your camera stalls.

cameras, music players and computers. Now Memory Stick slots can be found in at least some models across Sony's broad portfolio. The original Memory Sticks offered a moderately large-sized card and fairly modest capacities, but this was enhanced with the launch of the Memory Stick Duo (smaller footprint) and Memory Stick Pro (larger capacities). The latter also comes in "Duo" form, offering the smaller footprint.

Compatibility between card types is an issue – the cards feature controller cards and it is important to check that the more recent, larger-capacity cards will work in older devices.

Fig 38 – The Memory Stick family, including Pro, Duo and an adaptor to use with original format card-based devices.

FIXING YOUR PHOTOS

Even with years of experience, photographs never turn out quite as you expect them to. The weather may not be quite right or you totally overlooked an electricity pylon that now dominates your photo. Or the picture's too dark, too light or lacking in colour. Get to grips with image-manipulation software and you can make poor pictures OK, and good photos great. Here are some quick fixes you can apply in seconds:

RED-EYE

You probably know the effect. Stone-cold sober yet the photos seem to tell a different story. Eyes have a red, demonic look. It's called, naturally enough, red-eye and it's due to the light from a camera's flash reflecting directly off the blood-rich retina at the back of the eye. Most cameras have an anti-red-eye setting on the flash, which uses a series of preflashes to make the iris contract before the main flash fires. They rarely work.

Don't worry – fixing this with image-editing software is simple. In some cases, you will find a red-eye brush that you can move over the offending colour to remove it. But in most applications there is a correction tool something like this.

1. Here is the original photo. Children, and babies in particular, are more prone to red-eye as their eyes take longer to adjust to lighting changes (fig 39).
2. Select the Red-eye tool. This may be from a button, as here, or a menu command, depending on what application software you are using (fig 40).
3. Using the mouse, drag a selection over one or both eyes. In some applications, the tool works by taking away the red colour from the selected area. In this case you will need to make your selection of the areas just around the iris to avoid affecting the skin colour too (fig 41).
4. When you release the mouse button, the red-eye is removed instantly. The result is entirely natural. From devil to angel at a stroke (fig 42).

Pets also suffer from this effect, but the result tends to be green- rather than red-eye. Red-eye tools don't usually work with colours other than red, so if you want to correct the problem in a favourite cat or dog shot, you'll need to use the Paintbrush tool to paint over the green.

ADDING COLOUR

So we know how to remove colour where it's not wanted, but what if we want to add more colour? How many times have you returned from a trip or holiday and been disappointed by your pictures? Somehow the photographs never look as colourful

Fig 42

Fig 41

Fig 39

Fig 40

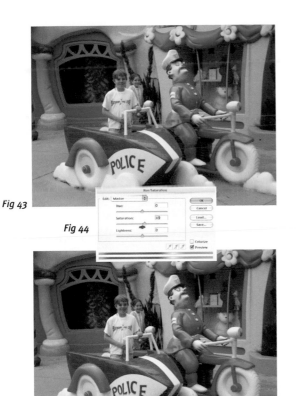

Fig 43

Fig 44

Fig 45

moving the Hue slider by just 2 per cent it was possible to make the sky less cyan and more blue in colour (fig 45).

BETTER COLOUR

Sometimes the colour recorded by the camera is not entirely as you expected. It is not that the colour is pale or weak, as has been described above, rather that there are colour casts present. Sometimes casts occur because you set the wrong white balance on the camera (see page 44) or there were natural colour casts due to overcast skies during the day or low, reddish-coloured light in the morning or evening. Whatever the cause, there is a simple fix. It's called Auto Levels in some applications or Auto Enhance in others (figs 46, 47).

This useful cure-all analyses your image and determines if the spread of colours, brightness and contrast need to be adjusted in order to match those that would be expected in an "average" photograph. It can work wonders on most photos, adding a little sparkle missing in the original.

It's probably worth pointing out that this control does not work every time. Where you may have strong colours in the scene, Auto Levels can sometimes overcompensate and remove them. In these cases, stick with the original or explore some of the manual correction tools on offer.

as you remember the real thing. But it's simple to boost the colour – either selectively or across the whole image – to produce a result that will make you the envy of your friends and family.

1. Here's a typical photo anyone might take. Although it's actually a pretty accurate representation of the scene, the colours are not vibrant. Wouldn't it be better if we could adjust them and make them more saturated, perhaps like those we see in travel brochures (fig 43)?
2. Using the Hue/Saturation control, it's possible to make our adjustments. This lets you increase or decrease the colour saturation of a photo. In this case, the slider control was moved to the right to increase colour saturation. It's important not to overcorrect – if the colours become oversaturated, they will look artificial and also produce problems when printing (fig 44).
3. Here is the finished image. By increasing the colour saturation by less than 10 per cent, a much more punchy result has been achieved. And by

Fig 46

Fig 47

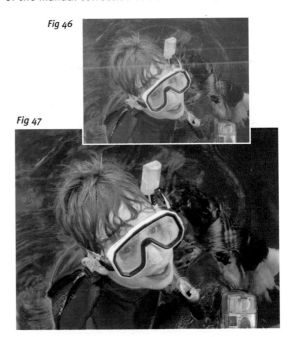

CROPPING

The great thing about zoom lenses is that they allow you to frame your subject with a flexibility simply not possible using a fixed lens. You can zoom in and remove any distracting surroundings to your portraits, for example, cropping out distractions that might otherwise mar results, or zoom back and show your subject in its proper context.

The trouble is, the framing of the subject in the camera's viewfinder – even that of an SLR – is only approximate. The same applies to the LCD preview screen. The good news is that both viewfinder and LCD tend to err on the side of caution and show you less of the image than is actually recorded. So you can make your final crop of the image later. Here's how to do it:

1. It's all down to the Crop tool. Here you can begin by selecting the area of the image that you want to retain (in some applications, such as Photoshop Elements, you will need to select the crop tool first). In this case, the area outside the selection, is lightened (fig 48).

2. Hit the Crop button to effect the crop. If you make a mistake and have taken away too much, don't worry. In virtually every application you can select the Edit menu and then Undo or Step Backward to restore the image to its original state (fig 49).

3. Here is the cropped image. Superfluous detail has been trimmed away and you can concentrate on the girl and the prized ticket in her hand (fig 50).

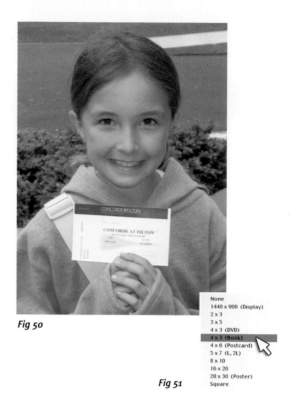

Fig 50

Fig 51

Sometimes it is necessary to crop images to a particular ratio. For example, you may want to trim an image to fit a photo frame or the dimensions of a television screen if you are preparing images for inclusion in a multimedia presentation. The Constrain feature lets you select an aspect ratio. When you drag your selection with a chosen ratio, the crop will be automatically scaled (fig 51).

ART EFFECTS

Most image-manipulation software includes a range of software filters that can transform your images into subtle works of art or something more eye-popping in nature. Used with care, they can make your photos really stand out.

"Use with care" is something to bear firmly in mind when using photo filters, as some are so crude in their effect that they immediately betray the fact that they have been used. There's a fine line between art and kitsch.

Here (Figs 52–60) are examples of some of the more effective filters. Remember that you can play around with these and just hit the Undo button if the effect is not what you want.

Fig 48

Fig 49

Fig 52 – The original image.

Fig 53 – Palette Knife simulates the effect of using a palette knife with acrylic or oil paints.

Fig 54 – Dry Brush applies a subtle brushed effect.

Fig 55 – Waterpaper gives the impression that the image has been painted on to absorbent watercolour paper.

Fig 56 – Posterize reduces the number of hues in the photo to leave areas of well-demarcated areas of flat colour.

Fig 57 – There is no mistaking the Solarization effect, which essentially reverses some of the colour and tone

Fig 58 – Conte Crayon, with a canvas base texture, produces a subtle, hand-drawn appearance.

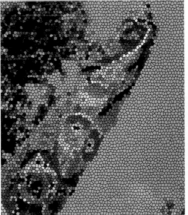

Fig 59 – Stained glass breaks the image into small cells of even colour and adds a border to each.

Fig 60 – Craquelure is ideal if you want to make your photos look as if they are printed on a highly textured surface.

IMPROVING REALITY

Perhaps the most startling of image-manipulation tricks involves the Clone tool. Sometimes called the Rubber Stamp, this is the tool that can be used to hide unwanted elements, move subjects (even between different photos) or copy selected parts of your pictures.

Here the clone tool has been used to cure a problem that occurs all too often. The girl in this photograph blinked at the crucial moment. In this example, the eyes of the girl's brother are open, so we can clone these across (figs 61–63).

Fig 62 – The boy's left eye has been cloned over the girl's left eye.

Fig 63 – Now both eyes have been cloned. It is not as good as catching the girl with her eyes open, of course, but it certainly rescues a shot that would otherwise be consigned to the computer's trash can.

Fig 61 – The original image showing the girl's eyes closed.

Fig 64

Fig 65

Here is a more extreme use of the Clone tool. This photograph of a cottage in a Cotswold village is undoubtedly picturesque, but from the photographer's point of view it is cluttered by cabling and other ephemera of contemporary living (fig 64). With some subtle use of the clone tool we can replace unwanted parts of the scene using material copied from elsewhere (fig 65). To achieve this effect is painstaking and time-consuming, but not difficult.

MONTAGE

In digital photography anything, it seems, is possible. Once you begin to explore all the tools and features embedded in even the most modest of software packages you will come to realize the truth of this. Some call it cheating, others creative, but there is no doubt that montage is one of the best ways of creating new images from parts of others. Here you will see how to create a scene that never existed in reality.

1. Let's take this girl and astronaut and place them against a new background, the Mission Space pavilion at Disney's Epcot. Here are both the original images (figs 66, 67).

2. The first step is to cut out the girl and astronaut. We can use a selection tool called the Magnetic Lasso to do this. You drag it around the edge of the parts of the image you want to select and it automatically aligns itself. Alternatively, you can use the Eraser tool to rub away the background. As in darkroom photography, digital photography often gives you several ways to achieve the same effect (fig 68).

3. We can now place our cut-out selection on the new background. Simply use the Copy command to copy the selection from the original image and then, in the new image, use the Paste command (fig 69).

That's all there is to it. Of course, it doesn't always work out as easily as this. If the two source images have a different resolution (for example, if they were taken with different cameras) or different colour balance, you would have to adjust the images accordingly to marry them together seamlessly.

Fig 66

Fig 67

Fig 68

Fig 69

PHOTOGRAPHY WITHOUT WIRES

When you own a digital camera, at some point you will need to connect it to a device to download images. But this physical connection is increasingly irksome to users – now that computer peripherals, such as keyboards, mice and even printers, can work wirelessly, why can't our cameras? The answer is they can.

Using both Wireless and Bluetooth (see pages 30), you can download images (remotely or locally) and even print. Bluetooth print adaptors will transform a compatible printer

Fig 70 – By building Bluetooth communications into a CompactFlash memory card for printers designed to accept such cards, they can instantly be converted into wireless printers. Devices featuring Secure Digital memory cards (SD) can also be equipped with a Bluetooth-enabled card – you can then print direct from a PDA camera or (at a more mundane level) print out documents directly from your PDA.

into a wireless device that can (subject to the usual "ifs" and "buts") print photos directly from a computer, a phone or a PDA (figs 70, 72, 74), if they also have Bluetooth. This is a convenient way of printing out all those casual photos taken with your cameras without the hassle of having to download them to your computer first. True, you are a little limited in the way you can manipulate photos (limited to the controls on the printer itself), but for getting prints to hand around to friends and family, it is a great solution.

Bluetooth media players are an even better way to enjoy photos with your friends. With one of these attached to your television, all you need do is display photos on your phone and ensure that Bluetooth is on. Then create a live slideshow direct from your phone – or your friends'

Fig 71 – Media players, such as this one from Anycom, make it simple to transfer media from a mobile phone or camera directly to a television using Bluetooth. The small media-player unit simply connects to an input in the same manner as a set-top box or camcorder.

Fig 73 – Concord Camera's WIT – Wireless Image Transfer – makes it simple and fast to transfer images from a camera via email.

conventional mobile phone with GRPS. Even video transfer becomes more viable using this method of transmission.

This option is brilliant for downloading images from your camera's memory card without the need to take a computer laptop with you, or even a portable hard-disc storage device. You can spend your time away from home safe in the knowledge that your images will be waiting for you in your email inbox.

Ultimately, expect to see this technology included in some cameras. The extra expense and bulk that an integral device like this would add mean that we are unlikely to see all cameras equipped with it, but as an option in mid-market and professional cameras it is sure to be a winner.

Fig 72 – Converting virtually any printer to Bluetooth operation requires only a simple adaptor connected to the USB socket. With this attached, data from a Bluetooth-enabled device is interpreted in a form that the printer can understand, as if directly connected to the device.

phones – to the screen (fig 71).

Although not commonplace, some cameras can also communicate directly with a printer – or a media player – via Bluetooth. Again, it's a simple way to get prints fast without the need to connect cables.

If you are further afield, you have had the capability for some time of using your mobile phone to connect to laptops and cameras to download images, but often the logistics and costs involved limit this option to professionals only.

For the rest of us, there is a solution in the WIT from Concord Camera Corporation (fig 73). The small, palm-sized unit connects to a camera's USB port and allows images to be transmitted wirelessly using fast 802.11g standards. Using this, a 5-megapixel image can be transferred in well under a second – 1,500 times faster than using a

Fig 74 – With a compact printer (such as the HP model shown here) and a Bluetooth adaptor (either built into the printer or connected via USB), a portable printer becomes much more viable.

CREATING WEB PHOTO GALLERIES

Web photo galleries are a great way to show your photos in a virtual album. A gallery is also a versatile medium: you can save your album to CD or DVD, on your computer's hard disc, a virtual disc or on the web itself. Anyone who has access to the disc or web can use a web browser, such as Internet Explorer or Safari, to view and explore your gallery.

Here you will see how to create a gallery using Photoshop Elements.

1. Gather together all the photos you want to use in an electronic folder. This will be your Source folder. If you want to edit your photos – say, trim them or correct any other problems – do it now. You will also need to create a second new Destination folder. This is where all the processed images and web page files will be placed (fig 75).

2. In Photoshop Elements, choose File menu ····⟩ Create Web Photo Gallery. The creation is automatic; you just have to configure the dialogue box to get the results you want. From the Styles pull-down menu, choose a style. This will give a look to the web page (a thumbnail image indicates the appearance of each selection). Also in this dialogue box, enter a Banner name in the Options menu. The banner name will be displayed across the top of the page. Optionally, you can enter the photographer's name, date and even a contact number or site (fig 76).

3. In the Folders section, use the Browse button to

Fig 75

Fig 76

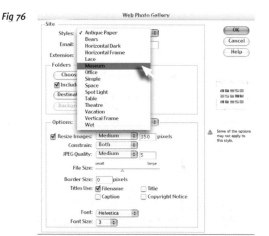

Fig 77

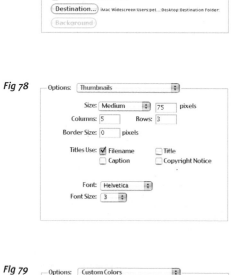

Fig 78

Fig 79

select the Source and Destination folders. These can be placed anywhere, but the Destination folder must not be within the Source folder (fig 77).

4. Image Display. You can choose how images are displayed, along with those of the thumbnails. The thumbnails are the small images that, when clicked on, will display corresponding larger versions. If this is your first time, use the default settings already in place; you can always return later and alter them to get the precise look that you want (fig 78).

5. You can personalize the gallery further by choosing a colour scheme using the Custom Colors selection from the Options pull-down menu. Try not to be too radical in your selection. The web page should be a backdrop to your images, not compete with them for your audience's attention (fig 79).

6. Click OK to start the web page generation. This will take a few minutes, but you can monitor progress on screen, seeing the thumbnails and web images being generated. Once complete, the web browser will open and display your web gallery (Fig 80)

PUBLISHING A GALLERY WITH iPHOTO

Creating and publishing a web photo gallery with iPhoto is even simpler. Begin by selecting your images from the Photo Library or an Album. Then click on the HomePage button. Choose a theme, enter captions and hit Publish. Job done. Limitations? You'll need to have a .mac account and you are limited to

the dozen or so themes. But you can have your page on the web in minutes – great for showing off your day out.

Fig 80

DIGITAL VIDEO

IN THIS CHAPTER WE DISCOVER:

- The roots of digital video.
- Get to grips with the features and tools of modern digital video cameras.
- Look at how to take an informal video you can be proud to show to family and friends.
- Learn how simple it is to edit and embellish your movies using your computer.

THE MODERN CAMCORDER PROVIDES EXCEPTIONAL PICTURE QUALITY, IT IS EASY TO USE AND HAS AN IMPRESSIVE TECHNICAL SPECIFICATION. EFFECTIVE AUTOMATIC EXPOSURE AND IMAGING MODES MAKE FOR GREAT MOVIES UNDER A WIDE RANGE OF CONDITIONS, WHILE THE DIGITAL NATURE MAKES IT SIMPLE TO EDIT AND ENHANCE THE RECORDED FOOTAGE. SOME MODELS EVEN LET YOU EMAIL MOVIE CLIPS DIRECT FROM ANYWHERE IN THE WORLD.

THE WAY WE WERE

Go back just a few years and you would things rather different. First, there were no camcorders as we now know them. You would be restricted to using film-based cine cameras. Though smaller, more compact and easier to use than those used in commercial film-making, they were by no means pocketable. This led to the second difference: movie-making. Even on an informal level, such as recording family events, you definitely needed to be an enthusiast.

Once the film was processed, you would need to labour at an editing station to trim the movie footage and reassemble the component shots into a logical sequence. Your audience could then sit around the projector and enjoy (or, in most cases, endure) the performance. And a running commentary, rather than soundtrack, would be necessary to add to the atmosphere.

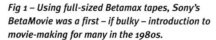
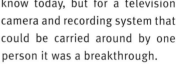

Fig 1 – Using full-sized Betamax tapes, Sony's BetaMovie was a first – if bulky – introduction to movie-making for many in the 1980s.

The dawn of portable video

When Super-8 cine cameras – those that used convenient film cartridges and could be described as the most user-friendly – were at their most popular, around the late 1960s, the first steps towards a convenient, portable video format were being taken. The Sony PortaPak was not portable in the sense we know today, but for a television camera and recording system that could be carried around by one person it was a breakthrough.

Within a few years, the cameras became smaller and smaller and, moving on from the early monochrome systems, colour cameras and recording became possible.

The video tape cassette

Nineteen seventy-one saw the next breakthrough: U-Matic tape cassettes. Until then, video tape recording had followed the basic format of audio recording, with reels of tape being fed through the machine (except the video tape's path through the

Fig 2 – Semi-professional video cameras offer a ragne of facilities similar to those of a professional television camera.

recorder was more cumbersome than that of audio tape). With U-Matic, narrow, half-inch tape was contained within a cassette that was simply dropped into the recorder.

Soon Sony revealed that it was working on another format destined for the consumer market. This would offer even smaller cassettes and longer recording time for only a modest decrease in picture quality. This was the format ultimately known as Betamax. In parallel, JVC was developing its own format, dubbed the Video Home System (VHS) – the same one that we still use – if in ever-decreasing numbers – today.

Both formats quickly established themselves for home recording, timeshifting and the replaying of pre-recorded tapes, but it took a little time for portable versions to appear. The first were two-piece units, aping those of a decade earlier. A video camera comprising imaging tubes (rather than the CCDs) would be connected to a substantial shoulder-mounted recording unit. The latter was very similar to its domestic counterpart in size and weight, but often without the timer and tuner features to save weight and cost.

The camcorder is born

In 1982 both Sony and JVC launched single-piece video camera recorders, a name that was rapidly contracted to camcorder. Sony's version was Betamovie (fig 1). A small (for its

Fig 3 – Sharp virtually invented the LCD panel viewing screens with its analogue Viewcams. The ability to shoot overhead or at extreme angles was a hit that eventually saw all makers adopt the system. Sharp's Viewcam format – with the screen on the back panel – is now offered in digital form.

day) camera that was generally shoulder-mounted contained a full-sized Betamax tape and recording mechanism. As another first, it also featured an electronic viewfinder.

JVC's offering promoted a compact version of the VHS cassette, VHS-C. Although models that used

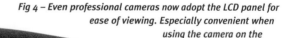

Fig 4 – Even professional cameras now adopt the LCD panel for ease of viewing. Especially convenient when using the camera on the move.

full-sized tapes were offered, they were too large for general use and required the same dedication on the part of the user as had been demanded of the old cine photographer.

Inevitably, size and weight decreased as more and more of the mechanical and electronic components were rationalized and miniaturized, but

the next breakthrough would come from an unexpected source. Early in 1984, Kodak announced a new series of camcorders and home recorders based on a new format, Video 8. Sony, one of the co-developers of the format, released its own version. Suddenly, shoulders were liberated as camcorders became devices that could truly be hand-held.

Throughout the 1980s the cameras became increasingly complex and more reliable. And they continued to shrink. New recording formats based on a higher frequency of recording produced images

Fig 5 – When MiniDV swept the camcorder world and cameras got smaller and smaller, Canon bucked the trend with its XL1. Built with no compromise on image quality or features, it was aimed at the serious enthusiast rather than professional user.

VIDEO FORMATS COMPARED
Digital

MiniDV: The most widespread format, it records pictures and audio virtually to broadcast quality. Uses MiniDV tapes that offer recording, at best quality, for up to an hour (longer recording times are possible using slightly lower quality). Video and audio are compressed but recordings can be easily edited.

Digital 8: This is a similar recording format to MiniDV, but uses a tape cassette similar to analogue Video 8. Larger tape cassettes (compared with MiniDV) lead to larger camcorders.

MicroMV: A tiny tape format introduced by Sony to enable subcompact camcorder design. Records in MPEG-2 format, similar to DVD. The compression regime can compromise editing but quality remains high.

DVD: Uses small recordable (or rewrite-able) DVD discs to record MPEG-2-quality video. DVD discs can be replayed by most DVD players and virtually all DVD-equipped computers. Editing and copying can be more problematic than with MiniDV or Digital 8.

Analogue

Video 8: Sony format designed specifically for camcorders and portable devices. Uses tapes similar in size to audio cassettes. Picture quality is average, on a par with VHS.

VHS-C: Compact version of VHS, using similar-sized tape in a small-sized cassette. Can be replayed in a domestic video record with an adaptor.

Hi8 and SVHS-C: "Hi-band" versions of Video 8 and VHS-C offering substantially improved picture quality, but still inferior to digital formats.

Fig 6 – Sanyo's Xacti camcorder uses flash memory to store good-quality video and record stills images. It also uses the MPEG-4 format.

of better quality. As users demanded better results, Hi8 and S-VHS appeared.

By the early 1990s the LCD panel appeared on a camcorder for the first time. In a still-bulky Sharp camcorder, video photographers now had the opportunity to photograph subjects successfully from extreme angles and no longer needed to squint through a restrictive eyepiece (fig 3).

The arrival of digital

All these formats shared one common feature: they were analogue. We had to wait until 1995 for Panasonic and Sony to release the first digital camcorders. Promising higher image quality – nearly up to the standards of broadcast quality if you were to believe the advertising – and smaller camcorder sizes, they first appeared at the premium end of the market. Again, it was the enthusiast who recognized some of the then-hidden virtues of a digital format. First, the great image quality did not deteriorate in the same way as analogue formats. Play an analogue tape a few times and the quality starts to drop. Copy an analogue tape between two recorders and image quality quickly deteriorates. Now, in the digital domain, no such compromises were inevitable – you could replay your clips indefinitely and edit them to your heart's content without losing the original's quality.

Now, digital cameras exist throughout the price and feature ranges, from basic to semi-professional models. Editing on the computer has become simple and, thanks to new recording formats, you can even email video files. Through this chapter we will explore more about the digital video camera and what can be done with the media. And, now that it's so easy to gather movie footage, we will also take a look at the basic techniques of the video film-maker to see how to apply them to our own productions.

Fig 7 – Samsung's DuoCam uses separate optical systems to record stills and video images. As a result, it can record high-quality digital video footage and 5-megapixel stills images. The discreet optical systems are precisely matched to each imaging mode. For good measure, it can also record short MPEG-4 clips.

Fig 8 – This pocketable MPEG-4 camera can record 2.1-megapixel stills images as well as video on a Secure Digital memory card.

CHOOSING A DIGITAL VIDEO CAMERA

There's no doubt that digital video cameras are immensely affordable, and the choice of models is enormous. But how do you make the right choice? You need to establish what you want from your camera. Here is a guide to help you through the maze of options and possibilities. With an eye to the future, you will also learn about the emergent new digital video format – HDV – that will allow us all to produce high-definition video programming.

Fig 9 – This enthusiast's model boasts three CCDs for improved image quality and a cracking lens – but it is not the type of camera that you can slip into a pocket.

The following information looks at a range of needs and wishes with respect to:

- The imaging chip – with consequent impact on size and quality
- The lens
- Handling
- Features

The imaging chip

The core of a digital video camera, like its stills equivalent, is the CCD imaging chip. These come in a range of sizes and resolutions, which have an obvious impact on the detail recorded when shooting both movies and stills images. Think first about what you will want to record with your camera.

The chip that does so well for stills images does not fare quite as well when pushed through the punishing regime of recording the many images per second demanded by video. Shortcomings in the electronics (which for all intents and purposes are rendered invisible for stills images) become all too clear. Three-chip cameras can overcome most of the problems. They work by dedicating each chip to record one of the three primary colours – red, green or blue. The drawbacks are that the cameras tend to be physically larger than their single-chip counterparts and, because they are made in smaller numbers, they are also more expensive.

Fig 10 – Once, a camera like this would have been regarded as tiny. Now, this miniDV model is average sized. But it is fitted with a Zeiss lens and can provide excellent-quality movies.

So how do we analyse the quality of the CCD? One way is to read all the reviews of the shortlisted cameras, but this doesn't really address the subjective elements that are particularly important. The best way is to equip yourself with a DV tape (of a format appropriate to your intended purchase) and ask your photo store if you can shoot some footage with each of the prospective purchases. Of course, some stores will say no, but perseverance will pay off and you will eventually find a store that values good customer relations.

Shoot similar footage with each camera. Try to include indoor scenes as well as outdoor ones, making a continuous transition between the two if possible. While outside, take some shots of foliage on trees and also power or telephone lines. The reason will become clear shortly.

With your footage recorded, it is time to study the results. Replay the recording on a television and a computer. Of course, this demands that you have a DV camera already; if you don't, beg or borrow one from a friend for a couple of hours. Check the following:

- *Colour accuracy* Is the camera reproducing the scene as you remember it? Are colours faithfully reproduced or are they washed out or even changed? CCDs are often poor at reproducing

blues – introducing colour shifts and noise – so pay particular attention to skies and water Reds, too, can be problematic, becoming oversaturated and lacking in detail compared with other parts of the image.

- *Tone* Certain cameras have colour characteristics. Sony cameras are well known for (when using default settings) veering towards cold, blue tones, while Canon models can be biased towards warm reds. Some models have onboard compensation for these, and it is possible (as with digital stills photos) to correct this later, but nothing beats getting a result that looks good (to you at least) in the camera (fig 11).

- *White balance* The automatic adjustment of the CCD recording characteristics to the lighting is crucial in getting quality, authentic results. Test the accuracy of this by recording areas of white under different lighting conditions to see if they exhibit a tint on playback. Test skin tones, too. Do they look natural when you review them?

- *Sharpening* The output from a CCD can be rather soft and this softness is made worse when

Fig 12 – The oversharpening of digital movie images can produce artificial-looking results, as shown in this image.

Fig 11 – Different digital video cameras interpret the same scene "normally" in quite different ways. Here, one camera has a warm tone, the other a cold tone.

Fig 13 – Even at night, most cameras are capable of giving very good results, maintaining detail until the light levels fall very low.

displayed on a television screen. Taking a cue from television cameras of all vintages, digital video cameras artificially sharpen the images they record so that they appear more detailed when displayed on a television screen. This often has a very positive effect, but the degree of sharpening can sometimes be too extreme and give movies an overprocessed look. Check for this when you review your test tape on both computer and television screens. This is where your footage of foliage and cables can come in useful. The cables will show light halos either side if they have been oversharpened, while foliage becomes very pixelated (fig 12).

- *Sensitivity* More so than digital stills cameras, digital video cameras can work in very low light levels and still produce acceptable results. If you plan to shoot indoors, after sunset or in any other gloomy conditions, check your camera's

performance. How do colour and noise (displayed as graininess on the movie footage) change with decreasing light levels? Not all cameras react in the same way. And if you want to work in total darkness, you can even choose a camera that will work with (virtually) no light, using image-intensification techniques (fig 13).

The lens

The CCD may be responsible for ensuring picture quality at an electronic level, but the lens delivers the optical quality. Most digital video cameras feature fixed (that is, non-interchangeable) zoom lenses. These are invariably of very good quality and perform to very high standards. Assessing the lens – to tell a good one from a great one – requires that you look again at the footage you recorded. This time you need to pay particular attention to these characteristics:

Fig 14 – Flare, to a degree, is a natural consequence of complex lens structures. To avoid it spoiling your images, ensure that the sun is always behind or to the side of the lens.

- *Flare* We all know the effect – when a camera turns towards the sun or a bright light, internal reflections produce blurred images of the light source. Often used to dramatic effect, some lenses are more prone to this than others. Although the effect does look pictorial, it is best to avoid lenses that produce the most flare. The net result of flare is a reduction in overall image contrast (fig 14).

- *Distortion* Does the image become distorted as you change the zoom from wide-angle to telephoto? Many (if not most) lenses tend to produce some distortion, varying from pincushion (in which rectangular shapes bow outwards like the edges of a well-stuffed cushion) through to barrel (in which the edges of the same rectangle swell like those of a well-rounded beer keg). Don't dismiss a lens that demonstrates distortion such as this, though clearly, if your main subject area is videoing architectural subjects, then this type of distortion will be more evident.

- *Vignetting* This is a name for uneven lighting. In the past, lenses on cheaper cameras of all types used to produce images in which the centres of images were brighter than the edges (the corners particularly). Modern lens design has

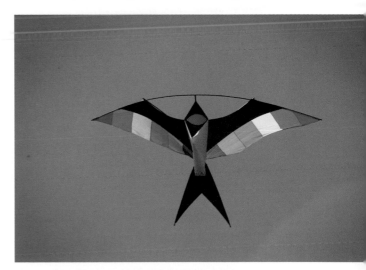

Fig 15 – Vignetting looks most obvious against a plain background. Here, the sky is obviously darker in the corners.

MAKING AN INFORMED CHOICE

Choosing the right camera needs a little planning and consideration before you rush off to your local photographic store. Here are some points to bear in mind:

• If you want movie clips that you can share with friends over the web or by CD and quality is not of paramount importance, just about any digital video camera will do. The caveat here is that to transfer movies to a computer for editing and conversion, you will need to ensure that the camera has a DV-out connector. This may be marked Firewire or iLink. It is pretty much an essential feature – if not now, then it will be at some point in the future.

• If you are working to a budget, don't worry about three-chip cameras. They cost disproportionately more than single-chip models for only an incremental increase in performance.

• If you want to be discreet or always want to carry a camera with you, aim for one of the small miniDV or microMV models (fig 16). As many of the compact digital cameras currently available are so small, they can safely be carried with you at all times.

Fig 16 – To illustrate just how small some cameras can be, this microMV model is smaller than a Hi8 cassette.

• If you shoot – or plan to shoot – indoors or in dark conditions, check the low-light performance of your shortlisted cameras. Digital video cameras are adept at shooting when darkness falls, but some are more efficient than others. Some will even offer a total darkness mode, which uses image-intensification techniques to shoot in minimal lighting.

overcome the problem, but you may still find occurrences (fig 15).

• *Focusing* Lenses today focus automatically. Some focus precisely all the time while others tend to hunt for the point of focus – oscillating backwards and forwards. Hunting increases as light levels fall.

Remember, too, the advice given regarding digital stills cameras and digital zooms. If anything, digital zoom ratios on digital video cameras are even more extreme and equally to be avoided.

Handling

No matter how good the optics or the CCD, they mean nothing if the camera is cumbersome or difficult to use. Handling quirks may seem superficial when you first examine a camera, but if they inhibit smooth operation it will be your movies that suffer as a result.

Once you have analysed the recordings made with your shortlisted cameras, you need to return to the store to make your final decision. Have a play  with your favourite camera. Does the zoom lens control fall easily under a finger or thumb? Can you operate it smoothly? Most zoom lenses now are pressure sensitive – the more pressure you apply, the faster the zoom operates. This is useful – if only to ensure that you never zoom too fast. As any good video photographer will tell you, the zoom feature should be used sparingly when the camera is running, and then only if the zoom is slow and smooth.

Next, listen to the camera. How well does it record sound? The in-built microphones can often give very acceptable results but their potency can also be their downfall: they can often record the sound of the tape moving through the camera and that of the zoom mechanism, which is another reason for not using the zoom while filming.

As well as these specifics, just hold the camera. You'll get that instinctive feel if the camera is right for you.

Features

Digital video cameras are loaded with features. Some – sepia toning, mosaics and the like – are quite superfluous. If you want effects like this you can achieve them later when you edit the movie on your computer. Others need a closer look.

It is worth reiterating here the need to have a DV-out connection. This, as has already been mentioned, is essential for getting digital video out to your computer for editing. It is also useful, too, to have DV-in. This will allow you to copy the edited video footage back on to video tape.

Most cameras are compatible with most movie-editing software. But if you have a particular camera in mind and already own software, it is wise to check compatibility.

Here are some other features worth considering:

- *Image stabilization* We hand-hold cameras most of the time, so anything that makes this simpler is to be welcomed. Image stabilizers ensure that any unsteadiness in our hands is not recorded by the camera.
- *Manual controls* Although auto-everything cameras are great for those grabbed scenes, there are times when we need more creative

Fig 17 – Not all digital video cameras use tape. An increasing number use recordable and re-writable DVD discs.

control. This might be for exposure (to preserve low light levels) or focus (to keep the focus on the principal subject) or colour balance (for eithercreative or technical control).

- *Still images* Camcorders have long been able to record stills images, but more recently they have been able to vie with low-end digital stills cameras in terms of quality. Some offer 2 megapixels or more, and most offer the option of storing those images on a memory card that is easily downloaded to a computer.
- *Progressive scan* Many cameras feature this, but few users understand it. In progressive scan mode each frame of a movie is scanned from top to bottom in one go. Traditionally, only the odd-numbered lines of a frame are scanned in one go and these are then followed by the even-numbered lines. The two frames are then interlaced to produce a single frame. Progressive scanning gives a better approximation to the look of film.

DO YOU REALLY NEED A DIGITAL VIDEO CAMERA?

You may want to record digital video, but do you really want to carry a digital video camera with you everywhere? If you already habitually carry a digital stills camera with you, it will probably be capable of taking good video movie clips. If you want to record some movie scenes (rather than create a jaw-dropping blockbuster), this may well be all you require. Quality falls a little short of true DV, and you will be limited in the amount of manual creative control you have, but this feature does come free so why not give it a try?

HDV: DIGITAL VIDEO FOR THE HIGH-DEFINITION AGE

All the video formats we have explored so far have one thing in common. Although they may vary in quality and purpose, they are all designed for displaying on a standard-definition television, or the computer-monitor equivalent. Yet, as we shall see in Chapter 6, television itself is taking a leap forward. Not just migrating to the digital world, television is moving into the world of high definition, offering sharp, detailed pictures that do justice to large plasma, LCD and projection screens.

High-definition television is seen by many as the preserve of the major studios – both television and Hollywood – but is that really the case? In fact, no. Creating high-definition movies is something we will all soon be doing.

Enter HDV: a new video-recording format for consumer digital cameras. It has been dubbed the "high-definition format for the masses", as it offers the opportunity to record true high-definition-quality movies but uses the same humble miniDV cassette that has been the mainstay of consumer digital video since its inception.

Fig 18 – The HDR-FX1 was Sony's inaugural HDV-format camera. Not the first HDV camera (that honour goes to JVC's GR-HD1), it was both the first to offer three – CCD imaging and a keen price point that puts it within range of enthusiasts. With critically sharp lens performance, it also permits the recording of a standard DV signal as well as HDV.

Fig 19 – One for the more well-heeled enthusiast, Apple's Final Cut Pro has an enviable position in many television production suites and with the major networks Final Cut Pro HD makes the powerhouse application compatible with high-definition editing.

HDV was born, so far as we are all concerned, in 2003, when four of the largest video camera manufacturers – Canon, JVC, Sharp and Sony (fig 18) – agreed the format and the common standard that defines it. Since then, other companies have climbed aboard, most notably Adobe, Canopus and Ulead, which are big names in consumer and enthusiast video-editing software.

The decision to use an existing tape format is, historically, an unusual one, but it is also rather clever. By using the same cassette, tape speed and recording tracks as the basic format, the mechanical assemblies used for miniDV can also be employed, capitalizing on the all-important, cost-saving economies of scale. For a format that is – to a degree – specialized, but needs a large number of users ultimately to adopt it if it is to be successful, this is crucial in containing costs. It also means that the general market for accessories and add-ons can be shared.

So what does HDV have to offer? It can record either of the two common HDTV formats (based on 720 or 1080 vertical lines of resolution) compatible with both NTSC and PAL television broadcast and replay (though, as a digital format it is strictly independent of these broadcasting standards). Video is recorded in MPEG-2 format, the same as that used for DVD, with the sound recorded in MPEG-1 Layer II format. The latter offers better than CD audio quality.

Interestingly, although HDV is a high-definition format, it is still possible to record one hour of video on a 60-minute miniDV tape, the same as with DV itself. Compare this with the amount of data recorded when recording video from a high-definition television station: on average, it requires six times the space of a conventional, standard-definition station.

Recording HDV is only part of the story. For it to be a successful format in the enthusiast market it needs to be editable in a form similar to that of conventional digital video. Prior to the announcement of HDV, editing high-definition material required computers equipped with potent video accelerators (high-speed versions of the graphics cards so prized by computer gamers), powerful workstations and professionally specified (and priced) software.

Within months of the announcement of HDV, key players in the software market had announced that they had, or would soon be, producing updates to popular editing applications that would process HDV video using standard Windows and Macintosh desktop and laptop computers.

One of the fundamental edicts of the HDV standard is that it must conform to existing desktop hardware. Hence the compression of the video and audio is such that it can be passed in real time over FireWire connections, in the same way as standard DV. There is no doubt that HDV will thrive in the coming decade. Cameras are now on sale and at the sort of prices that just a very few years ago would have been attached to high-end consumer DV cameras. HDV is not for everyone, but for those who need the quality and want to exploit the potential of all aspects of high-definition media, it will soon prove well-nigh essential.

VIDEO-EDITING SOFTWARE

If you already have a perfectly good analogue camcorder, why change to digital? I have already alluded to some of the reasons. Even if you have a hi-band analogue camcorder (using Hi8 or S-VHS-C), you will notice a huge increase in picture quality and stability. Digital video is often described as being of "broadcast quality" and while it might be splitting hairs to discuss why this is not actually true, the results you see on your television screen at home could be better than much of what you receive over the air.

But for many users, the key attribute of digital video is the ease with which it can be edited. No longer is video editing the preserve of the enthusiast and those with too much time on their hands; with digital video, editing is for everyone. Imagine recording your child's performance at a school play in the morning and distributing edited copies on CD before the end of the day. That's how easy the editing process is.

Video-editing software

Central to all video-editing applications are the same key functions:

- Uploading digital video recordings from your camcorder.

- Cutting your raw footage into individual scenes.
- Allowing scenes to be assembled on a timeline.
- Enabling the editing of audio and the adding of new soundtracks.
- Creating transitions and fades between scenes.
- Adding titles.
- Exporting your finished movie to disc, tape or whatever medium you choose.

And you may want some additional features such as:
- Filters and effects.
- The option of importing and converting video from other sources.
- Importing images for video slideshows.

Video-editing software, like image-editing applications, tends to fall into one of two broad categories: professional and consumer. The distinction between categories is rather woolly: many amateur users invest in professional-grade applications and a surprising number of professional users use consumer-level products for some of their projects.

Professional video editors

Professional products are characterized by cost and functionality. Like their image-editing counterparts, these applications will enable you to do just about anything. The trouble is, they are so well specified that for most of us just knowing what to do first can be a problem. So comprehensive are the features that simple activities can seem overcomplex. This, of course, is ideal for the more experienced user, or the user who is seeking to make a totally professional-looking movie. But for the rest of us, it is probably overkill. And the price will probably exclude

Fig 20 – Adobe's Premiere is a professional-level product and is demanding on users. But if you are serious about movie-making, it is a tool that will grow along with your skills.

Fig 21 – Featuring many of the key functions that makes Final Cut Pro a market leader, Final Cut Express will satisfy the needs of many serious enthusiasts who have graduated from consumer-level products, but can't financially justify going the whole way to a professional product.

them from your shortlist.

If, however, you have had experience of the consumer-level products and have been bitten by the movie-making bug, then do audition these professional applications. For the PC there is Adobe's Premiere (fig 20). Like its stablemate Photoshop, this is one of those applications by which all others are judged. It really does do just about everything.

If you are a Mac user, then it is Apple's Final Cut Pro (fig 21). This is another professional powerhouse of a program and one that is used extensively by semi-professional users through to the big studios and television companies. With an eye to the increasingly demanding enthusiast marketplace, Apple has produced a trimmed-down version of Final Cut Pro called Final Cut Express. It is a great halfway house, offering much of the functionality of its senior, but without the sobering price tag.

Consumer video editors

At the other extreme – in price terms – come the consumer-level video editors. Simplicity of use is the keynote to these applications, but that doesn't mean they are short of functions. You can expect to see all of the key features we noted above included as standard, and quite a few extras, too. The most popular of these applications, by virtue of being included with their respective operating systems, are Apple's iMovie (fig 22) and Windows Movie Maker (fig 23). There are also some great third-party products (from the likes of Ulead) that provide similar tools at a remarkably low cost. In fact, many digital video cameras feature such a product in the software bundle that accompanies them.

Fig 22 – It can't claim to have created the digital video-editing explosion, but Apple's iMovie has launched many people into a new creative hobby. Intuitive interface and logical operation make movie generation and distribution simple.

Fig 23 – Aping many of iMovie's features, Windows Movie Maker is a great tool for quick movie editing. The only drawback is that the slightly limited features list may stunt the creativity of users as they gain experience.

Fig 24

Fig 25

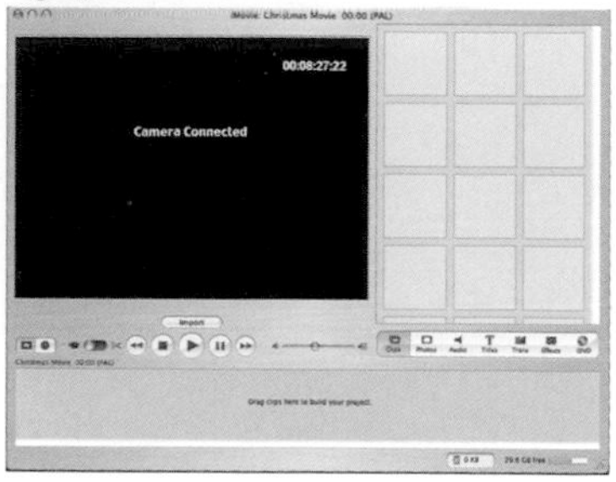

Fig 26

Editing your first movie

"Digital movie editing is simple." No matter how often it is said, most of us are cynical, often to the point of not chancing our luck. Part of the fear is down to the software. To the uninitiated, even simple applications look complex. But approach a project in a stepwise fashion and you will be convinced that the process really is simple. You will soon be attacking all those archived video tapes with fervour. For clarity, the following work has all been based on iMovie, but the general method of working will be the same with most equivalent applications.

1. Connect your camcorder. The importance of a Firewire connector on your camcorder has already been mentioned (see page 72–3). This is where you make use of it. Connecting the camcorder and computer by Firewire will enable the copying of the video data to the computer in real time. There is a great deal of data, so a fast, reliable connection is essential (fig 24).

2. Once connected, the software will recognize the camera and display "Camera Connected". This does depend on the software and the camera. Not all are immediately compatible, though even nominally incompatible pairings can often be "forced" in to communicating (fig 25).

3. The camera is now under the control of the software and you can download the video recording. Watch as the tape plays. The software will automatically identify each scene. Each scene is automatically saved as a separate movie clip (fig 26).

4. Once downloading is complete, you can begin editing. Note that at this time you don't need to have your camcorder attached. Drag the clips from the panel (sometimes called the shelf) on to the Timeline. The Timeline represents the finished movie. You can drag clips here in any order, so if you have shot scenes out of sequence you can reconstruct the storyline here (fig 27).

5. You don't have to leave each clip as you shot it. Chances are, you will want to trim off superfluous

Fig 29

Fig 30

Fig 27

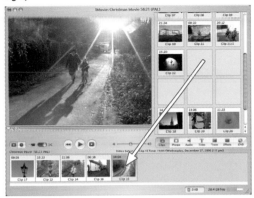

Fig 28

bits at the beginning or end. You can trim your clips precisely using the main window (fig 28).

6. You can improve the flow of your movie by adding transitions between scenes. Take a look at television programmes and movies. See how scenes flow together better when one scene fades into another, or when one fades out to black before another fades in. You can use the Transitions folder to add similar transitions yourself (fig 29). *TIP: Don't add too many transitions, and try to refrain from using some of the wilder ones. They may look novel the first time but your audience will soon tire of them.*

7. Add titles. Often the best titles can be caught on tape, by videoing, say, the programme for the play or musical you are recording or perhaps the entrance of a theme park, if your movie features a day at that park. But if you need to create your own, click on the Titles tab and make your choice. Again, go for simple, bold titles. Those that have too many words or use a difficult-to-read font

(typeface) tend to annoy viewers, who will struggle to read them (fig 30).

8. If you want to, or if your story requires it, add special effects. Special effects are many and varied, but can, for example, turn your movie into black and white (and perhaps give it a jerky, silent-movie look), or sepia toned, or give it a soft-focus appearance. These can be really effective when used appropriately, but can be equally irritating if used often or recklessly (fig 31).

9. Save the finished production. Give your movie a critical appraisal and, if nothing needs changing, save it. You can save it on your computer's hard disc, but as movies tend to consume large amounts of hard-disc space, a better bet is to record it back, at the original quality, to DV tape. You can do this by reconnecting your camcorder and recording to a new tape. Never delete or record over the original footage – you may need to recompile a video later and will then need this source material (fig 32).

Fig 31

Fig 32

Sharing your movie

Exporting your finished movie ensures that you preserve it at the highest possible quality. DV provides the optimum quality for your work but it is not necessarily the most effective for sharing. How you share your production will depend on the audience. Here are the options:

- VHS video
- DVD
- CD-ROM
- Email

VHS video

Although recordable DVD is rapidly replacing the humble VHS video recorder as our recording tool of choice, the wide user base and our enormous collections of video material will ensure that the VCR remains with us for some time to come. You can copy your movie to VHS video tape in two ways.

The first method uses the DV recording you made back to the camcorder. You can now hook up the camcorder to your VHS video, using the cabling that is normally supplied with the camcorder (or replacements that are widely available). Set the camcorder to play and the VHS video to record simultaneously. With the television set to the video output, you can monitor your recording while it is in progress.

The second method requires a digital-to-

ANALOGUE-TO-DIGITAL CONVERSION

The digital-to-analogue converter already mentioned for making VHS copies of your DV videos can also be used in reverse – to make digital video copies of your VHS (or other) analogue videos. You can connect your video player (or even your television) to the input and then import the video in digital form. Many video-editing applications will recognize the converter as a camera, and import the recording in a similar way (Fig 33).

---

analogue converter. This connects your computer and the VHS video and the device will, in real time, convert the digital video output of the computer to analogue video that can be recorded on the videotape. It is fast and effective but it does require the additional hardware. These units are getting progressively cheaper, so it could be a good investment if you plan to make many copies of your movies.

Use: when compatibility with non-computer users is important.

DVD

With DVD burners proliferating, you can easily convert your DV movie on your computer to DVD-

Fig 33 – Analogue-to-digital converters (such as the ADVC110 from Canopus, shown here) allow two-way conversions between digital video and analogue video. Connectors on the front and back provide pathways for signals in either direction.

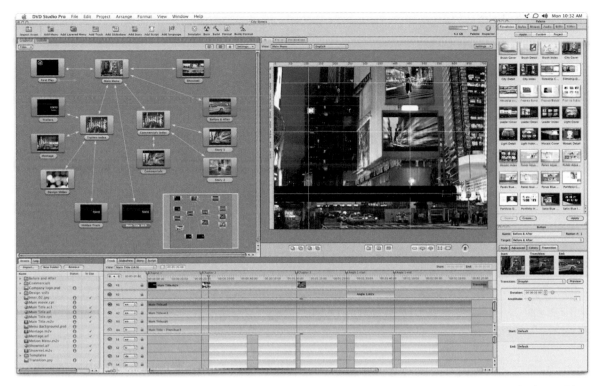

Fig 34 – DVD Studio Pro is a professional application for those serious about authoring DVDs. You can build in very complex interactivity and animated menus – if that sounds familiar, it is because this is the tool used by many studios in creating their commercial DVDs.

format media files. If you have used iMovie, you can click on the iDVD button to compile these directly. Otherwise there is a range of applications that will produce the respective files for you. You can even add animated menus, chapter breaks and submenus, just as in a commercially produced DVD. Compiling the media files can take some time (there is some serious reprocessing to be done), but the result is a DVD that best displays the quality of digital video.

If you have a DVD recorder attached to your television and that recorder has a Firewire link (iLink), you can even record directly from your computer to the recorder. This is a great option if your computer does not have a DVD burner, but it doesn't give you the option of adding menus and breaks.

If you have a CD burner on your computer and your movie is short, you can make a Super Video CD or miniDVD. Take a look at page 101 for more about these obscure but useful formats.

Use: when quality is paramount.

CD-ROM

If you don't want (or need) the highest of quality, you can record your production to a conventional CD. Your image-editing application will have several qualities on offer – usually encoded into Quicktime format – from which to choose. If you are distributing your production by CD, it makes sense to choose the best quality that will fit on the disc.

Use: when maximum compatibility with computer users is essential.

Email

The most compact of the Quicktime formats produces a small, compressed version of the movie that is ideal to email to people. Such email-quality movies can still be quite large so you will need to establish that your recipients can receive large attachments before sending. Or you could try using a format like DivX (see page 84), which can compress a video to a much higher degree than other formats without significant loss of quality.

Use: for the delivery of the smallest possible file size.

TIPS FOR SUCCESSFUL (AND WATCHABLE) DIGITAL VIDEOS

Whether you are new to digital video or an old hand, you will be in no doubt about the superlative quality of the medium. But does that make your movies watchable? Often the answer is "No". Even your closest friends will feign illness or book a holiday to avoid an invitation to see your latest production. Here are some tips for making your movies stand out – for the right reasons.

Be dispassionate

What you consider the best bits of your movie may not be what others enjoy. Your children are lovely, and photogenic, but friends may not want to see them onscreen for hour after hour.

Tell a story

Whether you are creating a blockbuster, documentary or even recording a sporting event, you need to tell a story. People expect a storyline no matter what the subject. Scribble a storyline first. Even if your subjects don't obviously suggest a story, begin by noting down your aims, objectives and intended conclusions. Making a documentary? You still need to set the scene and describe your intentions, then, at the end you'll need to wrap up the production with some form of conclusion.

Think first, shoot later

The beginning of a movie project is characterized by a high level of enthusiasm; as the project progresses, it becomes more workmanlike. This is unfortunate because the audience picks up on your enthusiasm, or lack of it. When shooting, think about what the audience will appreciate. If you are shooting a long stage production at your children's school, for example, vary the shots so that you don't simply have a view of the whole stage all the way through. Shoot cutaways – shots of the audience smiling and applauding. You can intersperse these in your recording if you need to trim out sections without loosing the continuity (fig 35).

Keep still!

There is a terrible temptation with any movie camera to move the camera around while shooting. Nothing is more certain to induce vertigo and motion sickness in your audience. Unless there is a real reason to move the camera, perhaps to follow a moving object, let the subjects create the motion. If your camera does not have an image stabilizer, or

Fig 35 – Audience shots and other peripheral scenes are great for cutaways – scenes that can be used to link two other shots, usually where you have deleted parts.

Fig 36 – Poor-quality shots such as this have no place in the finished movie, no matter how much they mean to you. Cut them.

you don't have a particularly steady hand, or you are using the zoom at its furthest extension, consider investing in a tripod or other support to minimize unwanted camera shake. Improvise using a wall, fence or even a chair if you are caught without any custom support.

Think sound

When shooting movies we tend to labour over the images and neglect the sound. Until you come to edit, you don't realize how much superfluous noise there is or, worse still, how little valuable ambient noise you have recorded. Consider an accessory microphone. These will ensure better sound quality and many models let you "zoom" with the lens to record relevant sound rather than too much of the distracting environmental noise.

Consider, too, the sound that you want to use as a soundtrack later. You can add any music at the editing stage but it can be useful to record some movie footage purely for the sound. Street carnivals, the beach and sea, even city noise can all add to the atmosphere of your finished movie.

Cut the dross

Quantity is no substitute for quality. When you tell a story, remember that it is the essence of the story that is important. If you want to convey your journey to a distant country, shots of the departure lounge, aircraft and arrival are quite sufficient. There is no pictorial, emotional or storytelling benefit in endless footage of airport terminals – even if you want to tell

everyone about the interminable wait you had. Any blurred, badly composed or irrelevant shots? Cut them. You'll still have the shots on the original tape if they are important to you, but the tightly cut finished movie will run so much better without them (fig 36).

Don't shoot the movie in-camera

Many video photographers aim to shoot the whole movie sequentially, in-camera, thinking that it will save work later. In fact, the amount of work saved is minimal – you will still have to trim shots and delete some altogether. By shooting in a linear manner you can compromise the content; be prepared to shoot elements out of sequence and reassemble later.

Shoot visual titles

Shoot scenes that imply what you would otherwise need written captions for. Wordy titles can be used sparingly but if you can achieve a similar inference with a visual, go for it. A shot of the sun rising, for example, or a caption saying "Morning" (figs 37–39). Which do you think your audience would prefer?

Fig 37 – A scene like this implies morning.

Fig 38 – Effective, but dull.

The Big Day

Fig 39 – It may be the wedding day, but the scene implies morning again.

DIVX: MP3 FOR MOVIES?

Once MP3 became the standard for digitally distributed music, it semed inevitable that an equivalent system for video media would appear. And it did. It is called DivX (note the capitalization – it becomes important later) and, like MP3, it enables high-quality files to be produced from original media that are substantially compressed. With DivX encoding you can squeeze a DVD's worth of movie material on to a standard CD-ROM disc.

DivX achieves its impressive compression by employing MPEG-4 (see page 182) rather than the MPEG-2 used in DVDs. Like MP3, the compression is substantial – files are between 12 and 20 per cent the size of the original. Also like MP3, software for DivX encoding is freely available on the web.

What you need for DivX

Take a look around the web and you will see not only encoders but value-added tools that make the process simpler. If you want to enjoy DivX content (and there's a lot of it about), all you need is a DivX codec. You can download one from www.divx.com for any computer platform. Unlike some codecs – the software applications that replay video media – this basic and free installation will play back absolutely any DivX file. It acts as a plug-in to Quicktime (or other media players) and will replay your movies in that player, giving you all the control you're used to.

You don't have to stop with simply replaying existing DivX media. You can create your own DivX movies from your own movies. Encoding is virtually as simple as replaying. Read the blurb on DivX and it will extol the power of the format and how you can enjoy your movies without loss of quality. A little caution is required, however. With MP3 there are audiophiles who will immediately detect and point out shortcomings that limit the audio quality. Likewise, those with a keen eye will spot visual compromises brought about by the compression. But for most users, this will be a small price to pay for the amount of hard-disc space that is liberated.

Spreading the enjoyment

It is likely that you will use DivX extensively on your computer, but you can also enjoy DivX-encoded discs throughout your home using one of the increasing number of compatible DVD players. Just as CD players can, increasingly, also play MP3-encoded discs, so it is the same with DVD players. You can enjoy a DivX-encoded disc in the same way as a traditional DVD. Expect to see this functionality spread and, in the same way that MP3 music can be shared around the home from your computer, wireless and Ethernet connections delivering DivX directly from your computer's hard disc. You will also find an increasing number of PVRs (see page 89) offering the option of compact DivX recording.

CREATING YOUR OWN DIVX RECORDINGS

Once you have downloaded the free DivX encoder you really are ready to go. Here is the encoder dialogue box from DivX Pro (fig 40). You can refine the encoding by altering the parameters (though most encodings will be fine using the default settings). You can use DivX recordings across a range of devices, ranging from hand-held PDAs through home theatre television systems and high-definition television. Make sure you click the appropriate button for optimum performance.

Fig 40 – The main screen of the DivX encoder.

Fig 41 – Make your encoding suitable for the replay device by clicking on the appropriate button.

DivX & MPEG-4 FREQUENTLY ASKED QUESTIONS

Q: What do I need to play DivX movies or programming?

A: You'll need to install a DivX codec on your computer. These are available for all computer platforms at websites such as DivX.com or DivXmovies.com. Some computers now come preloaded with DivX players. You can also play DivX movies that have been written to CD on many compatible DVD players, direct to your television.

Q: Will any computer play DivX movies?

A: Assuming the codec is installed, most computers will play back programming. The better specified, the better the overall quality will be. DivX experts suggest that a Pentium 300Mhz Windows PC and a G3 Macintosh are the minimum-spec machines.

Q: Can I find DivX programming and movies on the Internet?

A: Yes, there are a number of resources available. Try a Google search for some suggestions. You'll also find sites like DivX.com featuring showcases of programming. Take care not to download illegally encoded material, however!

Q: How long does it take to download a movie over the Internet?

A: It will depend on your connection. Cable modems will download 2 minutes of movie in 1 minute; other connections will take proportionally longer.

Q: What is H.264?

A: Not a memorable name, but H.264 is another MPEG-4 codec that can offer quality akin to that of MPEG-2 but at only half the data rate. It is a scalable format which means it can be used in devices with limited bandwidth (such as 3G mobile phones) though to high-definition television broadcasts.

Q: Is H.264 the same as DivX?

A: Not quite. They are both derived from the MPEG-4 standard but the coding is slightly different. H.264 is sometimes known as AVC or JVT.

Q: Who uses H.264?

A: You will find H.264 in Quicktime 7. It has also been made mandatory for the Blu-ray and HD-DVD formats, assuring that it will be a key feature of the future developments in movie formats.

Q: How do DivX, MPEG-2 and H.264 compare?

A: Here's a visual demonstration of the qualities of each. Don't worry if you don't see major differences in quality – each is very subtle and overall quality ranges from very good to excellent (fig 42).

Fig 42 – DivX, H.264 and MPEG-2. Differences are clearer in detailed areas (such as foliage) that are the most difficult to encode fast.

VIDEO & AUDIO RECORDING

IN THIS CHAPTER WE:

- Explore the evolution of video-recording formats from early reel-to-reel systems through to today's PVRs.
- Examine different formats for recording sound and audio at home.
- Look at how simple it is to produce DVD video recordings of treasured video tapes and even off-air programming.
- Look at the future of recordable media.

THE VIDEO CASSETTE RECORDER WAS, FOR SEVERAL DECADES, A PIECE OF "MUST-HAVE" TECHNOLOGY. WITH IT WE WERE FREED FROM THE SHACKLES OF THE TELEVISION SCHEDULES, AND IN A WORLD WHERE THERE WERE ONLY A HANDFUL OF TELEVISION STATIONS, IT PROVIDED THE MEANS TO PLAY ALTERNATIVE PROGRAMMING.

THE DAYS OF THE VIDEO CASSETTE RECORDER NOW SEEM NUMBERED AS NEWER TECHNOLOGIES SUCH AS RECORDABLE DVD AND PERSONAL VIDEO RECORDERS – PVRS – BECOME COMMONPLACE. BUT THE NEED, THE RATIONALE, OF VIDEO RECORDING IS AS IMPORTANT AND SIGNIFICANT NOW IN OUR WORLD OF SEVERAL HUNDRED TV CHANNELS AS IT HAS EVER BEEN.

VIDEO ON FILM

In the 1950s the only viable option for recording television pictures and sound was the Kinescope, often called the telerecording. This was a specially constructed 35mm and 16mm movie film camera whose speed of shooting was precisely matched to the frame rate of the television monitor, mounted in front of the lens. Today, this seems a remarkably

Fig 1 – Looking for all the world like the reel-to-reel audio recorders of yesteryear, the first video recorders aped their audio cousins. These models from the 1960s used 1-in magnetic tape to record in black and white (in the case of the Ampex) and colour (the Sony). The size and cost limited use to professional and semi-professional studios.

Fig 2 – Combined DVD and video machines allow users to access their library of media and make th best possible recordings of contemporary programming.

crude system but it was one that survived for many years, even after video recording on to tape became viable. For the studios it allowed overseas sales: often overseas markets were able to screen 16mm film stock but not video tape.

Surprisingly for a system that notionally demands a very professional configuration, there was a thriving enthusiast market for telerecording equipment. And "enthusiast" was a very apt term. Unlike the essentially passive nature of video recording today (where the recording activity takes place in the background and does not influence our live viewing preferences) telerecording required that the television screen used for the filming be shrouded in a box or curtain that excluded all external light. This would make the television programme impossible to watch live.

There's evidence that organisations like the BBC were still making telerecordings in the early 1980s because it was often cheaper – at the time – than using one of the handful of quality video recorders then available. Ultimately telerecording gave way to the use of domestic video recording techniques for those recordings that did not demand the highest quality.

GETTING IT TAPED

But what of video recording itself? We explored the broad chronology of video with regard to digital video in the previous chapter. The story of off-air video recording (that is, recording broadcast, or pre-broadcast programming) is much the same, though the highlights are somewhat different.

The first high-profile use of a colour video tape recorder was in 1958 when manufacturer Ampex took a unit to Moscow to record a meeting between Richard Nixon and Nikita Khrushchev. The recording was aired in the US on their return. Prior to this, monochrome systems, using 13mm reel-to-reel video tape was used with moderate success in the training films market. Similar systems were used to distribute programming to schools and colleges well into the 1970s. Connected to a suitable television (one of the rare "studio grade" monitors offering direct video out signals) it was even possible to record television programmes manually.

Around this time, as we've already seen, Philips introduced its original video cassette format. Although the recording time was only one hour, this compared favourably with the reel-to-reel systems. The crucial difference (apart from the obvious one of the simple-to-use tape cassette) was that these domestic units featured a tuner. Users could now set the timer to switch the recorder on when a programme was due to begin and record that programme unattended (or at least until the tape ran out). With analogue timers (which owed more to the timer units found on kitchen stoves than electronics) and a paucity of prerecorded tapes, take up of these machines was limited.

FORMAT WARS MOVE INTO THE HOME

It would be the end of the decade before Sony's Betamax and JVC's VHS became widely available, joined latterly by Philips's V2000 format. The former two formats entered the fray with large, cumbersome machines that often featured mechanical rather than electronically based controls. Timers were digital but still limited. Often they would offer only one programme-recording option, requiring any user to preselect a channel to record from.

Despite its clear technical superiority, Betamax languished in the sales tables, up against the marketing muscle of the VHS camp. Although it survived as a minority format for some years (and longer still in the USA) it eventually – and rather quietly – disappeared, supported only by a few devotees. Many reasons are quoted for the success of VHS

At launch it offered longer recording times – essential for recording long programmes and a more economic option.

Marketing – JVC licensed many companies to produce VHS machines, allowing marques ranging from the prestige through to the budget to produce equipment. More market sectors could be catered

for yet JVC would get their royalty payments all the same. Sony, by contrast, only had limited licensing that essentially only included Sanyo and their respective affiliates.

VHS offered the largest library of prerecorded programming. Video stores were loathed to stock multiple copies of each title in two formats so tended to skew their stock towards the biggest selling format, adding pressure on those buying new machines or upgrading

In reality it was a combination. Yes, Beta was technically better, but for many consumers price was the most important issue. Average television screen sizes at the time were around 18 in (45 cm) and many were badly tuned. Performance gains owing to Beta would be largely lost.

Ironically, quality did become an issue with an increasing number of users. JVC's answer, as we've seen, was the higher (but not high) definition of Super VHS. Sony had also released – on a more limited basis – similarly engineered improvements to the Beta format, Super Beta and, best of all the analogue formats, Extended Definition Beta. But for the declining format it was too late. Although quality was promised and delivered, by now most users had cupboards and shelves full of VHS recording they needed to replay.

VHS'S DIGITAL EDGE

For the digital age, aiming to ensure that VHS survived the impending DVD recording formats, JVC announced yet another variation on the VHS theme: Digital VHS. Backwardly compatible with VHS and Super VHS – ensuring that people's tape collections were not

Fig 3 – Sticking with VHS to the bitter end, DVHS gives the edge of Digital to a format that has been in use for decades.

disenfranchised – Digital VHS can support high-definition broadcast recordings (see page 109) and can store up to 49 hours of recording (standard resolution) on a single tape.

No manner of embellishments to VHS could stave off the onslaught of DVD. Cheap, robust media, easy access to content and compactness meant that the day of DVHS was shortlived, again save for the devotee market.

DVD, then, seemed to have a clear run. And it would have were it not for the rise of an interloper: the Personal Video Recorder, or PVR.

Not personal in the sense of a personal CD or MP3 player, PVRs are video recorders that use computer hard discs to record on. There's actually nothing novel in that (you can record DVD quality video and audio to and from your computer hard disc) but the "personal" element comes to the fore with the programming capabilities. Rather than the problematic timing programming offered on conventional tape or DVD recorders (how many of us technophiles have recorded the wrong programme, wrong station or failed altogether?), PVRs offer intelligent programming that can, from historical data, predict programming we like and automatically record. We'll look at these in more detail shortly.

GOODBYE TO TAPE?

So does it mean that tape – as a recording medium – is about to enter the history books? Quite possibly. Tape – and the same applies to audio tape as to video tape – is a reasonably robust medium that can, when looked after, provide many years of great service. It has the benefit of being cheap: you can

store many gigabytes of data (or the equivalent of many gigabytes of data) for far less than you could an equivalent amount using, for instance, solid state memory chips.

Tape, though, has lost its competitive edge in other areas. One, as we have observed already, is access. We are used, today, to being able to access a specific track or recording on a CD, DVD or hard disc, in just a matter of seconds (and often less). The need to wind tape and then detect a recording's start position takes far longer. In the modern world we no longer have the patience!

Being a contact medium, tape also wears, resulting in continual degradation. Video recorder manufacturers have been particularly adept at minimizing the wear of tape (and, indeed, the recording heads themselves) by careful use of air flowing over the heads to provide a microscopically fine "air cushion". Even so, after repeated recording and playback cycles, or playback cycles alone, tape does wear.

In analogue recordings this means the picture gets steadily worse, with softer colours, lower contrast and noise. Digital recordings survive better to begin with: error correction and digital techniques ensure that playback quality is maintained for as long as possible. But, ultimately, the recording will fail – completely. When it becomes impossible for the error correction to correct worn parts of the recording, it gives up. The screen goes blank.

So, for our consumer recording formats, expect to see disc and solid state memory card based recording see us through the next few decades. The day of tape recording is fast coming to a close.

CREATING YOUR OWN DVDS

Creating your own DVDs – with all the features that you would expect from a commercial product – is now simple and provides an excellent way to present your old movies, photos and even television archives.

The process can be split into simple steps:

1. Collecting media and starting the project.
2. Choosing a theme.
3. Adding a movie or programming.
4. Creating menus.
5. Optional additional resources.
6. Burning the DVD.

Collecting media and starting the project

Think of those commercially available DVDs. They usually comprise a movie or, perhaps a television series. Then there will be the extras. Perhaps a "making-of" documentary, out-takes and even a gallery of stills images. When you prepare to create your own DVD, you need to gather the corresponding resources. These may comprise a movie (or movies), photos and even audio files.

These will need to be in a format that the DVD-authoring software will accept. Often this is the same format used for the conventional storage of such media, such as DV for digital video, JPEG for images and MP3 for audio (MP3 is defined, after all, as the audio component of DVD video).

It makes good sense to gather all these resources together in an electronic folder. Prior to this, you need to ensure that you have edited the video to your total satisfaction and manipulated your images so they are as you want them to look.

Now you are set to start creating your own DVD. Here, iDVD is being used. This is a simple application that actually behaves in a very similar manner to other applications and follows on logically from iMovie (see page 77).

Fig 4

After opening iDVD you are prompted to open a project or, if you have no saved projects, to create a new one. Choose a location to save your project (which will include all your media, ultimately) and click Create.

Choosing a theme

When you play a commercial DVD you rarely play the main feature movie directly; instead you are presented with an often-animated front-screen menu. In the world of DVD creation this page, its menu and any submenus are described as a "theme". You could spend a lot of time creating your own, unique, theme but it is often easier to choose one of the many preset themes provided with DVD-creation applications.

Fig 5

Fig 6

Fig 7

AUTOPLAY MOVIES

Back to those commercial DVDs. Remember how some have a short movie that plays before the menu appears? Sometimes it is an all-action highlights trailer of the main movie, sometimes a promo for other titles from the same studio. You can add your own movie that plays automatically when the DVD is put in a player – it is called an autoplay movie. Only some themes include the option to feature an autoplay – these are indicated in iDVD by the disc icon in the top left-hand corner of the theme thumbnail.

pane. You can choose, from the pull-down menu, Audio, Photo or Movies. If you choose movies or photos, you can drag a selected item, or items, to the area on the theme window labelled "Drag movies or photos here". This is known as a drop zone. If you choose photos, you can select more than one image to be displayed; they will then play in the window as a slideshow. Here, three images have been selected and placed into the drop zone (Figs 8, 9).

• Some themes feature multiple drop zones. These can be useful for displaying a clip from different parts of a movie, but don't go overboard. Make it simple for your viewers to navigate your production.

Adding a movie or programming

Adding a movie or other programming material to the DVD is also a matter of dragging and dropping.

• In iDVD you can see the available themes in the Customize drawer. Click on the Customize button to open the drawer and then the Themes button at the top. To see all the available themes, click on Choose All.

• Some of the themes contain animations, slideshows or even movies. Click on the Motion button to see these features in action accompanied, where configured, with an audio soundtrack.

• Select a theme. In this selection, Fish One, there is an animated background (the fish) and a photo frame (Fig 7).

• Click on the Media tab at the top of the Customize

• Drag the movie (or rather, the movie icon) from the folder to the theme window, taking care to avoid the drop zones. You will see the file name of the movie appear in the window. Two buttons are then created: a Play button (which lets you play the whole movie from the start) and a Scene Selection button. This will link to the scene-selection menu (which will be examined more closely in a moment) and will ultimately allow you to choose individual scenes in the movie.

Fig 9

Fig 8

Fig 10

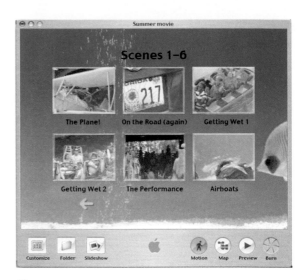

Fig 12

- Scene selections are possible only when, in video-editing software, you have added chapter marks. Increasingly more and more video-editing applications provide this option; alternatively, some DVD-creation applications allow you to add breaks retrospectively. Here are the chapters created for this movie, generated from iMovie (Fig 10).
- Where there are no chapter marks you will usually see only one button with the same title as the movie. When you click on this, the movie will play in the same way as if you had clicked on the "Play" button described above.
- If you now click on the Scene Selection button, you will see buttons for each of the chapters that were created in the movie, each named according to the name that you gave the chapters when

compiling the movie. Again, depending on the theme, you can display images to correspond to each chapter; these may be stills images dragged from a photo folder or could be stills image thumbnails taken from each of the chapters. Here is the same scene menu using two different themes, one with thumbnails, one without (Figs 11, 12).

- Want to give your menu window some background music? Click on the Media tab again and choose Audio. You can now pull in an audio file from the folder containing your resources. In this case, with iDVD you can also access the iTunes library of music (Fig 13).

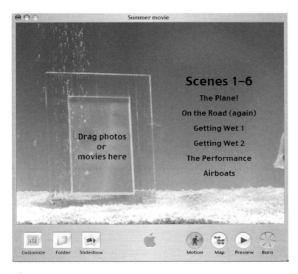

Fig 11

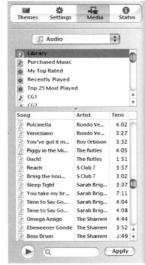

Fig 13

- It is worth making mention here of copyright. If you are creating a DVD of family events for your own enjoyment, there is no practical restriction on the resources you can use. But if you want to show your production – even to close friends – including copyrighted music might be illegal. Make sure that you use copyright-free or royalty-free music (often produced specially for the purpose) to avoid any possible litigation.

Creating menus

Themes make it simple to get great menus fast, but often you will want to refine them slightly. Perhaps the text size is too small or maybe an inappropriate (to your movie) colour. Some changes have already been made (by adding music), but here are some other personalizing options:

- To add more text to the window (a description of the options, some helpful hints on which button to press, perhaps) click on Project ····} Add Text. Text will appear automatically and, by clicking on it, you can overwrite it with your own words (Fig 14).

Fig 15

Fig 16

Fig 14

- In the Settings pane of the Customize pull-out you also have the opportunity to change the text colour, font and size. Here, a subtitle has been added, the poorly visible white colour is now black, and the font of the title has been changed to a more informal Comic Sans (Fig 15).
- The Transitions option on the Menu option's sub-window of the Customize panel will let you control

the way the menu and movie (or menu and submenu) link together. You can choose from a number of transitions akin to those you might find in a video-editing application or a PowerPoint presentation. It is a good tip to choose something simple, such as Dissolve. You want your audience blown away by the content of your movie, not assaulted – in visual terms – by the special effects leading up to it (Fig 16).

- Should you wish, you can now change or add an audio file, too. Click on the Preview button below the main menu window to see how the results will look when the DVD is compiled. Click the Preview button again to leave this mode.
- Anything you do in the main menu, you can repeat for the submenu; you don't have to use the same theme for the submenu, but you will find that the movie hangs together better if you use the same or a similar theme throughout.

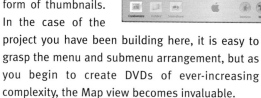

MAP VIEW

The Map button displays your DVD project in the form of a flow diagram. It shows each of the individual stages that you have added to the project in the form of thumbnails. In the case of the project you have been building here, it is easy to grasp the menu and submenu arrangement, but as you begin to create DVDs of ever-increasing complexity, the Map view becomes invaluable.

Fig 17

Fig 18

Optional additional resources

You have added your main movie and assigned section breaks to it so that viewers can rapidly navigate to selected passages. You may want to add additional movies or, in the case of this holiday DVD, you might want to append the best photos you took. You can add additional movies to your main menu in the same way you did with the original. Adding

photos, which will take the form of an automated album, requires a slightly different process:

- Click on the Slideshow button at the base of the screen to create a new entry (labelled "My Slideshow") in the main menu. Select this text and type in your own title, such as "Photo Album", as here.
- Double click on the title to open the slideshow creator. You can now drag images from a folder on to the workspace. Thumbnails of the selected images will be created, but be warned: this can take some time, particularly if your original photo files are large.
- At the base of the screen you can see the slideshow parameters. These are largely self-explanatory, but here is an overview of the options:
- Click on the Loop Slideshow box to let the slideshow play continuously.
- Clicking on the Display ⟨···· ····⟩ during the slideshow places left and right arrows on the screen so that viewers can move manually from slide to slide, forwards or backwards.
- If you want to add copies of the original images (rather than the reduced-size images), click on the Add original photos on DVD-ROM button.
- Use the pull-down Slide Duration menu to set a time for each slide's display.
- Use the Transition pull-down menu to create a transition between each slide.
- Drag an audio file (or multiple files) to the Audio button to give the slideshow background music.

Once you have added any movies of photos and provided a soundtrack, you have just about completed the project. It is a good idea at this point to select File ····⟩ Save Project to save all our hard work up to this point.

Burning the DVD

The simple stage: click on the Burn button, drop a blank DVD into the drive and wait. It is a good idea (no, it is essential) that before doing this you preview your production. Once the burning process begins you can't stop and change anything. If something is wrong, you will have wasted time and the cost of a blank disc.

While the burning is taking place, consider what you want to do next with your project. Like a movie you have created, you may want to preserve it for future use, perhaps to burn another copy (remember, DVDs are not indestructible and are prone to failure). If so, you need to make an archive copy of the project. This ensures you have a repository that contains all the resources used in making the DVD, along with all the links and theme modifications.

In iDVD, once the disc has been burned and ejected, click on File ···⟩ Archive Project. A dialogue box will open and advise you of the size of the archive and give you the option of including the themes themselves and also saving encoded files. If you save these, it will save you time when it comes to assembling the DVD next time.

And finally

You should now have a DVD you can put in your domestic DVD player and have friends and family watch and enjoy. But what if the disc doesn't play? Check these possible causes:

1. DVD-authoring and burning applications designed for consumer use tend to use low data rates (low bit rates) for encoding to enable two hours of material to be recorded on a 4.7GB DVD. Some DVD players don't play low-bit-rate DVDs. You will need to ensure that either the DVD players are compatible (by burning a test disc) or else burn a shorter length of material at standard bit rates.

2. Many DVD players (particularly older machines) are not tolerant of recorded DVDs. Many will play DVD-R format discs but fewer will play the re-recordable DVD-RW or alternate format DVD+RW discs. Again, check compatibility with a test disc.

3. Fast-moving action requires higher data rates to record accurately and with good definition. Fast-moving subjects and heavy action scenes can appear soft-focused when recorded with low data rates.

DVD CREATION GOES WIDE AND HIGH DEFINITION

2005 saw many movie-editing and DVD-ceating software applications offer high-definition capabilities and widescreen.

From version 5, iDVD is compatible with HDTV. Even if you don't have an HDV video camcorder, you can produce breathtakingly detailed slideshows from your digital image.

DVD BURNING TIPS

• Always use high-quality media. Try out different brands. If you look closely, some cheap media have blemishes on the writing side. Give these a wide berth. When you find one that gives consistently good results, stick with it.

• Handle discs with care – before and after burning. Although DVD discs are resilient, fingerprints on the surface before burning will lead to a rejected disc; afterwards will make it difficult to read. It's also a good idea to keep discs in sleeves or cases when not used. This will keep them free of dust and other marks.

• Run only DVD burning on your computer when burning a disc. Other open applications can make demands on the computer's processor, interrupting the flow of data to the drive and causing the recording to be aborted. Even background applications can cause problems – including virus-checking software.

• Keep your hard disc tidy! Run a disc defragmentation utility to ensure that data is stored in a relatively contiguous way prior to being copied to the DVD. This ensures that the computer doesn't have to waste time jumping around your hard disc retrieving data and – possibly – interrupting the data flow again.

PERSONAL VIDEO RECORDERS

We mentioned earlier that the personal in Personal Video Recorder (PVR) actually relates to the content recorded. Once you have set up a few recordings, the system tends to know the programmes you enjoy and can even predict the type of programmes you might want and will record these, too. You can also pause live television, skip commercials and access, where available, interactive features.

PVRs are proliferating, but the names that started the trend include TiVo, popular in the US and with more modest penetration in Europe. More PVRs are now being bundled with digital television receivers. The biggest of these are the satellite television systems such as Sky+ in the UK (working with Sky distributed digital satellite) and the corresponding American system, DirecTiVo, which is an amalgam of the TiVo system and DirecTV reception.

The rationale behind PVRs was to make things for us, as consumers, as simple as possible. Despite all the attempts made to simplify the programming of video recorders, there is still a huge percentage of users who have never used timer programming; many of these have never even set the clock on the recorder and time shifted recordings merely mean setting the recorder going when leaving the house and capturing perhaps two hours of irrelevant material before the desired program is recorded.

Attempts to simplify the timer recordings have been made before, with VideoPlus being the most successful of these. But this requires a degree of familiarity with the programming system and also demands that you have the VideoPlus code (a list of numbers that the system interprets as start time, end time and station) to enter.

PVRs are much simpler. You can select a programme to record by choosing it from an electronic programme guide (these are offered, in the case of Sky or DirecTV, by the broadcaster or – with independent PVRs – via the box's manufacturer, often via a website).

Once you have set up for a programme, the PVR software will assume that you want to record further programmes in the series; if it is a daily or weekly serial, subsequent episodes will be recorded, too. But because each programme has a PVR code, which doesn't just identify the programme itself, but also the type of programme, the PVR will store programmes with a similar identifier. The hard disc basis of the PVR allows for extended recordings – far longer than a VHS video tape will offer – so there is little chance (unless you rarely view your recordings) of running out of space. And

Fig 19 – TiVo Central is the key to managing your television viewing. From here you can check the programmes to record, view live television or access other value-added features.

Fig 20 – No need to miss the action when there is a distraction. When the phone rings, or someone comes to the door you can just click on the pause button and live television is frozen until you are ready to continue. You can pick up the programme or event just where you left off. Courtesy British Sky Broadcasting.

intelligent management means that if you do run low on space, predictive recordings – those you haven't specifically asked for – will be sacrificed in favour of those you have requested.

In day-to-day use it is the ability to pause – even rewind – live television that is the most useful feature. So how, exactly, can you pause live television? In fact, what you pause is a live recording of your television programme. That programme is being recorded to the hard disc of the PVR and, when you pause, recording continues. Then when you are ready to resume, you can continue by playing back the recording from the point you left off. Like a computer hard disc, you can record and read from the same disc simultaneously. Using the same recording mechanism you can also rewind the "live" recording.

Fig 21 – The Sky+ Planner, an extension to the electronic programme guide, helps you keep track of recordings, identifying those you have already viewed and those that have been recorded automatically.

SKY+

Like DirecTiVo, Sky+ doesn't make that much reference to the term PVR. And that is deliberate. Sky+ is designed to make life simpler for viewers, but it is considered that mentioning "PVR" might compromise the perception. With Sky+ you can:

- Use the electronic programme guide to plan your recordings.
- Pause and rewind live television.
- Record a series of programming automatically.
- Use one-touch recording.
- Record interactive services.
- Record enhanced sound (such as Dolby Digital 5.1) broadcast with the programming.
- Record one (or, ultimately, several) satellite stations while viewing another.
- Watch one recording while starting another recording.

Fig 22 – Sky+ replaces a standard set-top box for digital satellite and includes all the functions that you would expect, in addition to the PVR features. Courtesy British Sky Broadcasting.

Moreover, the software that controls the box can be automatically updated by using a digital data stream broadcast via the same satellites used for programme distribution. So, as new facilities become available they are automatically delivered to the box. You can also enjoy recordings from the Sky+ box in another room while those connected directly to the box watch another (this requires the Multiroom upgrade).

YOUR COMPUTER AS PVR

You may have worked out by now that a PVR is essentially a cut-down computer, featuring a hard disc and controlling software. So it should not come as too much of a surprise to hear that you can use your computer as a PVR. There are numerous software solutions that let you use your computer's hard disc to record programming, but the most effective solutions combine this with some auxiliary software.

You will find there are different options. For example, El Gato and Hauppage make solutions that cover

Fig 23 – The EyeTV 400 solution for digital terrestrial broadcasts. The box provides the necessary decoding of the incoming signals.

Fig 24 – EyeTV 500 offers a PVR compatible with high-definition television broadcasts.

simple television replay on your computer through digital terrestrial PVRs, digital satellite and even high-definition systems.

Just as with stand-alone units, you can pause live television, repeat a selection or fast forward through the commercials. The electronic programme guide for a computer-based PVR is typically accessed through a website. Often this gives you the added benefit of being able to schedule a recording using an Internet connection remotely. Great for recording those shows you forgot to schedule before going away.

Another benefit of using your computer is that the programming that you do download can be treated in much the same way as digital video downloaded from a digital camcorder: you can edit the output and save it to an external disc. EyeTV (and many of its equivalents) include simple editing software that will allow you to trim scenes and, for example, make your own highlights programme from a sporting event or concert.

Once you have edited the material, you can transfer it to DVD, Video CD or Super Video CD to archive it.

Like stand-alone PVRs, you can also record high-quality sound (Dolby Digital 5.1) and receive updates to the software (in this case, via the Internet). This means, as television technology evolves, your hardware and software can keep pace and you won't be left with redundant equipment, as can so often be the case. Drawbacks? You may be limited with regard to the encrypted channels available (most systems offer access only to the unencrypted "free-to-air" channels). A conditional access module (CAM) can be fitted to some units to allow the conditional access smart card to be fitted to authorize those stations.

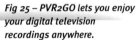

Fig 25 – PVR2GO lets you enjoy your digital television recordings anywhere.

MOBILE PVRS

A PVR essentially creates its own television schedule that you can watch when you want. But what if the cabling were to be dispensed with so that you were able to watch when and where you wanted? That was the inspiration which lay behind the Mobile PVR. From the set-top box manufacturer Pace comes PVR2GO, a portable television viewer which allows you to view down-loaded content and programming while on the move.

The unit offers all the features of a PVR – pausing, rewinding and selecting programming – and it can also handle standard MPEG (2 and 4) recordings and deliver its content to a large-screen television. For use on the go, you can use the in-built speakers to produce a 3D sound stage. PVR2GO will also decode all conditional access programming that the owner has personal access to. This makes it ideal for recording encrypted services for later viewing on the move or in the office.

Fig 26 – Computer-based PVRs include their own interface for setting recordings, but these are often augmented with a link to a website for programming. In the case of EyeTV, this is Titan TV in the USA and TVTV in the UK and mainland Europe.

SECRETS OF THE SILVER DISC

CDs and, latterly DVDs, are now widely used for music and video distribution and have, to all intents and purposes, usurped the compact cassette and VCR. But the ubiquitous silver disc has other strings to its bow. Hidden under the glare of CD and DVD are other disc formats. Some are useful in that they allow those of us without DVD burners to produce DVD content that we can share. Others address acknowledged shortcomings with the audio on CDs. Let's take a look at some of them.

DVD-Audio

When people talk about "DVDs", they generally mean DVD-Video – the format used to distribute movies and TV series. There is also an audio-only version that uses the enhanced capacity of the DVD (compared with CD) to deliver very high-quality sound, including surround-sound options. It can also provide video and image replay and even limited interactivity. DVD Plus discs, sometimes called Dual Discs, are double-sided versions of DVD-Audio discs that have a standard CD version of the audio content on the "B" side of the disc. DVD-Audio players will play standard CDs but they also have, optionally, Internet connections to enable track and other information to be downloaded.

Fig 27 – New technology – Super Audio CD – needed new expression. The Shanling Super Audio CD "Tube Disc" player makes an obvious statement visually but also ensures that the ultimate quality is delivered

Fig 28 – The Super Audio CD format required new methods of recording. The first DSD recorder was released by the UK-based audio pioneer, Genex in the shape of the Genex GX8500 shown here

Super Audio CD (SACD)

Super Audio CDs are audio-only discs (though limited video content or interactivity has been offered on some discs) that give very high-quality sound. These are generally offered as twin-format discs, with a standard CD version of the audio provided for those listening with conventional CD players.

The benefits of SACD is a recording and reproduction system that better represents the original music. It is a process called Direct Stream Digital and it follows the waveform of the audio being recorded rather than sampling the waveform, as in the case of standard CD audio recording.

Video CD (VCD)

Video CDs are based on a standard CD, but contain video and audio. A standard 700MB CD can accommodate up to 80 minutes of full-motion video and stereo sound. This is recorded using the inferior MPEG-1 format that was superseded by MPEG-2, the format that requires greater capacity but offers better quality and is used for DVD video. Video CDs are rarely found now because we, as consumers, demand the better quality of DVD. Video CD's MPEG-1 offers picture quality on a par with VHS video. The format is still hanging on in the Far East, where you can even find dedicated Video CD players. Note that Video CD is not the same as CDVideo. The latter format is based on analogue video and digital audio. CDVideos offer great picture quality but limited capacity – perhaps five minutes on a CD-sized (gold) disc.

Fig 30 – Now that DVD has become the de rigueur standard for video, Video CD has become something of a fringe medium used, as here, for bootleg recording

Fig 29 – Many innovative artists – such as Jean Michael Jarre here – were amongst the first to adopt new formats such as Video CD

Super Video CD (SVCD)

Similar to a VCD, though with a slightly reduced capacity (up to 60 minutes on a 700MB disc), SVCDs use the MPEG-2 recording format to offer enhanced video quality. SVCDs can be produced using appropriate software on computers that don't have DVD burners, and the discs can be replayed on most DVD players (as well as computers). Menus and chapters can be included (as with DVDs) on discs, and discs can be produced that include photo slide shows. Many of the more popular CD-burning applications can produce SVCD-format discs.

CVD

The Compact Video Disc is essentially an SVCD that has been recorded using a slightly lower video resolution. By using a lower resolution you can record higher data rates (reducing the possibility of

pixelation-type artifacts), but the result is a slightly softer image.

Extended SVCD (XSVCD)

This system uses higher data rates and higher resolution than SVCD to give the best video quality. XSVCD discs can be played on many (but not all) DVD players. Some DVD players are not able to read data sufficiently fast from a CD disc, although they can read at the required data rate from DVD. Most computers can read XSVCD discs but some will need the installation of a software VCD/MPG player.

miniDVD

The miniDVD is not the DVD equivalent of a mini CD, a recording made on an 8 cm (3 in) disc rather than a 15 cm (6 in) disc. Rather, it is DVD content that has been recorded in DVD format on a CD. These are sometimes called Compact DVD or cDVD. Because it uses the highest quality throughout, miniDVDs tend to have running times of around 12–15 minutes. Discs can be played on a very limited number of stand-alone players – many DVD players are not configured to read DVD data from a CD disc.

DivX

This is an MPEG-4 recording format that is looked at in more detail on page 84–5.

DVD: THE NEXT GENERATION

When recordable CD-ROMs became widely available they were a revelation. True, power users had for some time been using Zip discs and magneto-optical discs, but for the rest of us it was the 1.44MB floppy disc that was the most widely available recording medium. The enormous headroom provided – 650MB – was regarded as excessive for many. Soon, however, as digital photographs and MP3 music libraries blossomed, disc makers squeezed even more onto each disc – up to 700MB – to satisfy demand.

Those who had enjoyed the benefits of CD-ROM were quick to jump aboard the recordable DVD format. This afforded for those who needed to back up their libraries a convenient medium. Better still, this medium, by virtue of its "Versatile" nature, could also be used for producing programming and video content to be played on DVD players. As a result, it is rapidly overtaking VHS as the preferred video-recording format.

Now, with high-definition television and with digital video and images increasing in their file sizes, even the DVD is proving too small for many demands. Although the DVD format allows multiple layers and two-sided recording, there is still a ceiling of 18GB. This capacity, once only dreamed of, is now considered too small.

Recording the blues

So enter a new generation of disc-based recording formats, spearheaded by Blu-ray. Designed originally to support the recording of high-definition television programming, it is now seen by most manufacturers and industry pundits as providing the definitive recording medium across digital technologies for the next decade.

Fig 31 – Blu-ray logo

The name "Blu-ray" describes the difference between this system and previous ones: it uses a blue laser to read and write. Blue lasers have shorter wavelengths, allowing the beam to be focused with greater precision than the red lasers of earlier devices. Data can thus be more precisely packed on

Blu-ray

What formats are there?
- BD-ROM: a read only format for prerecorded content.
- BD-RE: a rewritable format for (principally) HDTV recording.
- BD-RL: a recordable format for PC data/media storage.
- BD-RW: a rewritable format for PC data storage.

Other formats are also planned.

What is the storage capacity?
- Single layer discs: 23.3GB, 25GB or 27GB.
- Dual layer discs: 46.6GB, 50GB or 54GB.

Four layer 100GB+ discs are currently under development.

How much can you record on a Blu-ray disc?
- On a 25GB disc you can record 12 hours of conventional, standard-definition television, or about two hours of HDTV.

Do you need to use a cartridge for discs?
- No. But rather like early CD-ROMs, early Blu-ray discs may require cartridges.

Can you replay DVDs in Blu-ray players/recorders?
- Yes, though individual models may not support DVD replay

Is Blu-ray the same as HD-DVD?
- No. Like VHS and Beta, these are two competing, incompatible formats. HD-DVD also uses a blue laser but records data in a different way.

to the disc. The word "Blu" in Blu-ray is deliberately spelled in this way to allow the copyrighting of the name. The good news for users and prospective users is that Blu-ray players and recorders will be backwardly compatible with the red laser discs, DVD and CD, allowing one machine to play back discs of all formats.

Fig 32 – Caddies will protect some Blu-ray discs from dust and fingerprints.

(you can record two hours of HDTV or 12 hours of standard-definition television on a 25GB Blu-ray disc), it will also feature in new PlayStation models. Sony, keen to promote the digital-hub nature of the PlayStation concept, sees new PlayStation models from PlayStation 3 using Blu-ray. This will give game designers more freedom in multi-threaded gaming but will also be used to stimulate interest in delivery of pre-recorded material, especially that from Sony's Sony Pictures subsidiary.

The other kid on the block

Now we are used to new formats getting a rough ride as competitors offer similar, yet incompatible, systems. Think back to the battle between VHS and Betamax video, DCC and DAT and, latterly, DVD-R and DVD+R formats. At one point there were no less than five formats vying to succeed DVD, but now there appears to be just one serious competitor – HD-DVD. More an evolution of DVD, it also uses blue lasers for increased capacity. HD-DVD (high-definition and high-density DVD) discs can hold 20GB on a single-side single layer.

At the time of writing, both Blu-ray and HD-DVD were working hard on getting the major film and television studios to back their respective formats. With the benefit of hindsight – from earlier video and disc formats – both camps have realized that it is the software that is crucial to a format's success. In this case, software means programming and movies.

By the beginning of 2005 Blu-ray remained the only format to have demonstrated – and sold – working players. By the time you are reading this there may well be a victor in the battle. But with so much to lose, don't expect either to throw in the towel without a major fight.

Fig 33 – Sony's BDZS77 was the first widely available Blu-ray recorder.

Although Blu-ray is able to store up to 50GB of data – an amount that will see it welcomed by many digital movie makers and archivists – it will be the proliferation of high-definition television services that will bring the format into the mainstream. When the format was originally specified, it was optimized for directly recording the digital television signals used globally, avoiding the need to transcode – the decoding and recoding required for DVD-based recording. This removes the need for extra processing and avoids the potential for quality loss. And like DVD-RAM, you can watch a recording while recording on another part of the disc.

Blu-ray for gaming

Although HDTV recording will be the primary aim of Blu-ray

DIGITAL BROADCASTING

IN THIS CHAPTER WE WILL:

- Discover the history and evolution of digital television – and radio.
- Look at the virtues of digital television.
- Explore how digital television works and how it can make life easier.
- Look at home cinema.
- See what digital audio broadcasting – digital radio – has to offer.

Fig 1 – How do you keep up with hundreds of TV channels? If you're a digital satellite broadcaster with a video wall like this. Courtesy of SES Astra).

FOR MOST PEOPLE, DIGITAL TELEVISION HAS BEEN THE MOST OBVIOUSLY PROMOTED DIGITAL TECHNOLOGY IN RECENT YEARS. ALTHOUGH CDS HAVE BEEN DELIVERING THE DIGITAL GOODS FOR A COUPLE OF DECADES, THERE IS NO DOUBT THAT DIGITAL TELEVISION HAS HAD THE BIGGEST IMPACT, PERHAPS REFLECTING THE SIGNIFICANCE OF TELEVISION IN OUR LIVES.

THE TWIN PILLARS ON WHICH THIS TECHNOLOGY HAS BEEN PROMOTED ARE EXTENDED CHOICE (MORE CHANNELS, GREATER INTERACTIVITY) AND BETTER PICTURE QUALITY. THE FORMER IS CERTAINLY TRUE BUT THE LATTER WAS NOT IMMEDIATELY OBVIOUS TO MANY PEOPLE. ONLY WITH THE INTRODUCTION OF HIGH-DEFINITION TELEVISION, HDTV, HAS THE PROMISE OF ENHANCED QUALITY BEEN DELIVERED. LET US NOW TAKE A LOOK AT HOW TELEVISION BROKE FREE FROM THE ANALOGUE WORLD AND HOW IT IS DELIVERED TO OUR HOMES, WORKPLACES AND EVEN OUR COMPUTER OR MOBILE DEVICES.

WE WILL ALSO TAKE A LOOK AT DIGITAL RADIO. BORN BEFORE DIGITAL TELEVISION, IT HAS BEEN DEVELOPING MODESTLY IN THE SHADOW OF ITS VISUAL COUNTERPART.

DIGITAL TELEVISION

It might be useful first to explain what we mean by digital television. The description for the purposes of this book applies to the transmission to our homes of television signals in digital form. This clear statement has to be made because, in fact, television studios have been working in the digital domain for some years. Studios and producers have long recognized the benefits of recording programming on digital video tape and editing digitally since the late 1980s. Even the delivery of programming to transmitters has often been digital. It is only more recently that the onward transmission to our homes has also been digital.

From the 1950s and 1960s analogue colour television has been broadcast around the world. There were two incompatible standards – NTSC in North America and Japan, and PAL in Europe and many other countries. A variation on PAL – SECAM – could be found in France and Eastern Europe.

The terrestrial broadcasting of television requires an enormous amount of bandwidth – the range of frequencies over which data is transmitted – which limits the number of television channels that can be broadcast to any one location without interference. As the demand for more and more channels increased, broadcasters sought other methods and techniques for broadcasting. Cable is a well-established method but for widely spread communities this is often not a viable option.

Satellite broadcasting was another. In fact,

Fig 2 – Dishes like this are now commonplace, distributing television stations and receiving signals from satellites. Courtesy NTL.

satellites had been used for some time to feed signals from studios and broadcasting centres to cable heads (Fig 2). Cable heads are the ground stations of networked cable that receive programming for distribution to their customers.

Direct broadcasting via satellite

Direct Broadcasting Satellite television (DBS) was something different. Unhindered by the constraints placed on terrestrial broadcasting, companies could explore new strategies. In the UK and across Europe,

Fig 3 – The ill-fated BSB Direct Broadcasting Satellite service introduced electronic programme guides and widescreen long before a true digital service rediscovered them.

a new pair of similar broadcasting standards were devised, D-MAC and D2-MAC, respectively. Although largely analogue, these formats (short for D Multiplexed Analogue Components) separated out the colour and brightness parts of a television picture and, along with a modest digital control signal, broadcast these components in a multiplex. Multiplexes allow large amounts of differing data to be combined and transmitted in a stream and then separated when received. The principal benefits of the MAC formats were clearer pictures and the opportunity to transmit digital data. This usually comprised basic (but, for the day, very welcome) electronic programme guides.

There was no doubt that MAC and DBS offered quality benefits, but they came at a cost. In Europe the MAC broadcasts fell victim to Astra programming. Set up to feed cable heads, the signal strength proved high enough to broadcast direct to homes (DTH). Based on the cheaper PAL and SECAM systems, Astra-based services dealt a fatal blow to D-MAC (Fig 3).

It seemed as if television broadcasting had also been dealt a technological blow, taking a big step backwards. But it proved only a momentary one. The insatiable appetite for new channels across Europe, particularly in the UK, the newly unified Germany and a liberalized Eastern Europe meant that a whole group of satellites were positioned along with the original Astra satellite (Fig 4). Still there was not

enough capacity. Rather than launch more and more satellites, the economics and logistics required that broadcasters and operators come up with a different solution. That solution was digital transmission.

A digital broadcast effectively takes up less space in bandwidth terms, allowing more channels to be broadcast in a similar frequency range. In fact, broadcasters use multiplexing, broadcasting five or more television channels using the space normally allocated to a single analogue channel. The nature of digital television is such that the amount of data transmitted for one channel can be varied: the more data that is transmitted, the more detailed and authentic the pictures. Transmitting a lower amount of data results in a less-detailed image that may show arteficing, digital effects that resemble pixelation, particularly on fast-moving scenes.

In some cases, ten or more channels can be squeezed into the space of a single channel, along,

Fig 4 – Satellite broadcasting is free from many of the technical constraints that affect terrestrial broadcasting. Courtesy SES Astra.

Digital text services make teletext transmissions look very dated, while the audiences of big sporting events have the opportunity to choose different camera angles or (for example, in the case of the Wimbledon tennis championships) any one of the games currently in play.

Additional services offer simple Internet-like facilities for shopping and banking using a telephone connection as the return path from the satellite.

Fig 5 – The rapid adoption of digital direct to home television services was driven by simple, easy-to-use equipment, such as these from Sky (UK) and DirecTV (USA).

sometimes, with some radio stations. Typically, mainstream networks (those with high audiences) use a higher data rate to deliver better-quality pictures. Those from minority channels use the slower (and cheaper) rates.

Digital satellite television (Fig 5) made its mark across the world – principally in North America and Europe – in the late 1990s, driven by simple dish and set-top box systems that made it easy to receive and easy to navigate the hundreds of channels that quickly appeared.

Since launch we have seen interactive services piggy-backing on the normal television services.

Digital cable

Not to be left behind, the cable companies went digital, too. Despite having the capability of delivering many tens of channels, this once-impressive number was now looking rather tame; digital cable can offer channel numbers on a par with those of digital satellite. Often faced with harsh competition from the satellite broadcasters (in the UK, Sky Television gave away satellite systems, charging only a nominal installation fee), cable companies have had to add additional services. Bundled telephony and broadband Internet connections are typically the unique selling propositions of cable, offering keenly priced packages.

Fig 6 – With hundreds of channels to monitor, the control room of a satellite digital television service is a busy place. Courtesy SES Astra.

THE DIGITAL ADVANTAGE

To sum up the advantages of digital television:

- Better image quality for a given bandwidth.
- The ability to broadcast multiple channels in the space of one analogue channel.
- Multiple delivery methods: satellite, terrestrial, cable, phone and Internet (Fig 7).
- Compatible with computers and computer-based devices.
- Greater interactivity options.
- Good audio quality, with the option for multiple languages.
- Reception more reliable and less prone to environmental interference.
- Upgrade paths to HDTV.

Fig 7 – Digital television blurs the boundary between television and Internet.

Digital terrestrial television

Digital broadcasting brings a new lease of life to the conventional airwaves. A digital multiplex, broadcasting in the bandwidth space equivalent to a single channel, can accommodate six television stations (in standard definition), and even more if a lesser data rate is used. Fortunately, for the crowded bandwidths found in most parts of the world, digital multiplexes are less likely to cause interference to existing stations, and can be placed closer together across the frequency band. In the UK, for example, in a crowded waveband that could accommodate no more conventional stations, four multiplexes offering 30 stations have been launched.

In its original incarnation, digital terrestrial television (DTT) included all the original free-to-air stations, new free-to-air services and a raft of subscription services. The original subscription service, Ondigital, later rebranded ITV Digital, made little headway in the face of competition from the digital cable and satellite broadcasters and closed down. Part of the lack of success was down to pricing – it cost about the same as the competing satellite service but offered a far smaller range of programming. It also offered poorer picture quality. But enhanced picture quality was one of the *raisons d'être* of digital television. Consumers were confused and opted not to subscribe.

Later, the DTT service was rescued and rebranded as Freeview. As the name suggests, it offers all the programming for free, comprising the free-to-air services from the original service along with some specially commissioned new stations. Freeview also allocated more bandwidth to many of the stations, so overcoming the hurdle of poor picture quality. This proved a winner. No subscriptions, and wider choice at no extra cost. Adoption of Freeview has been exceptional and proved a successful model for elsewhere in the world.

Ironically, Freeview has had a subscription service bundled with it, using up spare capacity. But unlike previous services, this offers only a small number of the most popular subscription stations for a nominal fee and without ongoing contracts. Again, another (if more modest) winner.

Fig 8 – Digital terrestrial broadcasts deliver digital quality from the same transmitters that deliver conventional broadcasts. Courtesy NTL.

Down the line

The nature of digital television also makes it possible to deliver transmissions in ways impossible for conventional, analogue signals, such as down a phone line. Using fast digital phone connections, you can have broadband Internet access along with digital television stations on demand. Services tend to offer a more limited choice than satellite or cable, but include free-to-air and the pick of subscription services. There are often unique channels offering local interest or specialized programming. You also have the option, found on some cable station, too, of replaying programmes from the most popular channels on demand – either momentarily after they are transmitted or for a full seven days afterwards.

Fig 9 – Though using only a standard telephone line, digital television by phone line offers a wide choice: here is just part of the portfolio offered by London-based Homechoice.

Video on demand (VOD) takes this one step further, by offering a bank of programming (which might include movies, drama, comedies, sport or news) and allowing you to select a feature to watch on demand. Just like selecting a DVD or video tape, but all at the press of a button.

High-definition television

So far, the rationale for digital television may not have appealed to the videophile. Greater choice, which digital television clearly offers, doesn't necessarily equate with better quality. The quality issue is now being addressed through high-definition television.

The concept is nothing new: Japan has offered HDTV services for some time on both analogue and digital television platforms, but now the digital version is spreading worldwide. For HDTV the vertical resolution (and hence the detail) in a television picture is increased from the 625 lines of PAL and SECAM systems or 525 lines of NTSC to between 720 and 1,080 lines (Fig 10). In this new format, all programming is produced in widescreen format (see pages 110–11) with Dolby Digital 5.1 sound (see page 114).

HDTV is increasingly important as we get used to – and demand – larger television screens. At 81 cm (32 in) we reach the limit at which a conventional digital or analogue channel (dubbed standard definition) can be displayed. Any larger and the picture becomes soft and less well defined. This rather negates the reason for large, widescreen televisions: being able to sit close so that the screen fills out peripheral vision. Increase the resolution by a factor of three or four and you get a much more detailed image that you can enjoy close, or closer up.

The drawback here is that HDTV demands a higher bandwidth. We are talking bandwidths on a par with conventional, standard-definition analogue stations. This means that the satellite – with its much broader bandwidths – has been the first to exploit the medium.

Fig 10 – The difference between HDTV and standard-definition television is marked. Examine part of an image in both (that indicated by the red frame), and the increased detailing is obvious.

UNDERSTANDING WIDESCREEN FORMATS

Although widescreen is not synonymous with digital television, it is the format that is now normal for digital broadcasts. But in a world where there are still conventional-format televisions and programming that was produced in this format, how are these represented on screen? And how are widescreen images presented on a conventional (or "narrowscreen") television?

A conventional television picture is produced so that the ratio of the width to the height, the aspect ratio, is always 4 to 3, or 4:3. So a television screen that is 45 cm (18 in) high will be 60 cm (24 in) wide. Widescreen television is produced with an aspect ratio of 16:9, so that a screen 45 cm (18 in) high will now be 80 cm (32 in) wide.

VIEWING WIDESCREEN ON A CONVENTIONAL SCREEN

Until widescreen broadcasting is the norm, not all programming will be compatible, in terms of making best use of the picture area, with our televisions. Often the set-top boxes used to decode digital television pictures (whether from a digital satellite, terrestrial or cable) allow us to switch the display format to match that of the television being used or to optimize the picture. Take this original widescreen image. This is the shape of the television picture being sent to the television (Fig 11).

Fig 11

If we watch this on a conventional-format television, it clearly won't fit. One option is to enlarge the centre area of picture so that the height of the picture matches that of the television screen. Because the picture is wider, parts of the image to each side will be lost, as here (Fig 12).

For most programming, this option is perfectly adequate. Most of the action, whether in sports, drama or documentary, takes place in the central

Fig 12

region. With only a limited loss, then, most viewers will be happy with this compromise.

Increasingly, however, film-makers in all genres are learning to make the best use of the whole frame. Where this is the case, you have the alternative of displaying the picture in total. To accommodate the full width, the height is reduced and the characteristic letterbox view is produced. This is familiar to many of us – it is the way widescreen cinematic movies have been presented for many years (Fig 13).

Fig 13

VIEWING A CONVENTIONAL PROGRAMME ON A WIDESCREEN TELEVISION

Fig 14

Watching widescreen programming on a widescreen television makes the maximum use of the format, filling the screen at all times. But what about displaying a conventional image, such as this? (Fig 14)

Fig 15

We could choose to display the picture in its entirety. This involves displaying the full height of the picture. Now the picture is not sufficiently wide to fill screen so rather than letterboxing, you see side banding (sometimes called pillar boxes) (Fig 15).

For those who have invested in widescreen televisions, this option is often not acceptable, presenting a picture about 25 per cent smaller than the screen is capable of delivering. So you could zoom in, making the width of the picture the same as the width of the screen. Now, you lose parts of the picture along the top and bottom (Fig 16).

Fig 16

This gives a successful full-screen image, but with a couple of problems. For people who need subtitles, the text will often be lost or truncated when the picture is zoomed in this fashion. In addition, when viewing conventional-format news programmes, the newsreader's head is often trimmed at the top of the screen. Many televisions avoid either of these drawbacks by offering additional picture modes that move the displayed part of the picture up or down accordingly.

Back when there was little widescreen programming, it was customary to offer an additional picture mode variously described as "wide" or "stretched". This involved keeping the height of the picture the same but stretching the width to that of the screen.

The result is obviously stretched (although smart stretching modes, which stretched the less-important edges of the picture more than the centre, are often used) and did the progress of widescreen in the consumer market no favours in the early days. But if you don't mind the compromises, it is a good way to get the immersive experience of widescreen with your collection of pre-widescreen media (Fig 17).

Fig 17

MORE FORMATS

Television stations that broadcast in conventional format (often an analogue station simultaneously broadcast with a widescreen digital one) often use a 14:9 aspect ratio. This gives a mild letterbox effect, but ensures virtually all the important action is displayed. The modest letterboxing is also less likely to provoke complaints from viewers feeling short changed by narrower letterboxes.

Fig 18 – A 2.35:1 movie compared with widescreen format (white rectangle) and 4:3 (black rectangle).

Some theatrical movies are produced in wider aspect ratios than 16:9. At 2:1 or greater, these will appear letterboxed even on a 16:9 widescreen television. Some televisions allow zooming, but this can often compromise image quality. For most widescreens, however, the loss is a good trade-off when enjoying the sweeping panoramas.

HOME CINEMA

Creating a home cinema can be exciting, but it needs a good deal of forward planning. Here is a stepwise approach to its design and implementation, along with details of some of the key components.

First, what is needed to create a home cinema? The term tends to be bandied around a lot and gets applied to everything from a mini-theatrical cinema to a simple television with extra speakers. For our purposes here, the concept is being based on a large-screen television, a source (or sources) of high-quality programming, an audio amplifier and a set of speakers.

Budget and space

Your first considerations need to be practical: budget and space. If you have a modest budget, it might not be inappropriate to consider a home cinema; a high-quality television with DVD player may be a better option even if it does not provide the full theatrical experience. Similarly, if you don't have a lot of space, your aspirations may also be curtailed. A home cinema does require enough room to accommodate all the hardware elements with sufficient space for the speakers to project their sound.

Vision

Assuming you have met the relevant criteria, a good place to start is with the television (we still tend to call it a television, even though in some set-ups it may not be connected to a television tuner – it may receive its input from, say, a DVD player). For the true cinematic experience, you need a screen that is as large as possible so that the images fill as much of your vision as possible.

The traditional route of a large conventional television is falling increasingly out of favour on account of cost (alternatives are more viable these days) and bulk. About 91 cm (36 in) is the biggest conventional screen size that can be accommodated and the cabinet that houses it will be colossal. Already a large part of your prospective cinema's floor space is lost just to the television.

Nowadays, it is more likely that you will opt for a projection television system or a flat-screen monitor. Projection televisions have come on in leaps and bounds in recent years and are capable of projecting images up to 1.5 m (5 ft), even in a brightly lit room. The drawbacks are that the screen is still not as bright as you would find with other options and projector bulbs can be absurdly expensive to

Fig 19 – The purist will demand perfect geometry of their home cinema layout, as in the case of this Jamo system. © Jamo.

FLAT-PANEL SCREENS: LCD VS PLASMA

Criteria	Plasma	LCD	Best
Screen size	91–152 cm (36–60 in)	25–127 cm (10–50 in)	Plasma
Refresh rate (ability to display fast-changing action)	Equivalent to conventional television	Slower, but technology is improving	Plasma
Viewing angle	Wide (155°)	Wider (up to 170°)	LCD
Life expectancy (based on 24/7 use)	Up to 30,000 hours	Up to 60,000 hours	LCD
Durability	Fragile	More robust	LCD
Weight	Heavy	Lighter	LCD
Burn-in (stationary images leaving a mark on screen)	Susceptible (but improving)	Not susceptible	LCD
Contrast ratio (ratio of light to dark areas on screen)	250:1	400:1	LCD
Thickness	7.5 cm (3 in)	5 cm (2 in)	LCD
Perceptual image quality (what viewers prefer)	High	Moderate	Plasma

Fig 20 – Plasma TV caption to go here Plasma TV caption to go here Plasma TV caption to go here

replace: up to 40 per cent of the projector's cost. But if you have a room where you can dim the lighting and want a really big picture – beyond 1.5 m (5 ft) – this is the ideal solution.

Flat-panel televisions have been the stuff of science fiction for decades. Now they are a reality and make it possible to hang a large television on your wall in the manner of a painting. Two technologies offer flat displays – plasma and LCD. Time was when plasma was the obvious choice, but LCD has been making up ground fast. The differences are highlighted in the table here (see above). It is best to audition your shortlisted screens and see how they compare: in qualitative tests, plasmas tend to score higher, size for size. But with the technology evolving continuously, benchmarks can quickly become out of date.

Audio

Getting a great quality screen for your cinema is crucial, but, as many enthusiasts will attest, the sound is of equal importance. Again, you have choices. On the one hand there are all-in-one systems that deliver all the audio components (and often a DVD player, too) in a single package. Everything is perfectly matched and all you need do is make some simple connections. This can be a very effective solution, especially for novices. This is also a great solution when your home cinema has to serve other purposes, such as be a family room. Compact and unobtrusive speakers will not compromise your lifestyle.

By the same token, modest speakers rarely

- Dolby Digital: Formerly known as AC-3, Dolby Digital is a lossy (data is compressed with some data lost) audio system. The lost data, thanks to perceptual coding, is generally inaudible sound. Used for high-quality sound on DVDs and digital television (including HDTV), but only in the United States and some other countries. Offers five full bandwidth channels, left and right front, left and right rear, and centre channel along with a low-frequency effect (LFE) channel (to provide the low frequency sounds essential for special effects). This sound stage is normally described as 5.1.
- DTS: Digital Theater Systems, first used with the release of *Jurassic Park* in 1993, and the chief competitor to Dolby Digital (though often DVDs are encoded with both and DVD players can decode both). DTS's chief attribute is that it normally requires lower data rates to encode similar sound.
- Dolby Pro Logic: Uses three audio channels to create the sound output from five speakers. A little long in the tooth now, but it has been included in VHS video recordings for many years.
- Dolby Pro Logic II: An advanced sound system that can process conventional stereo sound to create surround-sound effects from five speakers. Useful for interpreting "old" sources, such as movies or CDs.
- Dolby Surround Sound: Predecessor to Dolby Pro Logic that used only right, left and rear channels. A good (rather than excellent) surround-sound effect, but with the sound being less focused (and dialogue less precisely defined) than in later systems.

Fig 21 – This Panasonic home cinema manages to integrate well into the owner's home. Here it is easy to see the 106 cm (42 in) screen along with front stereo speakers, centre channel and subwoofer, but none of the elements intrude visually on the room. Courtesy Panasonic.

essentially ensures that voices appear to come from their on-screen images), and a subwoofer, which gives the omnidirectional deep sound that adds "body". These are all connected to an amplifier that decodes the sound from the television or DVD into the separate channels. Today, cinema-grade sound is usually transmitted in Dolby Digital, DTS or Dolby Pro-Logic. This can be replayed in conventional stereo (or even mono), but when it is run through an appropriate decoder you can get the full range of sound channels that you can feed to the speakers.

Sometimes it can be cost-efficient (not to mention space-efficient) to get a television that includes an integral Dolby decoder. This removes the need for an external amplifier and (through the use of a single remote control) can simplify operation. At the other extreme, the audiophile will demand a two-stage sound processor. The first stage decodes the signal into its separate components and the second performs the amplification. But these cost serious money and demand a dedicated home-cinema room to appreciate the full effect. Likewise ,at the more rarefied price levels come decoders for more advanced sound systems, such as THX Surround EX, Dolby EX and DTS ES.

Speakers

If you are going for separates – that is, components from different manufacturers – you will next need to choose your speakers. A matched set is the best way to ensure that speakers are matched for their

(although there are exceptions) give the best in sound performance; nor do they help create the best "soundstage", the optimum recreation of the sound environment as the movie director intended.

Conventionally there are six speakers: left and right front, left and right back, centre channel (which

respective roles and that there are no incompatibilities. The most important speakers are those that comprise the front stereo pair. These will be put through their paces on every occasion, made to reproduce every type of sound across a wide frequency range. These will also be the speakers you use if you listen to the radio or conventional CDs through your system. Next in importance comes the centre channel. Reproducing realistic dialogue is the essential characteristic of this.

The rear speakers reproduce environmental sounds only and help to build atmosphere. We say "only", but that is still no excuse to compromise. They need to be of equal quality to the others or there is a risk of them detracting from the overall sound quality.

Finally, the subwoofer. Working at really low frequency, this speaker can really boost the sound quality of any movie, giving true floor-shaking sound. Big and often ugly, they don't have to be precisely placed in the room. At such low frequencies (20–100Hz), your ears will find it impossible to detect where the sound originates, so the subwoofer can be placed in a corner, behind a sofa or beside a cupboard.

Programming sources

Once you have built your system, you will need programming sources. DVD is generally the staple of home cinema, but with satellite and digital terrestrial television also now providing high-quality source material, these are gaining ground. It makes sense not to economize at this stage. You will need a DVD player that offers good video quality and also handles the sound system used by the DVD recordings and the audio system. Again, it is crucial that you audition the DVD players you have shortlisted. It is surprising how different units playing the same disc can look and sound.

Fig 22 – In this configuration it is easy to adjust the position of the television and front speakers. This flexibility works well when the room needs to accommodate different uses (and different numbers of people) at different times. Courtesy Panasonic.

Fig 23 – This Gateway Media Center PC features a plasma TY style monitor and – the obvious giveaway – a remote control to allow easy access to all the features.

WINDOWS XP MEDIA CENTER: A BOLD STEP TOWARDS DIGITAL CONVERGENCE

Windows XP Media Center Edition is an extension to the standard Windows XP operating systems. Taking a step beyond Windows XP, it lets you extend your computer's power and resources to home entertainment. Rather like Apple's iLife, you can store, play and share digital music, photos, video and even, by virtue of an onboard PVR, TV.

Windows XP Media Center Edition, the operating system, is installed on Media Center PCs – it doesn't normally come installed on conventional Windows computers. Nor is it available as an upgrade to standard-edition Windows. Media Center PCs come equipped with all the additional hardware and components required to make the Media Center live up to its name and act as a digital hub.

Inside the Media Center PC

So what is it that makes a Media Center PC? Included in the package you'll find:

- A computer unit equipped with high-speed processors – essential for handling video and television.
- A large amount of RAM memory: an amount normally substantially higher than that provided in conventional computers.
- DVD drive. Most models now feature a DVD recordable drive to enable video and television programming stored on the PC to be downloaded.
- Top performance hard discs for supporting the recording of high-speed data.
- Uniquely, a full-function remote control. This gives the same functionality that you'd expect from multi-device remote controls.
- An advanced graphics card optimized to deliver the best performance when replaying games, television programming or video.
- A TV tuner. This can be a tuner designed for terrestrial, satellite or cable television transmissions.
- A Hardware encoder. This converts the incoming televisions signal or video input (say from a video camcorder) into a digital data stream that can be recorded to disc.

Fig 24 – Part computer, part home-cinema kit, this Media Center PC comes with all you need to install an impressive digital resource.

Extending your Media Center

One of the reasons that Internet-through-TV has not taken off to the degree that the proponents of the technology have often expected is down to the nature of the TV-Internet system. Offering Internet access through the TV can be confrontational. What happens when one member of the family wants to surf the web and others want to watch a movie? A conflict in which there is always one loser. Unless you have a very capitulatory family, it's a recipe for family strife.

This limitation becomes more marked in the modern home where we are used to multiple TV and computerr installations each capable of obeying different commands. So it will come as no surprise that Microsoft has come up with a solution that means the capabilities of the Media Center PC can be enjoyed around the home (it goes by the name of a Media Center Extender Set-top box, or 'Extender' for short):

• Access to all the resources on, or accessed through, your Media Center PC, wherever there is an extender unit installed.
• Enjoy one Media Center PC resource in one room, whilet others are using different resources in another. An end to conflicts!
• No need for special TV or monitors. The extender box will link up to almost any TV or TV system.

You can have up to five extenders feeding off one Media Center PC. Extenders feature simple and intuitive installers that make local configuration simple. You can even exploit any wired or wireless networks you may already have installed to distribute the signals around your home.

For devotees of Microsoft's Xbox, there's an extender pack designed to stream content from your Media Center PC directly to a remote TV attached to an Xbox. This is not a set-top box but rather a software application that is loaded in exactly the same way as a conventional Xbox game. A remote control – and receiver – ensure that you get exactly the same functionality and convenience with your Xbox as you would with a dedicated extender box.

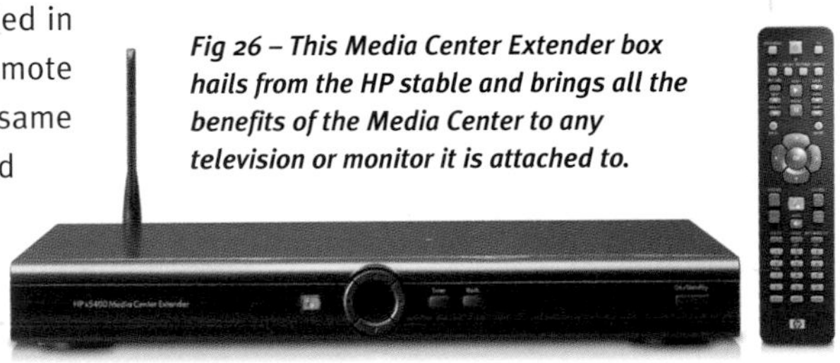

Fig 26 – This Media Center Extender box hails from the HP stable and brings all the benefits of the Media Center to any television or monitor it is attached to.

• A TV and Audio output. This lets you output your video and audio to an external television and hi-fi system.

Virtually all Media Center PCs also feature more "lounge friendly" styling, designed to make them more suitable placement at the heart of the home. The workmanlike beige or industrial grey styling of typical Windows PCs is eschewed in favour of more curvaceous designs or those that ape conventional audio video components.

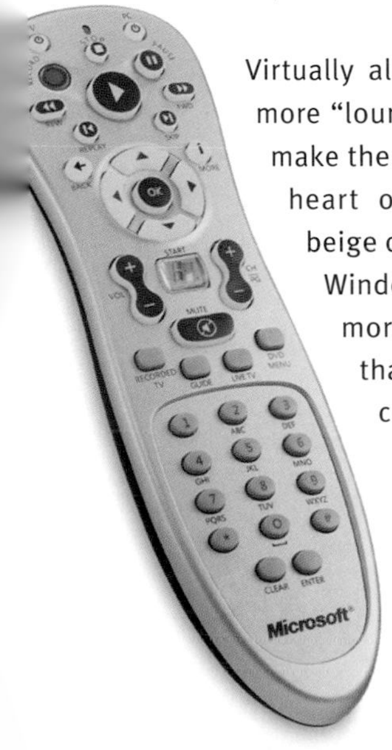

Fig 25 – The Media Center PC remote betrays its origin by virtue of the centrally located "Windows" button.

Media Center PCs in the Home

So how does a Media Center PC fit into your home and into your life?

Normally, computers find themselves, probably with deference to their styling and purpose, relegated to the study or den. As ostensibly a learning and communications tool, this is an ideal location in many ways. When we use the computer for composing and creating letters, we need to refer to correspondence files in our filing system. Likewise with our accounts. Often this is also where we'll find our Internet connection entering the house too.

For a Media Center PC the balance of use is tilted away from these more prosaic roles towards home entertainment. Suddenly, the computer is at the heart of our leisure time pursuits. It can now graduate to the lounge!

Placing a computer – no matter how aesthetic the styling – in your key living space will probably need a little more than cursory consideration. It will need to fit into your daily life and not jar with it; it also needs to conveniently offer its enhanced capabilities to users. Previously exclusive features of the computer – Internet access, word processing, image editing and movie making are now combined with the corresponding entertainment tasks: television watching, listening to music and video recording. The former require us to use a keyboard and mouse, while the latter are conducted via a well-specified remote control from the comfort of our favourite chair.

Most users find that the new experiences of the Media Centre PC are also enjoyed from a comfortable seat, using a large-screen television as the central informational display. This, though, is not always ideal. Many large-screen televisions lack the crisp resolution that we've come to expect from even a mid-range computer monitor. This can make it difficult to read computer-generated text across the room.

In many practical installations a large-screen television – used to enjoy the television programming, video recording and still images stored on or accessed through the Media Center PC – is best accompanied by a large computer monitor. This makes it possible to get the best from your movies and images but also retain all the benefits of a conventional computer monitor. It's simple to configure the computer to relay images to both screens simultaneously.

Much of you entertainment – whether web surfing, streaming video, PVR programming or humble email – will depend upon a broadband Internet connection. A hard-wired connection to the computer is ideal but a wireless connection is often more practical.

Now we need to make sure all the other connections are made. When you unpack your Media Center PC, you'll find a plethora of familiar and unusual cables and devices. Here's a quick guide to what goes where.

USB Cables: use these to connect the keyboard and mouse. If you opt for the flexibility of an infra-red keyboard and mouse, you'll need to use the USB cables – and extenders – to place the infrared receiver at a convenient location. Somewhere reasonably adjacent to where you'll be using the keyboard most often.

SVG Cable: use this to connect a conventional monitor to the Media Center PC.

SVGA, Composite, SCART, RCA Cables: You'll have a choice of these, depending on your computer and where you live. Use the appropriate set to connect your PC to the TV monitor.

Coaxial Cables: for connecting your computer's tuner to a television signal source (satellite, cable or terrestrial aerial).

Infrared keyboards and mice give you the same flexibility of use for these devices as a remote control. Don't expect either to have the same range as a remote control, though. In larger rooms it may pay to invest in a Bluetooth-enabled keyboard and mouse. These don't just have greater range, they are also more robust, signal wise, and less prone to interference or disruption.

Sound is often the Cinderella in any computer-based entertainment system. Media Center PCs often come with better-quality speakers than a standard computer. But if the Media Center PC really is going to be the pivotal home entertainment device, it makes sense to use the best possible speakers. And these will be those that you currently have on your hi-fi system. You could connect the speakers directly to the computer but connecting via your hifi will often be a more practical solution. Hooking up in this way will also let you enjoy "legacy" formats – such as vinyl albums or cassette tapes – which don't feature in the Media Center PC's arsenal.

Opposite: If you subscribe to Instant Messaging you can be alerted to an incoming message by a discreet flag over the TV or video programme that you are currently enjoying (Fig 28)
Like TiVo or Sky+, the Media Center PVR lets you instantly access previously recorded programming and schedule future programmes for recording (Fig 27)
Your collection of photos and videos can be reviewed using these simple access screens. When you've found your chosen media, you can replay the video or review the photos at will (Figs 29, 30, 31)

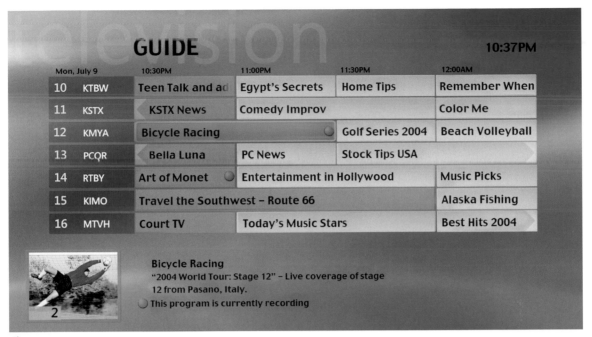

Fig 27

Fig 28   *Fig 29*

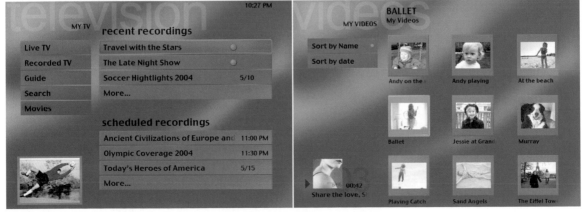

Fig 30   *Fig 31*

LOOK NO SPEAKERS! DOLBY'S VIRTUAL CINEMA

More and more people are building home cinemas with high levels of quality and great attention to detail. Most of us, however, don't have the luxury of the space or the budget. But that does not mean we have to settle for second best. In fact, even if we don't have the space to install even a modest home cinema, or if the room does not lend itself to one, we can still enjoy glorious theatrical sound, thanks to the genius of Dolby Labs.

Dolby is a name that crops up time and time again when talking about television and cinema sound, and in its Virtual Speaker Technology it has provided something special indeed. Dolby bills its Virtual Speaker Technology as a practical alternative to multi-speaker systems. Using new techniques made possible by digital technology, you can simulate surround sound with just two speakers.

Although you may have doubts, Virtual Speaker Technology really can deliver a soundstage akin to that normally provided by a five-speaker system. The good news is that it can be applied to many sound systems, including those of a television, a DVD player, PCs, personal speaker systems and,

of course, home cinema. This technology works alongside Dolby Digital and Dolby Pro-Logic II decoding (two of the most popular sound-encoding systems) to give the surround-sound experience whether the source is high-grade 5.1 sound from a digital satellite or "old" audio CDs.

Dolby is keen to promote the many-fold benefits of the system. These include:

- *Only two speakers* Cost savings are obvious but, more significantly for many users, it negates the need to install additional speakers and rearrange a room to make the best use of them.
- *Spatial cues and localization* There are no compromises in the sound, so the result is a realistic and detailed soundstage that replicates the original audio environment.
- *High sound quality* The original sound

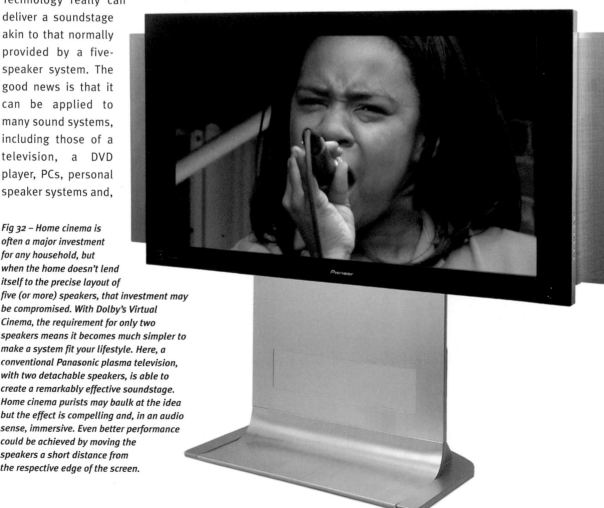

Fig 32 – Home cinema is often a major investment for any household, but when the home doesn't lend itself to the precise layout of five (or more) speakers, that investment may be compromised. With Dolby's Virtual Cinema, the requirement for only two speakers means it becomes much simpler to make a system fit your lifestyle. Here, a conventional Panasonic plasma television, with two detachable speakers, is able to create a remarkably effective soundstage. Home cinema purists may baulk at the idea but the effect is compelling and, in an audio sense, immersive. Even better performance could be achieved by moving the speakers a short distance from the respective edge of the screen.

DOLBY HEADPHONE

Dolby has been successful in removing the need for additional speakers beyond a conventional stereo pair. But the company did not stop there. Its next target was headphones. Headphones have always been something of a compromise: they offer us private listening, or listening on the move, but in audio terms they have not been able to deliver a three-dimensional soundstage that compares with that generated by conventional speakers.

Much of the advanced-modelling technology employed in the Virtual Speaker has been used to overcome the key problem with headphones. Unlike speakers, which use the acoustics of the room in which they play to create depth and width in the soundstage, headphones deliver sound direct to your eardrums. This direct delivery prevents any spatial information being conveyed.

By using powerful and very advanced digital-signal processing, Dolby Headphone processes the sound to simulate the echoes and delays that would normally affect sound delivered from speakers. The result is a sound that appears to come from outside your head and mimics the effect of five speakers. Not only that, it can also create a virtual subwoofer to ensure that the deep, booming tones are maintained.

Creating the signature of a room could be contentious. What room do you sonically recreate? In fact, Dolby chose to create three, which it dubbed Dolby Headphone (DH) modes 1, 2 and 3.

DH1 is a small room, rather like most living rooms, with soft furnishing to dampen echoes.

DH2 is what Dolby calls a more acoustically live room, where echoes and reverberation are sharper and more pronounced. This, apparently, is better for movies and general music listening.

DH3 is conceived as a "larger room", which we can interpret as a concert hall or commercial movie theatre.

Fig 33 – Dolby Virtual Speaker Modes: Reference Mode, left, Wide Mode, right.

quality is maintained despite the large amount of signal processing and filtering required to create the soundstage. The net result is natural and realistic without any audio artifacts.

- *Expanded soundstage* When Virtual Speaker Technology is used with stereo sources (rather than surround-sound sources), the system works in conjunction with Dolby Pro Logic II to create a realistic surround-sound environment. This can work with CDs, MP3s (and equivalent formats) and even with FM radio broadcasts.

- *Listening comfort* Because the original soundstage is faithfully reconstructed, the result is a restful listening experience. Other, inferior systems can produce artifacts that, subconsciously, lead to listening fatigue.

Dolby Virtual Speaker provides for two modes offering different surround-sound effects. Reference Mode produces the five-speaker surround-sound effect with the width of the soundstage determined by the actual width between the front speakers (see above far left). In Wide Mode you get the sonic effect of wider-spaced speakers, providing a broader soundstage (see above left).

In-car audio proved the salvation. Let's face it, for most of us it is in the car and on the move that we listen to most radio and, despite the benefits of RDS, reception can still prove problematic and discontinuous. This was the perfect opportunity for DAB. With prices still high, they proved their worth in the prestige car market where the quiet car interiors could demonstrably deliver the sound quality benefits.

Of course, it was not long until the prices fell and digital-only stations appeared, catering specifically for the specialized markets that DAB would need to appeal to. Now prices continue to fall and, by virtue of low-power compact chipsets – required to receive and decode digital radio – we have a choice ranging from top-end audiophile units through conventional radio sets to in-car units and even portable, Walkman-style receivers. In many areas you can also receive many more digital stations via digital satellite – either using a dedicated digital satellite radio receiver or via a digital television service, where the stations piggyback on the signals.

HOW IT WORKS

The audio signal picked up from a microphone – as in the case of "live" voice programming – or output from a music source is encoded in much the same

Fig 34 – Digital studio and transmission equipment provides the encoding of the analogue sound sources and then bundles several stations' output into a single multiplex.

DIGITAL RADIO

Digital radio, or DAB – Digital Audio Broadcasting – preceded digital television on to the airwaves, but for many of the more formative years of digital broadcasting it was seen as something of a Cinderella product. It was much easier to discuss and then show the benefits of digital television. Interference-free pictures, more choice and the ability to use existing televisions made an immediate impact.

The benefits of DAB were less easy to market. The core competences – interference-free signals, virtual CD-quality sound, more stations that are easier to identify and added informational services – were no less significant, but were lost to the consumer due to the high prices of early models.

way as music coded into MP3 on a computer, the format used by many digital music services and players. The digitized signal is then transmitted over the air to be decoded at the receiver. Because the signal is digitally encoded, it will not be degraded even if the signal is prone to interference. The receiver can filter any interference that might compromise the signal.

The key difference to the transmission method is that, like digital television, radio stations do not transmit on discrete, separate frequencies. Rather, a group of stations transmit over the same frequency in a multiplex with the receiver, again, filtering out the required signal from this complex composite. This means, again like digital television, that a larger number of stations can be broadcast over a limited number of frequencies and that cross-frequency interference can be eliminated. Since there is no frequency to find, DAB receivers can identify stations by name.

Reading the radio

Riding on the back of the audio signal is a text signal. This can be used (or not used, according to the station) to transmit additional information, and is displayed on the receiver. Information might include details on the current programme, song lyrics or contact details for phone-ins.

Fig 35 – Location-based databases are ideal for finding out the stations available from your home or workplace. This one is from the UK's Digital One multiplex operator.

A PVR FOR RADIO?

We are becoming increasingly familiar with PVRs – such as Sky+ for digital satellite – giving us the ability to pause live television, make automated recordings and flexible replay. You will find similar services offered on many DAB receivers. Hit a button when you have to leave the broadcast and you can then resume your listening when you return.

Some radios will record using a memory card, recording between one and four hours of content on a single card. Not only can you replay the recording on your radio later, but you can also transfer the card to a computer or PDA to listen when and wherever you want.

Reception is area-dependent, and the mix of stations also varies according to location. The digital nature of the signal also means that you will get very good reception even at the edge of signal areas. In the UK www.ukdigitalradio.com has an extremely effective system that will confirm your reception by entering a postcode. The Federal Communications Commission (www.fcc.gov) provides information on similar services in the United States.

DAB RECEIVERS

Like their conventional counterpart, DAB receivers come in an increasingly wide range of shapes, sizes and applications. As has already mentioned – and you have probably already discovered if you have the facility – digital television provides a convenient (if not portable) option. But when you take a look at dedicated receivers, you will find four key options: the portable, home, in-car and PC-based.

Portable receivers

In recognition that it comprised a major market segment, the portable receiver has been addressed by many manufacturers. Determined to differentiate DAB models from their analogue stablemates, digital models tend to be more dramatically styled than the tired-looking conventional models. Styling,

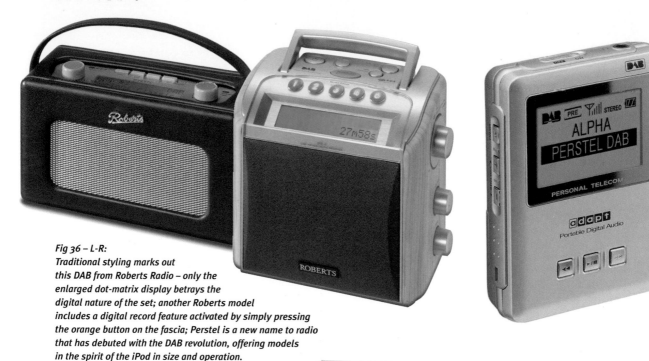

Fig 36 – L-R:
Traditional styling marks out
this DAB from Roberts Radio – only the
enlarged dot-matrix display betrays the
digital nature of the set; another Roberts model
includes a digital record feature activated by simply pressing
the orange button on the fascia; Perstel is a new name to radio
that has debuted with the DAB revolution, offering models
in the spirit of the iPod in size and operation.

to a degree, is determined by the need to provide a larger display and different controls, often including the "record" feature that lets you record or timeshift programming.

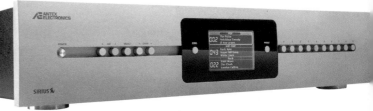

As the chipsets for DAB have shrunk, so have the receivers, with true pocketable receivers now commonplace. Some of these will also include memory – whether in the form of memory cards, in-built memory or a hard disc – allowing programming recording or storage of pre-recorded music.

Fig 37 – Apart from the comprehensive informational display, there is little to tell this Antex home receiver apart from a conventional tuner.

Home receivers

DAB debuted with home units, tuner decks designed to integrate with home hi-fi separates. Again, as a result of the decreasing size of the receiving components, DAB is increasingly integrated into one-piece audio and audiovisual equipment, with most major manufacturers offering the medium.

In-car audio

DAB reception is now only one of many functions offered by in-car units, along with, say, MP3 playback from CD, hard-disc audio storage (which allows DAB signals to be recorded for later replay) and more. In the United States and some other regions, satellite-based digital radio – rather than

digital terrestrial – is the norm for direct broadcasting and has given rise to receivers that can be used in the car and at home. A mobilephone-like car mount makes it simple to take the receiver with you.

More conventional digital car units can operate with services such as Sirius. Rather in the manner of CD changers, additional components for the reception of digital satellite radio can be housed elsewhere in the car and controlled from the dash-mounted head unit.

Fig 38 – A receiver suitable for car or home use was the motivation for this JVC Sirius model. You need to connect it to a suitable antenna when using it at different locations.

PC receivers

You can listen to digital radio via your computer. To listen to "real" DAB (rather than the broadcast feed of the radio station streamed over the internet) you need to fit a decoder card or an external decoder and install the appropriate software. Then you can either exploit the speakers of your PC or undoubtedly a better solution, connect the computer to a hi-fi system.

A unit such as Psion's Wavefinder (Fig 39) is essentially a signal receiver (which includes an antenna) and decoder. It

Fig 39 – Wavefinder incorporates an antenna and receiver in a simple, compact unit that is connected direct to a PC.

feeds the output directly to the computer where the Wavefinder software allows you to access a chosen channel via an electronic selection and programme guide. You can also see any text that is being transmitted along with the selected station. With a system like this you can also record – to the computer's hard disc – any content from the radio stations for later replay – as always, however, you need to be mindful of copyright considerations when doing this.

Modular Technology's DAB solution comprises a computer card and software. You will need to install its card inside your computer (not as difficult a task as it may sound) or have your dealer do it for you. Then connect an antenna, install the software and you are ready to go.

An elegant interface makes it easy to select stations, as with Wavefinder. Here, you can also tap into programme guides produced by the

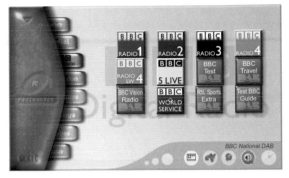

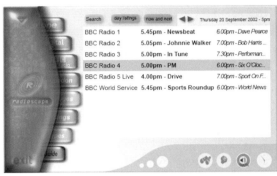

Fig 40 – An elegant interface makes it easy to select stations, as with Wavefinder. Here you can also tap into programme guides produced by the broadcaster to receive enhanced schedule and programme information.

broadcaster to receive enhanced schedule and programme information.

THE DIGITAL RADIO EVOLUTION

For a medium that is still in its comparative infancy, how will it develop? The nature of radio is such that we are unlikely in the short term to see the same pressure to drop analogue services, so "simulcasting" will carry on for some time, driven more by commercial than political pressure.

Technology will mean that the added services – currently text-based – can expand in scope to provide further supportive material. Pictures, maps and diagrams that could enrich a broadcast are possible now. Also possible – but not necessarily probable – is Digital Radio Mondiale (DRM). This is digital radio for the AM frequency band, bringing the benefits of digital radio to these wavelengths. Quality will be better than conventional AM but not up to the quality of FM. Good enough for speech and undemanding music-based services.

C IN THE DIGITAL AGE ... MUSIC .....

IN THIS CHAPTER WE WILL:

• Discover how the digital music you now enjoy came into being.

• Take a look at digital music devices and determine which is best for you.

• Look at what else you can do with music players.

• Study the iPod phenomenon.

• Examine how you can create and record your own music.

ONE MESSAGE IS EMERGING AS UNDERLYING THIS ENTIRE EXPLORATION OF THE DIGITAL WORLD: DIGITAL TECHNOLOGY EMPOWERS. THIS IS PARTICULARLY THE CASE WHEN WE TURN TO MUSIC. THE MATHEMATICAL MANIPULATIONS THAT ALLOWED US TO EDIT AND CREATE FANTASTIC IMAGERY IN DIGITAL PHOTOGRAPHY AND HELPED US CREATE PROFESSIONAL-GRADE DIGITAL MOVIES ALSO LETS US CREATE IMPRESSIVE MUSICAL PIECES. AND, THANKS TO THE MP3 RECORDING FORMAT, WE CAN TAKE, SEND OR DELIVER THAT MUSIC WHEREVER WE WISH. IF YOU HAVE EVEN A MODEST MUSICAL BENT YOU CAN UPLIFT YOUR PERFORMANCE TO NEW HEIGHTS. THE REST OF US, WITH NO COMPOSITIONAL SKILLS WHATSOEVER, CAN RELY ON CLEVER SOFTWARE TO INTERPRET THE MOST BASIC OF IDEAS AND DELIVER SOMETHING REMARKABLY TUNEFUL.

ONE OF THE REASONS FOR THE SUCCESS OF DIGITAL MUSIC HAS BEEN THE ONLINE MUSIC STORE. UNHEARD OF UNTIL THE TURN OF THE CENTURY, ONLINE STORES OFFER AN INTRIGUING MENU OF TRACKS AND ALBUMS THAT ARE EASILY DOWNLOADED TO A COMPUTER, TO PLAY ON THAT MACHINE, YOUR DIGITAL MUSIC PORTABLE PLAYER OR EVEN YOUR HOME HI-FI. IT HAS NEVER BEEN EASIER TO GET HOLD OF YOUR FAVOURITE TRACKS OR EXPLORE CATALOGUES FOR TITLES THAT YOU WOULD PROBABLY NEVER ENCOUNTER WERE YOU TO VISIT A TRADITIONAL MUSIC STORE.

MP3: THE STORY SO FAR

MP3 is a term that has become synonymous with digital music. This is slightly ironic as much digital music today is no longer in this format. But the history of MP3 is that of the development of digital music and recording and the technology also underpins other digital media. To cut through the jargon, MP3 provides the means for high-quality music and narrative to be delivered over the internet and stored in a fraction of the space normally required to store digital music.

Fig 1 – After the terrific impact of the iPod, the iPod Mini extended the concept and would be joined within a year by the solid state iPod Shuffle.

ENJOY THIS!

To commemorate the 75th anniversary of their celebrated car styling studio, Italy's Pininfarina created a special car, the Enjoy, to be built in a limited run of just 75 (Fig 2). The description harks back to the classic days of the Fiat Barchetta, but with the ability to adapt into an open-wheel race car in seconds. But all this was done with a modern twist that extended to the audio system. Within an interior styled by Louis Vuitton, Pininfarina chose to include the remarkable Beosound 2 MP3 player from Bang & Olufsen. Housed in small door enclosures, they provide driver and passenger with the ultimate in music entertainment on the go.

Fig 2 – Discreet Beosound units are housed in small enclosures in each door, surrounded by red leather. The his 'n' her devices can easily be removed and used on the go when out of the car.

The name MP3 is a contraction of the more cumbersome MPEG-1 Layer III, sometimes described as MPEG Audio Layer III. As such, it is an element of the multimedia standard MPEG defined by the International Standards Organization (ISO).

The development of what was to become MP3 began in the late 1980s at the Fraunhofer Institute in Germany as part of a European Union "Eureka" project, which was laying the foundations for digital audio broadcasting (DAB). The Fraunhofer Institute can be regarded as a European equivalent to MIT in the United States and has the same business-academic partnership at its core.

To tell the story of MP3 is to tell the story of the work of Karlheinz Brandenburg, a Section Leader at the Institute. The Eureka project (Project EU147) was originally concerned with ways of delivering high-

PERSONAL MUSIC: AN ILLUSTRATED HISTORY

In creating the original Walkman, Sony revolutionized personal entertainment on the move. Since then the market has flourished in scope and variety. Here's just a taster.

1980s
The cassette-based player is still popular on account of low cost and the amount of media that is still available.

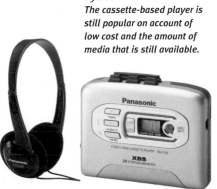

1990s
From a simple tape replay device, the modern tape Walkman has some of the functionality you would expect to find on digital music devices – such as the display panel on the earphone cord.

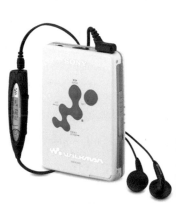

quality audio down a conventional telephone line.

The research of Brandenburg and his colleagues was based on creating a mathematical formula that could be applied to sound to compress the data without compromising the audio quality. They worked hard to determine how much of the data in a sound file could be removed before deterioration became noticeable. The embryonic formulae were applied to various sound files but the urban mythology suggests that it was Suzanne Vega's *Tom's Diner* that provided much of the working material. The quiet tracks, apparently, were the most problematic to compress and so provided an effective test. Although it is stretching the point a little, Suzanne Vega can claim to be the first recording artist to be represented in MP3.

The Fraunhofer Institute received a patent for MP3 as far back as 1989, but it would be a further four years before MPEG – the Motion Pictures Expert Group, a division of ISO involved in creating standards for digital video – incorporated it into the specification of MPEG-1. MPEG-1 was the first standard in digital video. Offering a quality similar to that of VHS video it achieved momentary success as the basis for video on the CD-I format in the early 1990s. But audiences' expectations had been raised and they were demanding more from video.

By 1995 MPEG-2, the format used in DVD video, was announced and this, too, featured MP3 as the audio component. Our demands for a high-quality video format had now been satiated and we would shortly see the results in the first DVD players, but the audio format was still lurking somewhat in the shadows.

Brandenburg was increasingly aware of the opportunities of MP3 and protected his creation – on behalf of the Fraunhofer Institute – with worldwide patents. But Brandenburg also realized the importance of open standards in advancing technology and thus his and, by association, the Fraunhofer Institute's approach to licensing was liberal and open. As a result, by the beginning of 1999 the first music tracks were being released on MP3 and rather than direct transmission down a phone line, they were being shared over the Internet. The market was ready for the widespread sharing of music over the web. All it needed was a catalyst.

The Napster age begins ...

That catalyst was Napster (Fig 3): a music-sharing system that allowed MP3 files stored on any computer connected to the internet and the Napster service to be shared with any other computer. The rise of Napster as a corporation was meteoric. It had tapped a latent need and filled it unequivocally. Huge numbers of MP3 files were shared on a regular basis as users of the free service passed files around the world.

Fig 3 – Napster: the site that kick-started the MP3 revolution.

Unfortunately for the Napster generation, and as was clearly pointed out by the music industry, "sharing files" was really a euphemism for "copying files". Rather than sharing files in some egalitarian musical nirvana, the users of Napster were being painted as copyright transgressors.

For some time there was something of a stand-off. The demand for MP3 music continued to grow while the music industry continued to flex its

1990s
Graduating from tape, CD-based Walkmans flourished in the 1990s. Now they offer enhanced performance and MP3 playback, giving 10 times the capacity of conventional CDs.

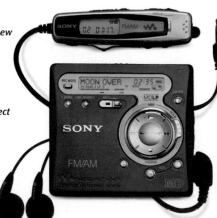

1996
Sony's pioneering of new media formats meant that it was inevitable that a MiniDisc player would appear. Before recordable CDs, the MiniDisc was the perfect medium for recording music from your own collection.

muscles. In late 1999 and through to 2000, court proceedings were initiated that saw the Napster operation shut down and then reopened. The music industry argued the case that free sharing denied legitimate royalties to the artists whose music was now passing freely across the net.

... and ends

Ultimately the industry had its way and Napster – or, as we should now say, the original Napster – closed down. But the public appetite remained unfulfilled and Napster wannabes came to the fore. File-sharing utilities such as LimeWire (Fig 4) found new followers in an MP3-starved world. Because it was not specifically designed to exchange MP3 files (but rather provide an easy exchange of any digital file), LimeWire escaped the same fate

Fig 4 – In the grey area of file sharing, LimeWire flourished.

as Napster because its file-sharing methods did not depend on a central interchange file-sharer – files simply passed from user to user.

Faced with this, the music industry changed tack. Realizing that it was the music listeners who were purloining services such as LimeWire, which had been created for the most innocent of reasons, it turned its attention to the downloaders of illicit MP3 files. After a few test cases, a shiver went through the downloading community that stopped trafficking

by all but the most committed and, dare we say it, foolhardy.

With an uneasy truce in place, some hard questions needed to be faced by all parties. MP3 music distribution was clearly in demand. But the music industry was strongly against unrestricted distribution. A solution needed to be found fast before another service, this time one that was more covert than Napster, could start trafficking again.

After many meetings, discussions and much planning – often behind closed doors – a new generation of music library began to appear. This time it would be legitimate, but it would come at a cost. A real cost: users would have to pay for their music either in the form of a fee for each track they downloaded or by subscription to the service. Moreover, the MP3 recording would be fingerprinted so that, once downloaded, it could not be freely or easily distributed onwards. Digital rights management would be introduced to ensure that the music downloaded by an individual could be enjoyed only by that person or their immediate circle of friends and family.

For the music downloaders, these restrictions seemed rather draconian; for the music industry, it had too many loopholes. But as a solution it was one that both parties realized they had to work with.

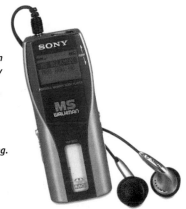

2000
Solid state memory – in the form of the memory card – overcame the drawbacks of disc- and tape-based systems. They could survive knocks and rapid movement while playing.

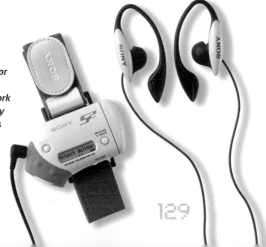

2004
Now, the ultimate for the active lifestyle. Sony's latest Network Walkman is not only totally digital but is designed for action sports use.

ALL ABOUT MP3 PLAYERS

Digital music players – sometimes known imprecisely as MP3 players – have in the space of just a few years become an essential lifestyle accessory. Conceptually they received a major fillip with the advent of legal online music stores, which make it possible to select and download music on demand, without the need necessarily to buy a complete album. The partnership of iTunes and the ubiquitous iPod (Fig 5) brought a level of simplicity to portable digital music that has won over many users not normally classed as technophiles.

The marketplace is now awash with digital music players offering a wide range of features. Manufacturers have been quick to recognize that there is no one-size-fits-all solution. So there is a diverse portfolio of units that you need to investigate in order to find the solution that best fits your lifestyle. Over the next few pages, you will be able to explore the different types – including multi-function devices – and compare specifications with the needs of different types of users.

As an aside, the term MP3 player tends to be used as a generic for these devices, yet many now also play alternate formats – but don't necessarily assume that every device will play all available formats. Formats and their differences will be discussed later, too.

Hard-drive players

If you are after maximum storage capacity, the hard-drive player is the solution. These are based on small computer hard discs of the type found in portable external computer drives. These drives are small and, for a mechanical device, particularly robust. Even so, most manufacturers advise against putting them through too much stress. Their large capacity also means that they can store other media – video files in some models – and can double up as an external disc drive for your computer. They are ideal for backing up or transporting large files between home and work computers.

Micro hard-disc players have a lower capacity and tend to be built around the 2.5-cm (1-in) IBM Microdrive (now produced by Hitachi and others). The maximum capacity of these players tends to be around 4GB.

FOR: High capacity, lowest price per megabyte of storage.
AGAINST: Hard drive requires more power and so tends to consume batteries faster, less suitable for power workouts.

Memory-card players

Using the same memory cards as you will find in digital cameras or other portable devices, memory-card players (or flash-card players as they are also known) have no moving parts and are, hence, more robust than hard-drive players (Fig 7). They are also much smaller – their size is often governed by the size of the battery pack. With several interchangeable memory cards you can store a large library of music but without the ultimate convenience

Fig 5 – Unlike its larger siblings, the iPod Shuffle uses a flash-card solid state memory to store up to 1GB of music.

THE SCIENCE

For most of us, the mechanics of getting music on to a digital player – whether it has been sourced from our CD library or online – is of little significance. The process is so transparent that we just select tracks and then enjoy the music wherever we may be. But let us spend a moment taking a look at how digital music systems deliver the goods.

Digitizing

The first process in delivering music digitally is digitizing. This is the conversion of the analogue sound (the singing, instrumental or narrative sounds) into a digital form – that string of numbers that a computer can interpret and manipulate. If you have bought your music on CD, then this process has already been done for you. Somewhere within the vast enclave of the recording studio – either at source or subsequently – an ADC (analogue-to-digital converter) has sampled the music. Otherwise you can now digitize analogue sound in real time using your desktop or portable PC.

Sampling involves measuring the volume, tone and pitch and assigning a numerical value to these parameters. The more samples taken per second, the closer the digital code is to the original analogue sounds. Of course, the more samples you take, the larger the amount of data and greater the size of the digital file that represents the original sounds.

Compressing

If you were to convert a digital file to CD-quality digital signals, you would find that each second of recording would take 1MB of space or even more. This would very quickly fill even a generous-sized hard disc with very little music. That is why the digital files need to be compressed to make them substantially more compact.

Compressing sound files is a process rather like that for compressing image files. It involves discarding some information (usually) but not so much that we would notice, except under the most critical of analyses.

Sound engineers and scientists called on the services of psychologists to help them produce compressed sound files. Together they investigated how we perceived sound. In particular, they examined which parts of a sound signal our ears (and brain) are most highly tuned to and which components they are not. This led to the creation of mathematical algorithms known as codecs that can be applied to a digital signal. This removes all those elements that we are unlikely to perceive when listening to music, but leaves the most obvious components untouched. Like image files, the greater the compression, the greater the degradation. But for sound files the bit rate – the number of samples per second – also has a bearing: the greater the rate, the better the quality. The box on page 135 explains more about the common file format codecs.

Downloading

Once the music has been compressed (the process is achieved automatically when the music is imported into iTunes, or an equivalent), we now need to download the files to an MP3 player. Again, this is largely an automatic process. In the case of the archetypal iTunes/iPod combo, synchronization ensures that when the iPod is connected to the computer, tracks are automatically downloaded.

For flash players – where the capacity of the player is likely to be far less than that of even a modest music library – you will need to use the software that accompanied the player to download selected tracks.

Replaying

With the digital files now resident in the player, how is this digital data converted back into high-quality sound? It is essentially the reverse of the encoding process, this time using a DAC – digital-to-analogue-converter. In an ideal system, this should lead to sounds similar to those recorded. In practice, the sound is compromised slightly by the compression but it is also coloured by the DAC circuitry and, once in analogue form, it can be prone to modest amounts of interference.

Fig 6 – Downloading songs to the MuVo is simple. Detach the memory unit and plug it straight into the computer's USB connection.

of having all your favourites on a single device.

FOR: Smaller than any hard-disc player, and as they have no moving parts they are more resilient to knocks and rapid movement. Expandable capacity using more memory cards and good battery life.

AGAINST: Expensive on a per-megabyte basis.

Flash players

Imagine a memory-card player with the memory card sealed for life within the player (Fig 6). That is the principle behind the flash player. It is a single unit – not expandable, but incredibly compact. Since there are no moving parts (not even a memory card to insert or remove), these can lay claim to being the most robust and durable.

FOR: Very small and very robust.

AGAINST: Limited, fixed capacity, limited power (small batteries to maintain small size).

Fig 7 – Freed from the Enjoy (see page 127), the Beosound 2 from Bang & Olufsen uses interchangeable memory cards to extend the capacity.

Multi-function devices

Many digital devices feature MP3 replay. Phones, PDAs (Fig 9) and even some watches have the option of using on-board or card-based memory for music storage. These devices rarely have the small size of a dedicated music player, but they have the advantage that, if you need to have a phone with you all the time or are never without your PDA, you don't have to carry a second device to enjoy your music library.

FOR: Need to carry only a single device.

AGAINST: Functionality may not be as comprehensive as with a dedicated music player. Some PDAs can be expensive if they are used primarily for music.

Fig 8 – The Beatman from Freecom is a CD-based MP3 player, but overcomes the usual associations of bulk by using small, 8-cm (3½-in) CDs.

CD-based players

Based on the portable CD player that has been around for years, CD-based digital players (Fig 8) will play conventional CDs and also CDs that have been recorded in MP3 format. These discs have a capacity for around ten times the music of a standard CD so it is quite possible to keep 12 albums on a single disc.

FOR: The cheapest player, compatible with CDs,

AGAINST: Also the largest of players, uses more power and can skip when bumped.

Fig 9 – PDAs let you organize your life – including music – in a single device.

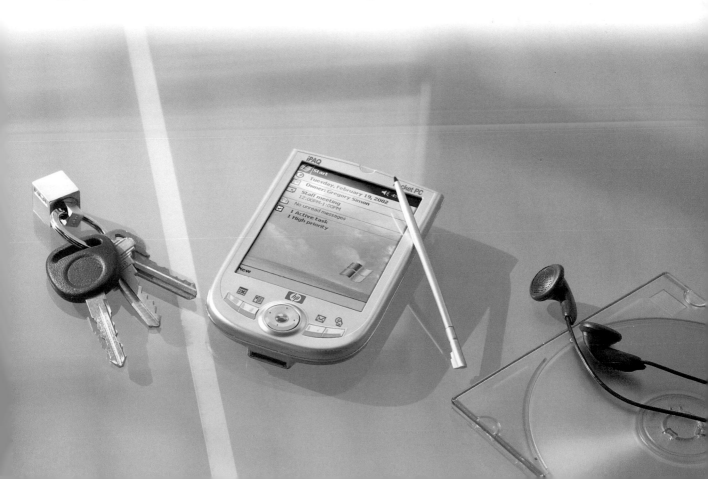

CHOOSING YOUR PERFECT MP3 PARTNER

As has been mentioned earlier, there is no single ideal MP3 player, but rather a range of devices each with powerful attributes and competences. This is just as well, because there is an equally diverse range of users. Here, users have been divided into different groups – to find the best machine for your needs, simply identify which category matches you most closely. If you straddle more than one group or inhabit two entirely different categories, you may need two devices.

The car driver

Spending most of your time in the car, you will not be too concerned about size. CD-based players will

Fig 10 – Although CD-based, the Beatman has great antishock facilities that make it possible to bend the rules and use a CD player while undertaking strenuous activity.

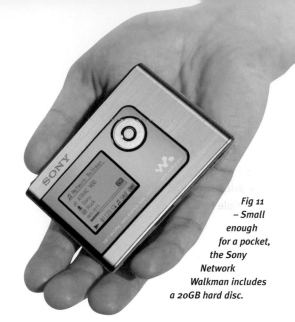

Fig 11 – Small enough for a pocket, the Sony Network Walkman includes a 20GB hard disc.

be OK and robust enough to use in the automotive environment. Hard-disc players will also be suitable. Some, such as the iPod, even have car kits (rather like those for mobile phones) that enable them to be mounted in a car and feed their output to the car's hi-fi system. If you listen to music only in the car, you may find it better to invest in an MP3 player/hard-disc recorder in-car unit.

The commuter

Those who use public transport or even cycle to work will want to look at something more pocketable (Fig 11), for both convenience and security (like mobile phones were a decade ago, MP3 players are now increasingly targets for street muggers). Mini hard-disc and flash players will be ideal. If cost is a principal consideration, you might do well to reserve a little more than you might otherwise for a good pair of headphones. Those supplied with even the top MP3 players tend to be poor at blocking external sound.

The jogger and gym freak

Jogging and gym workouts don't just put a high degree of strain on the body, they will affect your MP3 player, too. CD and hard-disc systems (Fig 10) are pretty resilient to the knocks and jostling that is inevitable in these conditions, but ultimately they will suffer. Flash systems are best in this situation. Even under violent motion, they will play on unhindered. But do take care of them – even the most robust player will succumb to repeated knocks.

DIGITAL MUSIC FORMATS EXPLAINED

MP3 virtually created the digital music genre, but it no longer has the field to itself. Other formats now vie for popularity, offering similar or better quality or added functionality. Most players can handle multiple formats, though not necessarily all.

MP3 Short for Motion Picture Experts Group Layer 3. The format was originally designed for encoding MPEG audio tracks for DVD video. It achieves a compression of around 90 per cent for most audio files with negligible loss of quality.

MP3PRO An "upgrade" to MP3 devised by the licensers of MP3 designed to give better sound quality at the same bit rate (in other words, with the same degree of compression). Not widely adopted.

AAC Advanced Audio Coding is the default coding used for iPod downloads. More compact than MP3, it also supports DRM coding – digital rights management – to prevent unauthorized copying of the files.

WMA Microsoft's Windows Media Audio offers a quality similar to MP3PRO and can also be encoded with copy protection.

AIFF The standard, uncompressed audio file found (mostly) on Macintosh computers.

WAV The standard, uncompressed audio file found (mostly) on Windows computers.

OGG VORBIS High-quality compressed audio format that is "open source". That is, the format is in the public domain so that users don't have to pay licensing fees to use it. Gaining ground as music vendors aim to cut costs.

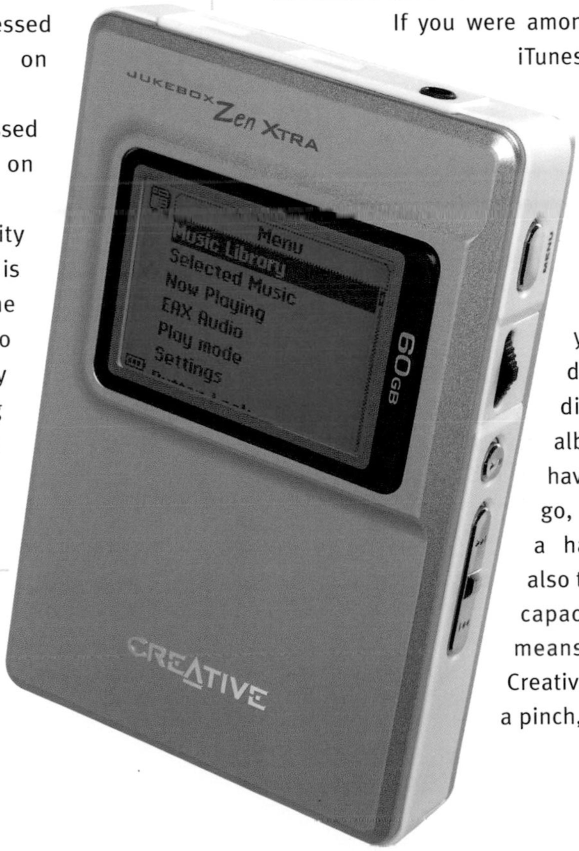

Fig 12 – Creative's Zen Extra Jukebox features a 60GB hard disc, which is sufficient for all but the largest of music collections.

The style guru

If appearance is the most important aspect – and with MP3 players all offering very good sound quality, this is not as trivial a consideration as you might think – there are really only two choices. First the iPod and second the Beosound 2. Both can claim style credentials through their associations with celebrity. But on a more practical level, both have been annexed by the fashion houses, which (especially with regard to the iPod) produce custom cases to be seen with.

The audiophile

Sound purists have rejected MP3 on the grounds that any form of compression will compromise sound quality. They would rather carry around two high-quality recordings than two days' worth of MP3. But, mindful that modern codecs do provide a very good representation of the original and that, on the move (in a car, plane, bus or even walking), it would be hard to get the best from a top-notch recording, they would most likely go for hard-disc players that have the capacity to accommodate high-bit-rate recordings.

The music devotee

If you were among the first to get an iTunes account and helped Napster flourish in the bad old days, you have probably found your hard disc is virtually dedicated to music; you will have copied your CD collection to disc and likewise digitized your vinyl albums. To ensure you have music wherever you go, you will need not only a hard-disc player, but also those with the highest capacity (Fig 12). That means something like Creative's 60GB models or, at a pinch, the largest iPod.

EXPANDING YOUR HORIZONS

As you might expect, in this digital domain, it is unusual now for a device to have just a single role. Phones can be PDAs, and vice versa; cameras can take still or movie images and even act as voice recorders. So what else can you expect from an MP3 player? Here's a rundown of some of the extended functions possible.

1. Radio

Remember how early Walkmans played cassettes and had a radio? Some MP3 players let you access radio, too. Mostly this is FM but digital radio (DAB) is now a viable alternative. In a useful crossover of technologies, some DAB/MP3 players will allow you to record radio programmes.

2. FM broadcasting

Sometimes you don't want to listen to your music though small headphones or earphones. FM broadcasters – such as Griffin's iTalk – connect to the MP3 player's headphone socket and broadcast the output over an FM frequency. This means that you can tune your car radio, portable radio, Walkman or even home receiver and (as long as you are within the very limited range of the device) and listen to your music library over the airwaves.

It is important to note that even though these devices are widely available, local regulations may limit or ban their use.

3. Voice recording

Although they are not suitable for high-fidelity recording of music and concerts, in-built or auxiliary microphones (Fig 13) let you use your MP3 player as a tapeless voice recording system. You can replay the files through the headphones or even transcribe them on your PC.

4. File storage

There is little difference between the memory in any MP3 player and that used in a computer, so you can treat your player as additional storage. Most commonly, people use their players to transfer files between home and office and also to store image files. The capacity of a modest MP3 player is many times that of the memory cards in a camera so, to avoid taking your computer away with you on extended trips, you can download your memory cards' contents to your MP3 player. Apple raised the stakes when it made the music iPod compatible with image libraries (Fig 14) (iPhoto on the Macintosh or Adobe Photoshop Elements on Windows PCs).

Fig 13 – use your iPod for note taking by adding this small microphone unit.

Fig 14 – iPodphoto allows storage and display of images as well as tunes. Fig 15 – The U2 iPod is signed on the back by the band.

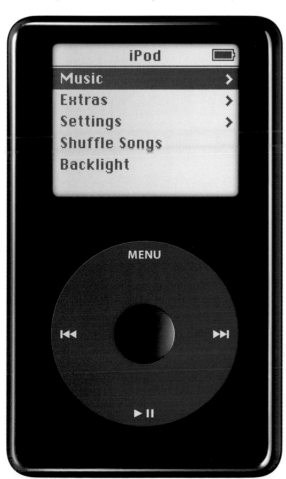

5. PDA

Nobody will pretend that your MP3 player can replace a PDA (though, to a degree, a PDA can replace your MP3 player), but many MP3 players store useful information that is downloaded from your computer when the two devices are synchronized. Phone numbers and contacts, along with calendars and appointments, are the most common data downloaded.

6. Hi-fi controls

One of the beauties of the MP3 player is its simplicity. It really lives up to the plug-and-play philosophy that so many digital devices promised but so few delivered. But there are still a number of controls that we have become familiar with from our other music players that are creeping on to MP3s. It is now possible – either straight out of the box or via a software upgrade – to create playlists on the go. Like the playlists created in iTunes and its peers, these are ideal for impromptu partying and DJ-ing.

Moreover, you can now also change the tone and sound quality to get the best perception of the sound, despite using headphones that can rarely be described as anything but average in their sound quality.

BUILDING YOUR MUSIC COLLECTION

When Sony released the Walkman, enjoying music was simple. You inserted a cassette and switched to play. If you had music on vinyl then you taped the albums – copyright permitting – and listened in the same way.

Then when tape gave way to CD, things got simpler. You stuck in a CD and enjoyed the music. You gained the benefits of CD music in terms of quality and functionality, but, with recordable CD out of sight, you were limited to your purchased music.

Now with MP3 there is a multiplicity of sources. And choice. you no longer need to accept what the big record labels decide that you should enjoy. Here are some of the opportunities now available.

A legacy collection

Chances are, you have a collection of MP3 or equivalent files already on your computer. When you install your MP3 player's software, it might well sweep your hard disc to retrieve files for you, and make them easily available to listen to or to download to your player.

Online music stores

There is no doubt the official music stores – typified by the iTunes Music Store (Fig 16) – have made music accessible to us all. Seamless integration of the store and downloading routines make it simple to identify, purchase and enjoy your favourite tracks. There will be some issues: for iTunes, for example, tight copyrighting and rights management restrict your use of the music (but not so any legitimate user need express concern). Also, iTunes is tightly integrated with the iPod – difficult if you prefer a different MP3 host player. Some stores charge a per-track price for songs, with a slightly cheaper price for album downloads. Other services offer a subscription basis, allowing a fixed or unlimited number of downloads for a specific monthly price.

Fig 16 – By virtue of making it available for Windows, PCs iTunes has garnered a massive following.

Remember, too, that different services don't just have different pricing regimes, they may also have different catalogues. If your favourite artists are carried on different services, you will need to subscribe to each.

Fig 17 – Artists' sites (this one is for the Danish band Swan Lee) are a good source of the more obscure tracks.

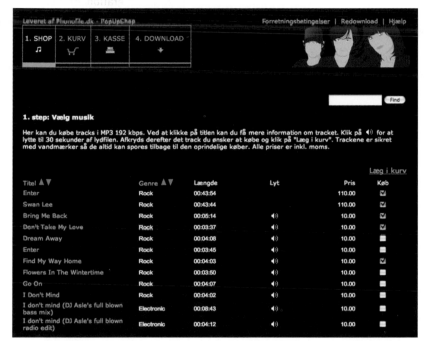

Leveret af Phonofile.dk - PopUpShop

Forretningsbetingelser | Redownload | Hjælp

1. SHOP   2. KURV   3. KASSE   4. DOWNLOAD

Find

1. step: Vælg musik

Her kan du købe tracks i MP3 192 kbps. Ved at klikke på titlen kan du få mere information om tracket. Klik på ◀) for at lytte til 30 sekunder af lydfilen. Afkryds derefter det track du ønsker at købe og klik på "Læg i kurv". Trackene er sikret med vandmærker så de altid kan spores tilbage til den oprindelige køber. Alle priser er inkl. moms.

Titel ▲▼	Genre ▲▼	Længde	Lyt	Pris	Læg i kurv Køb
Enter	Rock	00:43:54		110.00	☑
Swan Lee	Rock	00:43:44		110.00	☑
Bring Me Back	Rock	00:05:14	◀)	10.00	☑
Don't Take My Love	Rock	00:03:37	◀)	10.00	☑
Dream Away	Rock	00:04:08	◀)	10.00	■
Enter	Rock	00:03:45	◀)	10.00	■
Find My Way Home	Rock	00:04:03	◀)	10.00	☑
Flowers In The Wintertime	Rock	00:03:50	◀)	10.00	■
Go On	Rock	00:04:07	◀)	10.00	■
I Don't Mind	Rock	00:04:02	◀)	10.00	■
I don't mind (DJ Asle's full blown bass mix)	Electronic	00:08:43	◀)	10.00	■
I don't mind (DJ Asle's full blown radio edit)	Electronic	00:04:12	◀)	10.00	■

Official – and unofficial – artists' sites

Often you will find a limited number of MP3 files on the official websites of artists and bands (Fig 17). These may be direct transcriptions of recordings from CDs, new mixes or even new material that is unavailable elsewhere.

Unofficial sites can also contain material, but download it with caution. If the content is unauthorized, you may, no matter how inadvertently, fall foul of anti-piracy laws.

Compact discs

Your collection of CDs can easily be converted – or "ripped" – to MP3, AIFF, AAC or even OGG format in a matter of minutes and you can then import them to your player. But here are a couple of notes of caution. There is no problem transcribing your own discs for your own use, but encoding borrowed discs again means you fall foul of anti-piracy laws. Just

because you will never actually get caught does not make it legal.

Secondly, a few CDs have anti-copying technology built into them. At best, this means it will be difficult to rip them to MP3. In the worst case, you could compromise your computer's CD drive. There are many documented cases of CD drives becoming jammed or discs being trapped in drives due to anti-copying software. Keep clear of these CDs.

Old formats

Ripping CDs to MP3 is relatively straightforward. We are converting one digital format to another. But what if our source material is a cherished analogue recording on vinyl or tape? You will need software that can encode your recordings as they play out on your hi-fi along with suitable recording cables (Fig 18) to connect your computer and hi-fi. Some software will encode to MP3 directly, saving you considerable time.

You might even find that some applications can remove the inevitable hiss and crackle that you find on old records to give you a recording more pristine than you have ever experienced. Purists, however, will decry software that removes any interference. Their argument runs that, in the same way as the dust and scratch software used to process photographs scanned in a film or print scanner affects the integrity of the original, so, too, does the software that removes the unwanted elements from the sound of the music.

Fig 18 – A simple adaptor like this enables a conventional (and increasingly rare) turntable to be connected to the computer and record LP sound digitally.

THE iPOD INDUSTRY

Why has the iPod achieved such iconic status in a marketplace where technology of this type is normally more ephemeral? It is due in part to clever design. It looks sensational, but that look is not at the expense of function. Form doesn't so much follow function as run neck and neck with it. It also evolves, both physically and operationally. Beside the svelte latest manifestation, the first generations look ever so slightly bloated. Then there is the integration with iTunes. Closed systems – those that don't allow other hardware or software to interface – can be considered regressive, but in this virtually unique pairing you have a solution that makes it simple for anyone to collect, enjoy and take their music with them.

That the iPod is not transient is reflected in the industries that have grown up around the product, providing essential accessories and add-ons. Some of these, given the slightly delicate surfaces of the iPod, are cosmetic; others are more practical. And some are downright wacky. Here's a look – a snapshot if you like – of what you can do with your iPod.

Cases

Every variation of design, from soft neoprene through to hard, armoured protection, is on offer. Even designer names, such as Gucci, have confirmed the diminutive player's fashion credentials (Fig 19).

Radio frequency transmitters

These allow you to broadcast the output of your iPod to pick up on your radio at home or in the car. iTrip is a self-contained unit, whereas Roadtrip combines a transmitter with a charger that can recharge your iPod in the car (Fig 21), (see more on the next page).

Microphones

Ostensibly a replay device, the iPod can also act as a voice recorder. Discreet microphone units, such as the iTalk, let you record many hundreds of hours of notes and annotation (Fig 13).

Fig 19 – Every conceivable case design can be purchased for your iPod. With this one, you really can take your whole life with you in a single package.

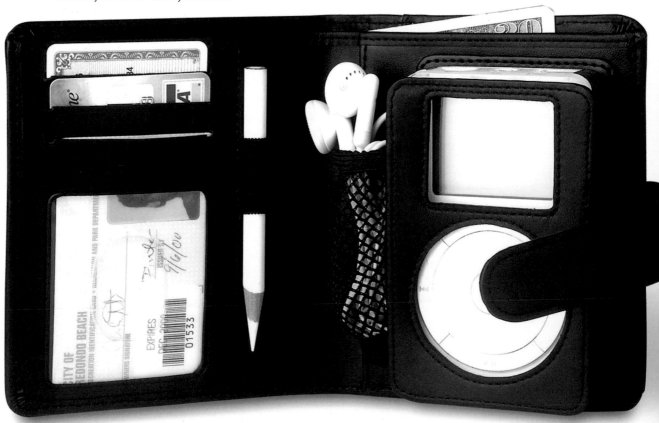

Fig 20 – The Harman JBL OnStage speaker system gives room-filling hi-fi performance and keeps your iPod fully charged.

Fig 21 – RoadTrip lets you play your iPod music collection wirelessly through your car's hi-fi system.

Speakers

It might be designed as a personal player but why not share your musical tastes? There is a range of speakers on offer (Fig 20) – some costing many times more than the iPod itself.

Lights

Turn your iPod into a flashlight? Not as absurd as it sounds. Plug in the iBeam and you can light your way to the front door at night or use your iPod as a laser pointer.

Memory card storage

Think of your iPod as a large hard disc and there are no end of the storage opportunities. Belkin and others have media readers that can be used to download your camera and PDA memory cards in the field (Fig 22).

Remote control

You don't always want to wear your iPod. But how do you operate it when it is connected to your hi-fi or external speakers? Simple, add a Navipod remote from Ten Technology. Looks the part, too.

Fig 22 – Before the iPodPhoto, Belkin's media card reader could also download images.

MAKING MUSIC

Listen to any aging rockers discussing how they got started and you will hear tales – no doubt embellished by the passage of time – of how they began in their bedroom or garage, recording on to reel-to-reel tapes. Tomorrow's rock legends (or their folk and pop equivalents) can still record at home, but now they have the capacity to produce polished productions. And even if your aspirations are more modest than this, creating music for your own pleasure, for example, or perhaps for a movie soundtrack, it can be great fun.

The hardware

Like producing movies or photography on your computer, music generation and production demands a well-specified computer. Below you will see that software exists for both Windows PCs and Macintosh computers, but whichever you use, make sure it is up to the job. If you are using a Mac, you will need to have at least a G4 running at 1GHz. PC users should be running with a 2GHz Pentium as a minimum specification.

If you are already practising the visual arts on your computer, you will know how important memory is. Well, it is just as important for audio. Don't be seduced into thinking that, with MP3 tracks clocking in at around 5MB and even the original CD-quality tracks at around 50MB, a modest memory allocation will be sufficient. Creating a five-minute musical piece comprising, say, five tracks, will consume more than 100MB of disc space. Processing that live needs lots of RAM. The software you choose will make recommendations but these tend to be minimum specifications. If you aim to have at least 512MB of RAM, you will be OK for all but the most ambitious of orchestral productions.

There are some useful parallels to be made with digital photography and movie-making. A multi-track musical piece is rather like a multi-layered image. The more layers, the greater the size. But music is a dynamic, a constantly varying medium, just like movies. So you will also need from your computer the means to read and write data quickly. This means the hard disc – something that we usually consider only in terms of the amount of data

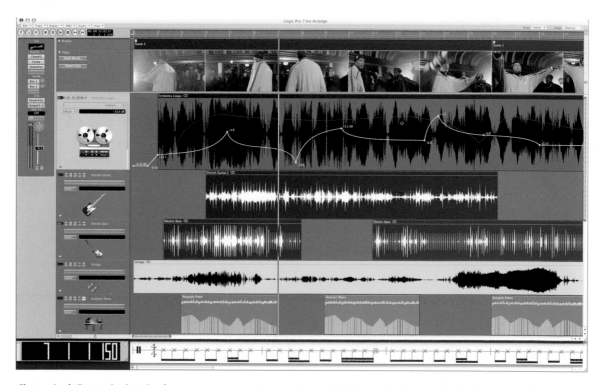

Fig 23 – Logic Pro can be daunting for anyone new to music production, but its interface is slick and effective. If you need ultimate control and versatility, Logic Pro is hard to beat.

MUSICAL PLUG-INS AND MP3

Applications such as GarageBand and Acid come with a good selection of loops that you can use to produce an almost infinite number of combinations. But you can extend your musical arsenal further with additional plug-in loops.

GarageBand (Fig 24), for example, has a number of add-on packs that you can buy and integrate into the host application. Some of these are produced by Apple, others by third parties. Third-party plug-ins tend to be more erratic in quality. That is not to say they are bad – just a little more uneven in quality. They are also less predictable, so if your musical tastes and ambitions are rather more eclectic, they can be a good source of inspiration.

You can also import other musical files in most formats (such as MP3, WAV or AIFF) and use these as part of your composition. There is no problem In using commercial music in your own compositions for your own use, but if the original material was subject to copyright (and most is) you will not be able to play the results publicly.

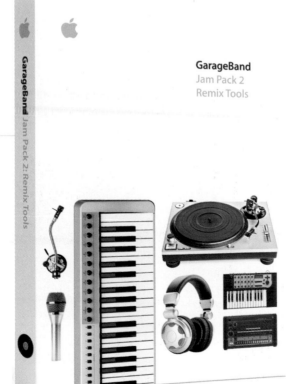

GarageBand
Jam Pack 2
Remix Tools

Fig 24 – Jam Packs offer extensive (around 2,000 per volume) additional loops to add to your GarageBand project.

it can store – must now be considered in terms of the speed at which data can be written to and read from it.

If you are serious about making music, it makes sense to use an external hard disc. You can reserve this for your music-making activities and leave your computer's in-built hard disc for more mundane (and less-speed-critical) activities. Go for a Firewire or USB 2 drive. These will give you the essential speed and performance that is required.

The software

The key to good music production is the software. Software needs to be able to interpret the music you give it, whether recorded by you or sampled from elsewhere, and allow you to arrange and manipulate it.

Again making the comparison with digital photography, there is a wide range of applications vying for our attention. Your choice will be limited by the type of music that you want to produce. For the serious musician and aspiring professional, that choice might be for one of the powerhouse applications, such as Logic Pro (Fig 23), the preferred software of many producers and musicians. As Photoshop is to photographers, so Logic Pro is to musicians. If you can't do it with Logic Pro, then it probably isn't worth doing. The latest versions even allow you to edit, in perfect synchronization, video footage to make music videos of your productions.

Logic Pro, and its Windows equivalent, Cubase, are professional tools and are professionally priced. They also offer so much functionality that it would be wasted on most of us. Fortunately, there are more keenly priced alternatives that, despite the price, don't inhibit creativity. Favourites are Sony's Acid (Fig 25) on the PC and GarageBand (Fig 26) on the Mac. GarageBand is part of the iLife suite, along with iPhoto, iMovie, iTunes and iDVD.

Fig 25 – Acid from Sony appears to be as cluttered as Logic Pro, but even a short association with it shows you that it is a very simple application to use.

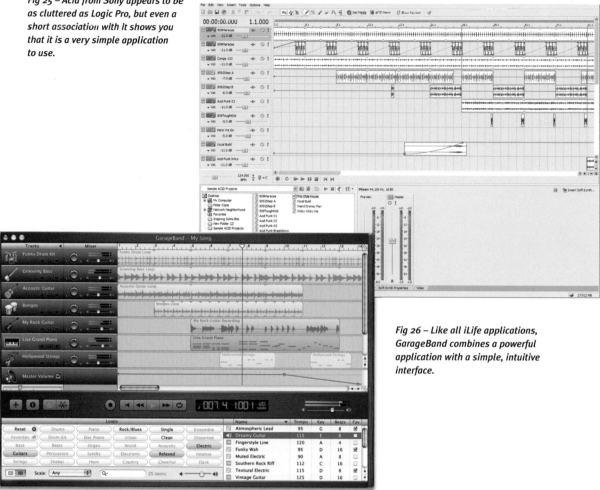

Fig 26 – Like all iLife applications, GarageBand combines a powerful application with a simple, intuitive interface.

These applications allow you to put together tracks of music created from the extensive raft of instruments provided. But once you have created your own tracks – or loops as they are more often called – you can add a rhythm track and even some recordings made with real instruments.

Electronically synthesized instruments have something of a bad name; they have a reputation of only sounding "like" the instrument that they represent. Musicians, being (by and large) perfectionists, want an authentic sound. The good news is that today's synthesized instruments sound very good indeed. Play them well and they will reward you well. But you don't need to be an expert musician to begin using these applications. You will find

libraries of loops that you can drag and drop to produce your own melodies. And yes, some of these

Fig 27 – The Prodikeys keyboard from Creative combines a conventional Qwerty keyboard with a piano keyboard and is the ideal solution for the enthusiastic music creator.

will sound truly awful, but soon you will get the hang of it and start to produce something that sounds good. In fact, many of the loops provided with these applications are designed to sound good together.

Here are some options for creating new music, based on your skills:

The complete novice: using loops

1. Begin by using the loop browser to gain familiarity with loops and how they sound (Fig 28).

Fig 28

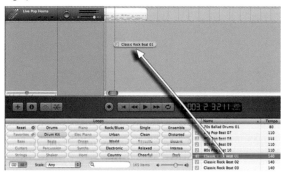

2. Add selected loops to the Timeline by dragging and dropping. You can add multiple loops if you wish, or repeat the same loop continuously (Fig 29).

Fig 29

3. Apply effects to the loop. You can vary the volume (say, to fade in or fade out) or add acoustic effects, such as reverberation and echo (Fig 30).

Fig 30

4. Listen. Your efforts may not get you recognized in the musical world, but they can be a great way to add a unique (and pertinent) soundtrack to a movie or multimedia slideshow.

The casual musician: keyboard magic

1. You can use an electronic keyboard to create and record your own music. When you create a musical track you can choose not only the type of instrument from the very many on offer, but also the characteristics of that instrument (Fig 31).
2. Record your music using the settings you have selected. This all happens in real time so it is up to you to ensure that you keep to the timing and rhythm.
3. Add more tracks. You can accompany yourself on another instrument or add a backing track. You can also select appropriate loops to add to your lead track.

The keen musician: real music

1. Using audio recording equipment (you will find details of what is needed with your music software), directly record your music. If you are part of a band, you can all record your respective tracks (Fig 27).
2. Add more tracks or loops if you need to embellish your own sound.
3. Add effects, manipulate the tone and volume and edit out any fluffs made by you or your fellow musicians.
4. Burn a CD and share your sound with friends.

Fig 31 – M-Audio Keyboard

GARAGEBAND

Over the previous few pages you have seen how simple it is to use an application such as GarageBand to produce music. Here is an overview of the GarageBand interface and its key elements. Even if you are using an alternate application (perhaps Acid), the key elements will be the same.

Familiarize yourself with just a few of the features and you will begin to understand the compositional process and, even without a traditional music background, you will be creating music yourself. Jamming has arrived on the desktop.

Fig 33 – The power of Garageband (and its equivalents) lies in the number and variety of instruments available. Some are shown in icon form, above. Each (or most) have additional variations and there are a number of melodies (loops) for each.

TRACK INSTRUMENT TYPE

INSTRUMENT NAME

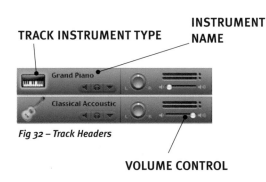

Fig 32 – Track Headers

VOLUME CONTROL

Fig 34 – Not satisfied with the countless default settings? In Track Info you can modify settings at will.

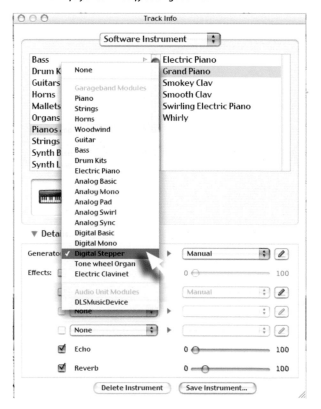

REPEATED LOOP

Fig 35 – Main interface

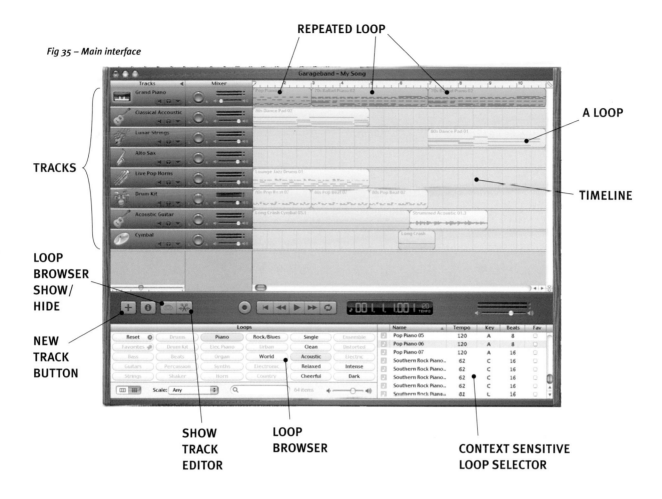

A LOOP

TRACKS

TIMELINE

LOOP BROWSER SHOW/ HIDE

NEW TRACK BUTTON

SHOW TRACK EDITOR

LOOP BROWSER

CONTEXT SENSITIVE LOOP SELECTOR

Fig 36 – Track Editor. You can create musical notes and times directly in the track editor. Option drag a note to the new position.

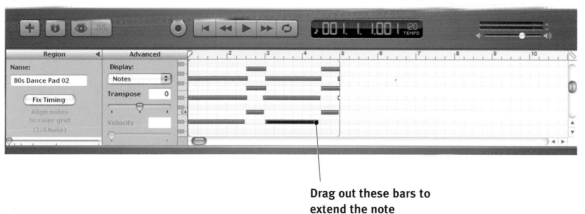

Drag out these bars to extend the note

PORTABLE LIFESTYLES

IN THIS CHAPTER WE:
- Discuss the remarkable history of the mobile phone.
- Examine the capabilities of the latest 3G phone networks.
- Look at how we can share images and video content by phone.
- Take a look at the PDA (personal digital assistant) and the difference it can make to our lives.
- Take a glance at how the game platform giants are muscling in on the portable marketplace.

IT SEEMS SLIGHTLY IRONIC NOW, WHEN WIRELESS COMMUNICATIONS IN COMPUTING IS THE NORM, THAT THE TERM "WIRED COMMUNITY" WAS LONG USED AS A EUPHEMISM FOR A CONNECTED DIGITAL WORLD. THE FREEDOM NOW AFFORDED BY TECHNOLOGIES SUCH AS BLUETOOTH AND WIRELESS ARE TAKEN FOR GRANTED AND EXPLOITED TO THE FULL.

BUT WE HAVE TAKEN MOBILE TELEPHONY FOR GRANTED FOR SOMEWHAT LONGER. FOR SOME YEARS WE HAVE HAD ACCESS TO PHONES FREE FROM WIRES. IN PRACTICE, WE MAY HAVE BEEN LIMITED BOTH BY THE TECHNOLOGY (WHICH, FOR A LONG TIME, FELL A LITTLE SHORT OF CUSTOMER EXPECTATION) AND THE COST, BUT THERE IS NO DOUBT THAT THE MOBILE PHONE IS NOW AN ALL-IMPORTANT TOOL AND ACCESSORY FOR MANY.

LIKE THE MOBILE PHONE, THE PDA (PERSONAL DIGITAL ASSISTANT) SUFFERED SOME BIRTH PANGS, BUT IT IS INCREASINGLY SEEN AS INDISPENSABLE BY MARKETS AS DIVERSE AS THE TIME-CONSCIOUS EXECUTIVE AND BUSY MOTHER. WITH ADDITIONAL FUNCTIONALITY – IN CAR NAVIGATION, MEDIA PLAYER AND EVEN AS A MOBILE PHONE – IT CONTINUES TO DEVELOP AND REINVENT ITSELF.

THIS CONFLUENCE OF FEATURES BETWEEN THE PHONE AND PDA MEANS WE NEED NOT LOSE ANY OF OUR CONNECTIVITY WHEN WE STEP OUTDOORS. WHETHER THIS ENRICHES OUR LIVES OR DEVALUES WHAT LITTLE TIME WE HAVE FOR OURSELVES IS ARGUABLE.

THE MOBILE PHONE: THE STORY SO FAR

The digital mobile phone today embodies some of the most advanced technology anywhere. The capabilities that are delivered in so compact a package are astonishing. It may come as a surprise, then, to discover that we can trace the origins of the mobile cellphone back to the grey days of the immediate post-war era.

The false dawn

Researchers in both the United States and Britain, equipped with potentially redundant electronic equipment developed since the end of the war, began to investigate how the existing radio communications systems used by emergency services could be improved. They realized that they could increase the capacity of the radio networks using a novel approach. By limiting the range of signal transmitters, rather than increasing their range and installing more of them over a geographical area, they could accommodate more communications over the limited frequencies allocated for broadcasts.

So the concept of the "cell" first appeared. The cell is a small area (which may be as little as a few hundred metres across in densely populated urban areas) over which a phone transmitter mast makes and receives calls. When a phone user moves to a

Fig 1 – Motorola's DynaTAC 8000X, launched in 1983 and weighing the best part of 1 kg (2 lb), was the first commercially available cellphone.

The dream is realized

It was not until the early 1970s that the call to arms was heard again. A low-key technology battle between staff at Motorola and Bell Laboratories ended with Dr Martin Cooper of Motorola calling his counterpart at Bell, Joel Engel. In a story that has become part of urban mythology, Cooper called Engel on the phone with the intriguing question: "... guess where I'm calling from?"

Although Bell had produced a cell-based communications network for the police, it was Motorola that delivered the first cellphone that could be used practically anywhere (and specifically, away from a vehicle). The new age of communications began. By 1982, within a decade of Cooper's phone call, the American FCC (Federal Communications Commission) finally acknowledged the technology and authorized commercially based cellphone services in the United States.

Portable?

The UK followed, with British Telecom and Vodaphone opening cellphone networks. These first-generation machines may have been mobile cellphones in name but they stretched the credibility of the term "portable". The early adopters, who, owing to the high price of the hardware and the calls, tended to be limited to city financiers and stockbrokers, were faced with handsets that were both large and heavy, drawing unkind, though not inaccurate, comparisons with house bricks.

Callpoint: a blind alley?

This was no mass-market device. They were perceived as prestige items that were impracticable for most users. But there is no doubt that – even then – they attracted the attention of a broader market. Both the cellphone networks and the conventional phone network providers were mindful of the opportunities ahead, but were restricted by practicalities. The result was the launch of the callpoint phone.

Callpoint phone networks were a curious hybrid of mobile phone and traditional payphone; the hardware was an equally curious cross between the compact cellphone we know today and a conventional cordless phone.

neighbouring cell, the call is seamlessly transferred to the transmitter in that cell.

The practical result of this is that many users can use phones in the same area and (for those with safety concerns) there is only a need to broadcast signals from a phone to a nearby transmitter.

But the cellphone was effectively stillborn when an application to create the first network in 1947 by AT&T in the United States was granted conditionally. The conditions made it impossible to create a network that would support more than 25 calls simultaneously. Even given the more modest take-up of the technology likely then, this was a non-starter.

Fig 2 – Another Motorola model formed the basis of some callpoint phones, and introduced the "flip phone" concept to an expectant public.

Handsets were cheaper than cellphones, but calls could be made only in range of a base station – there was no contiguous network of cells. Base stations were installed in rail stations, public areas and even in restaurant chains. The phones also worked as cordless phones when the owner reached home.

In the UK four networks were licensed: Mercury Callpoint, BT Phonepoint, Zonephone and Rabbit. But with the limited range of facilities alongside advances in cellphone technology, their impact was minimal. From the first launch in 1989, the last callpoint service ended just five years later in 1994.

Elsewhere, particularly in Asia, the networks were more long lived, with the discrete networks proving to be more cost-effective at the time than full-blown cell networks.

Mobile cellphones: the next generation

Before callpoint phones had got into their stride, cellphones were casting off their "brick" heritage and showing the first signs of a more inclusive pricing strategy. As cellular networks spread around the world, the potential for handset sales brought many entrants into the market. Rapidly falling prices and more creative tariffs widened the appeal and ownership of the mobile. Electronics shrunk in size and batteries – themselves a significant component of early models – also took on more diminutive proportions. The iconic

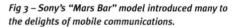

Fig 3 – Sony's "Mars Bar" model introduced many to the delights of mobile communications.

PHONE GENERATIONS

Mobile phone developments fall into "generations". The first generation was the original analogue network. Second, 2.5 and third generations describe those networks on offer today. Here is how they compare.

Features	2G	2.5G	3G
Type	Digital	Digital	Digital
Description	Basic mobile phone	Best non-3G services	High-speed data for phone PC and TV
Voice calls	Yes	Yes	Yes
Email	Receive simple	Send and receive	Send and receive
Web browsing	No	Yes	Yes
Navigation and maps	No	Yes	Yes
Upgradable*	No	Yes	Yes
Stills digital images	No	Yes	Yes
Movie clips	No	Limited	Yes
Video calls	No	No	Yes
Global roaming*	Limited	Limited	Yes
TV streaming	No	No	Yes
PDA integration	No	Limited	Yes, and PC
Data rate	10kb/sec	64–144kb/sec	114kb/sec–2Mb/sec
Download 1 min MP3	10–15 minutes	2–3 minutes	4–30 sec

Characteristics apply to the phone standard – networks or handsets may offer different services   *Depends on handset

phone of that age was the Sony CMH-333. As if to distance itself from mobile phone "bricks", it attracted the description of "Mars Bar" to describe its shape – and weight!

The digital dawn

As the customer base swelled, the networks were busy preparing the first digital cellphone networks. The conventional cellphones had all the problems of analogue networks – interference, poor sound quality and so on. So, alongside the existing networks appeared digital equivalents, holding out the promise of an enhanced service.

The needs of international travellers would be met by establishing worldwide standards – known as GSM, or Global System for Mobile Communications – letting travellers use their phones no matter where they were.

In the UK four networks launched between 1991 and 1994, including Orange – a phoenix that rose from the ashes of the Rabbit callpoint network. The parent company, Hutchison Telecom, later sold this network to concentrate on third-generation (3G) cellphones.

As the decade advanced, the cellphone entered the mainstream. Clever marketing, made possible as a result of continuing price reductions, made the

Fig 4 – Some mobile phones offer additional web browsing capabilities from within a compact-form handset that apes many features of a PDA.

cellphone a "must-have" accessory by the end of the decade as well as an indispensable tool in business.

A new age in mobile

Just when you thought cellphones were as feature packed as possible, along came the third-generation networks, often described as 3G. In 3G we see the true coming together of several digital technologies. Video calling, so often promised but rarely delivered, mobile videoconferencing, television and movies on the go and fast wireless networking are all on offer with 3G phone networks. That is what we'll take a closer look at next.

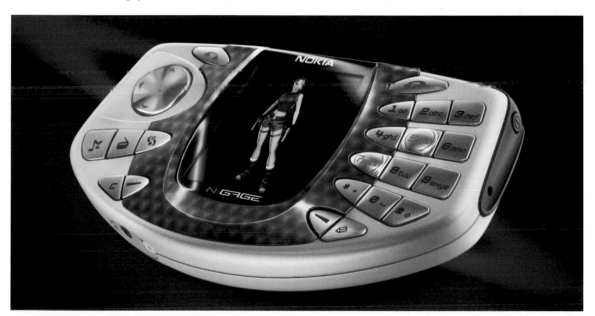

Fig 5 – ngage from Nokia not only allows games to be played on the handset (like many) but also competitive gaming between handsets, thanks to Bluetooth compatibility.

MOBILE COMMUNICATIONS: TALKING THE TALK

Mobile telephony has its own terminology and jargon that can baffle even the most ardent technophile. Here are some of the key terms and features you will be bombarded with in the mobile world.

Bluetooth

We discussed the mechanics of Bluetooth earlier (see pages 30–1). In mobile phones the key use of Bluetooth is to allow communications between a phone and headset. With this link you can use a discreet headset (rather like a modern take on a traditional behind-the-ear hearing aid) for talking and listening, while you keep the phone securely out of sight.

Some hands-free car kits also use Bluetooth: useful if you change your phone handset more often than your car. In addition, Bluetooth makes it simple to synchronize between computer and phone in order to store and back-up calendar or name information.

GSM

Global System for Mobile Communications is the most popular mobile-telephony technology, boasting more than a billion subscribers. It is the system that allows secure voice and data services with roaming and interoperability across different networks within one territory or across multiple countries. Different frequency bands are offered by different networks, but handsets typically operate on two frequencies, or all three.

GRPS (SHOULD THIS, THEN, BE GPRS??)

General Packer Radio Service, essentially piggy backs on GSM allowing data services based on conventional Internet Protocols (IPs). With GRPS, enabled connections can be "always open", rather in the manner of a broadband Internet connection, so that data can be sent or received on demand, rather than waiting for a dial-up connection to be established. Fortunately for consumers, costs are usually incurred only when data is exchanged.

i-Mode

An alternative to WAP (see below) that allows web browsing from a smartphone handset.

Instant messaging

Instant messaging allows the exchange of text messages, images or video clips between handsets. Unlike email messages (which reside on a central server until the recipient chooses to download it), instant messages are delivered to the recipient immediately.

Java

Java is a programming language originally devised by Sun Microsystems, but now implemented across a wide range of platforms. As such, it is platform-independent. In programming terms, it differs from

Fig 6 – Look, no wires! Bluetooth car kits make it easy to install the latest technology – and change that technology at will.

Fig 7 – An obvious antenna (which thankfully retracts) characterizes an Iridium satellite phone.

other languages in that it is not compiled but interpreted as run; this makes it fast. In mobile phones it is used extensively for games and also for on-board applications.

Mobile email

Mobile email services permit the sending or receiving of email messages from a mobile phone. Depending on the network, you may also be able to use your computer email address. Often, advanced email software can be employed to retrieve only selected parts of an email (usually the header) so that you do not incur costs downloading whole messages.

RFID

Radio Frequency Identification. A wireless barcode used to identify items uniquely, and in mobile telephony it is typically used to identify a phone handset securely in a way that cannot be reprogrammed. A small chip with a unique identifier is embedded in the antenna of some phones, from where radio frequency signals can be used to read the code.

SMS

Short Messaging Service. A method of sending basic text messages (which can include a limited range of special characters) of up to 160 characters in length between mobile phones.

Fig 8 – The Symbian OS makes it possible to build ever more impressive functionality into your phone handset. Here, BBC World news is delivered to your palm, thanks to the Nokia 7710.

PIE IN THE SKY? IRIDIUM'S LAST LAUGH

Imagine a phone system you could use wherever you were in the world. With no boundaries and not conditional on being within a cell? That was the promise of operator Iridium. It planned a network of satellites that would create dynamic "cells", enabling people to use their phones anywhere.

When the system launched there were major drawbacks Phone handsets were large (bringing back memories of the bricks), calls costly and – perhaps most damning of all – calls needed clear line of sight to a satellite. But the original concept has evolved, and the net of 66 satellites still provides a convenient phone network, which tends now to be marketed at those users who would be out of sight of conventional cellphone networks rather than aiming to compete with existing national systems.

Symbian

An operating system designed for mobile devices, specifically smartphones. In such phones the Symbian OS (operating system) drives all the applications and processes found on the phone and, being a standard, it is easily implemented on a wide range of handsets. It also integrates with GSM, GRPS, WiFi and Bluetooth.

WAP

Wireless Application Protocol: a secure communications protocol for displaying basic web content on mobile phones. It is optimized for the small screens of non-smart, non-3G phones and for simple one-handed navigation using the standard phone keyboard.

You will find a more extensive glossary of all things mobile on page 85.

CREATING MOVIE CONTENT FOR 3G PHONES

As 3G (third-generation) networks evolve and more features (included in the original specification) become accessible, it is becoming viable to create content ourselves and deliver it to family or friends over the network.

Here is how you can create a short movie using movie clips that might have originated on your 3G video handset, digital video camera or even your digital stills camera, when recording, using the movie mode.

Fig 9

1. Begin by piecing together the movie clips, stills images or camcorder footage as we did earlier when we examined digital video (see page 78–9). It is particularly important now to be ruthless with unwanted or material that is below par. When aiming to send a video to a mobile phone handset, you want only the best, and then only a précis of all the shots you have taken (Fig 9).

2. As most video-editing software won't feature an option to convert the video in a form that is

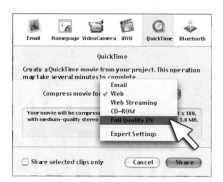

Fig 10

directly accessible to 3G telephones, save the movie in the best quality offered by the application. Here, the QuickTime option in iMovie, saved in DV quality, has been used. You don't need the highest quality, but since you will be exporting this content, it makes sense to start with the best quality you can realistically achieve (Fig 10).

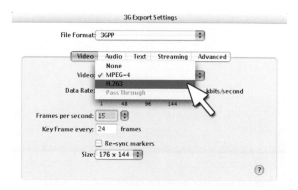

Fig 11

3. QuickTime Pro (PC and Mac) will let you edit your movies in a compatible format. It will also open your movie created elsewhere and allow you to export it in a suitable form. Select Movie to 3G from the drop-down menu. (Fig 11)

4. Select a video format. For most applications the default MPEG-4 is fine. (Fig 12).

Fig 12

5. Select a file format. Again, for most applications the 3GPP default setting is fine. If you have any

Fig 13

concerns, check a compatible handset and see which formats are used for video clips (Fig 13).

6. Repeat for the Data Rate and Video Size. Bear in mind that a greater data rate will give a better video result, but it could then take longer to send, thus compromising performance. A larger video size will also demand a higher data rate. For most telephone handsets, the smaller size is fine (Figs 14, 15).

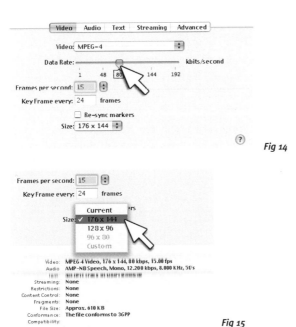

Fig 14

Fig 15

7. Select OK to export your movie. This may take a few minutes, depending on the settings chosen. When complete, the video will open in a new window. Check the performance and if necessary make changes to the settings and export it a. Aim to achieve the lowest data rate that gives good, watchable results (Fig 16).

8. Select Send to transmit your movie. You can se. it by email or as streaming content. Check the network preferences. You will find them in the

VIDEO ON YOUR MOBILE?

Do you really want to send a movie to a mobile phone and will the recipients really want to watch it? That is similar to a question that was asked about the sending and receiving of text messages: why would anyone want to use a mobile phone to send written messages?

So there is a clear precedent – 3G-handset users have demonstrated a wish to receive video clips and are avid savers of video messages, so the answer has to be "Yes" to both questions. Remember that you can save the video on your phone handset either by emailing it onwards to the email address you access from your computer or by making a direct PC connection and downloading it.

Fig 16

handbook that accompanies your handset (this is one occasion you will need to read it). Once received, your movie can be played and replayed at will (Fig 17).

Fig 17

TIPS FOR GREAT PHOTOS FROM YOUR PHONE

Although more serious photographers might scoff at phone cameras, you can still get some great pictures with them. You just need to exploit – rather than fall victim to – their limitations. The rules of photography we discussed earlier (see pages 54–9) still apply, but here are ten tips to help you get the best from your phone camera.

1 DISTANCE

Don't try to include too much in your shot. Small details, whether of a sweeping landscape or general views of activities or sports, just don't work. Instead, get in close, or closer, and concentrate on one part of the scene. Getting in close helps you capture, for example, expressions on people's faces that make for more interesting shots.

Fig 18 – Distance: closing in on your subject makes for a more powerful shot.

2 CLOSE AND CLOSER

Phone cameras often allow you to shoot very close up to the lens. This can lead to some fascinating perspective effects. Get to know – through practice or by referring to the manual – how close you can go.

3 RESOLUTION

Like digital cameras, phone cameras offer different resolutions. Remember, a high resolution will give better results but the files will be bigger (and more expensive to email from the camera). Choose a high resolution for those images you want to download later and produce prints from. Use lower resolutions for those grabbed shots that you will want to email straight away.

Fig 19 – Resolution: increasing resolution gives more detailed shots – but at the expense of file size.

4 LIGHTS, CAMERA, ACTION

Digital cameras tend to offer a range of sensitivities that allows successful photography in even very subdued lighting conditions. Phone cameras will struggle in low light, delivering blurred results where there is any subject movement – and that includes a shaking camera due to a wobbly hand. If your camera has a flash or auxiliary light, use it when the lighting level falls. Or, if blurring is inevitable, use it creatively, as if you meant to blur the shot.

Fig 20 – Low light: when the light levels fall, camera shake is inevitable. Modest flash light helps to restore sharpness.

5 KEEP IN THE LIMELIGHT

Or rather, keep your subjects that way. Unless you are being deliberately creative, keep the main lighting behind you so that it shines directly on the subjects. Phone cameras tend to react to backlighting by underexposing and rendering subjects in silhouette, which is rarely a flattering effect.

Fig 22 – Clean up: just one fingerprint can degrade an image.

6 BE SUPPORTIVE

Even when you have enough light, an unsteady hand can give results that lack critical sharpness. If you are already struggling with the light, use a convenient support when shooting. Rest the camera on a table or against a wall when you press the button. Simple but effective.

7 CLEANLINESS IS NEXT TO ...

The nature of phones means that they are being handled often and with little regard to the optical surfaces of the camera lens. Unlike those of cameras, phone lenses tend to be exposed most of the time and so are prone to picking up fingerprints from careless handling and fluff and lint when slipped into a purse or pocket. Use a soft, clean cloth to clean the lens periodically – or invest in a case that keeps the entire phone covered when it is not in use.

8 DISCRETION

Although your actions will be above reproach, people can still feel uncomfortable being photographed, especially when the camera is also a phone. It is perceived as being somewhat furtive. Be mindful of sensitivities, especially when there are children around.

9 SAVING FOR POSTERITY

Since there is only limited memory, download the images from your phone as often as you can. Use the connection cable provided with the camera or, if your phone has Bluetooth or infrared capabilities, use these. In this way, you won't just protect the shots you have, you will also ensure that you have plenty of memory in the camera for new ones.

10 EXPLORE

You have your phone with you all the time? What better way to experiment with photographs? Experiment with shots at odd angles, strange positions, and including subject movement. You will shoot some real howlers, but you will also get some jaw-dropping shots to send to your friends.

Fig 23 – Weird or wonderful: exploiting the camera's short-comings or using unusual angles can produce intriguing effects.

VIDEO TIPS

If you are recording video, then the tips given here for your camera phone will also give you great video clips. Remember, too, that you need to keep your shots interesting. Avoid long clips – around seven seconds is the best length (unless there is some activity in progress). And let your subjects move while you keep the camera still.

PODCASTING: PERSONAL RADIO SCHEDULES ON THE MOVE

Here is the solution for those of us who would love to listen to more radio, but find that our favourite programming is broadcast at inconvenient times. It is called "podcasting" and it has been described as a PVR – personal video recorder – for radio.

Whether commercial or public service, the biggest radio audiences are delivered during the so-called "drive time", the daily commute of millions of us from home to office and, at the end of the day, back home again. This is when commercial stations make their money, with the assurance that advertisers really are playing to large, essentially captive, audiences. But by the same token, in order to appeal to this crucially important mass audience, programming at these times can be a little ... bland. It is designed not to be controversial or highbrow; rather, it is easy listening in its most literal sense.

For many of us, this is the ideal wind-down time at the end of a long day, but for others it could be an opportunity to catch up with all that programming they might otherwise miss. This is where podcasting comes in. It gives you the opportunity to download selected programming to an MP3 player and enjoy the programmes you want, when you want.

The term "podcasting" is a relatively recent one. It first appeared in a British newspaper feature in 2004 as a concise term to describe the process. That process was one of identifying programme types that you want to listen to, pulling them down to a computer desktop in MP3 form and then downloading them to an MP3 player for listening to at your leisure. The "pod" in podcasting refers, as you might imagine, to Apple's iPod, though the medium is not exclusive to that unit.

Podcasting is essentially a value-added service that is a hybrid of broadcasting and webcasting.

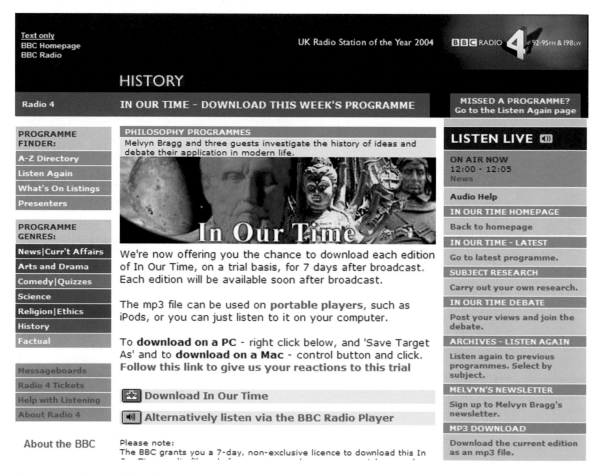

Fig 24 – In Our Time is a BBC Radio 4 programme that is now enjoyed around the world thanks to podcasting.

Unlike either of these services, both of which deliver content to the listener by pushing it out from their studios to essentially passive listeners, podcasting is a pulling process in which the listener drags the requested content from a website. This can be a fully manual process (rather like selecting MP3 tracks from a music site) or it can be automated so that a program on your computer will trawl selected sites automatically for preferred programming types and then download them for your consideration.

Anyone who has news feeds or stock market figures delivered to their desktop will be familiar – in operation terms if not by name – with an "aggregator". Aggregators automatically gather news and information from various websites and deliver them to you in a convenient package. You don't need to visit a website or log on to an email service.

Podcasting applications do much the same, but this time aggregating audio content and downloading it to your mobile device. It is a completely seamless operation – once you have configured your podcasting application, all you need do is place your device in its PC cradle each day for the most recent content to be downloaded. Then when you next get in the car and play, it is there for you.

Initially podcasting was seen as somewhat geeky, with most of the output derived either from unique programming or from selected Internet-only radio stations, but towards the end of 2004 a more mainstream option appeared. Offering at first only a trial, the BBC in London offered selected programming in MP3 format as well as streamed direct in real time over the Internet. The MP3 version of programmes could be downloaded and pulled straight into iTunes (for iPod users) or used with a generic utility, such as iPodderX, to podcast straight on to any MP3-compatible player.

Although promoted as a test, it was very well received around the world and has alerted commercial interest in what was, at its inception, a non-commercial venture.

It is probably also worth noting at this point that an MP3 file per se is not a podcast; to be a proper podcastable file it needs to be presented in a form that a podcasting application (like those you will find at websites such as www.podcasters.org or www.podcast.net) can handle. This usually means that it is provided as an RSS enclosure feed. But you don't have to worry about these technicalities – when you subscribe to a service, all these are taken care of for you. So, strictly speaking, downloading via iTunes is not podcasting, but to all intents and purposes, the process is identical.

As for the future, as well as commercial interventions, there is no reason why images and even movies could not be downloaded in exactly the same way. When this becomes viable, we might have the ultimate in truly personal PVRs.

Fig 25 – iPodder is a popular tool for gathering and downloading podcast programming.

Fig 26 – Popular podcasting sites let you select from a wide range of podcast material. This list is growing exponentially, carrying new and archived programming along with Internet radio broadcasts.

GAMING ON THE GO

No study of digital technology would be complete without at least mentioning gaming. Since the earliest days of Pong, through Space Invaders, Donkey Kong and Super Mario, video gaming has been in both commercial and social terms a massive ongoing success story.

We have seen now how games, of varying complexity, feature on devices as diverse as the ubiquitous Playstations and Xboxes to mobile phones and even watches. Like computers, gaming platforms (which are, essentially, optimized computers) continue to offer greater and greater power and ever-increasing flexibility. In this case, this upward progression manifests itself by offering better and better graphics capabilities and true-(or truer-) to-life visuals.

"State of the art" in video gaming today is arguably represented by Sony's Playstation Portable – the PSP. Forget the low-resolution graphics of older devices and the compromises over quality; this is a fully fledged gaming platform that makes no compromise in the quest for portability. Not intended as a successor to the Playstation 2 (more of an adjunct), the PSP inherits the same operational characteristics of its tethered siblings and offers a screen that, at a resolution of 480 x 272, gives a quality virtually unique in the portable gaming world. The inclusion of Wireless connectivity enables a whole host of new opportunities for

Fig 27 – The PSP handset clearly has a new look, yet the detailing – such as the buttons and controls – makes its heritage obvious.

connecting to other devices in the home, on external networks and also in the wider world. The immediate opportunity is the capability of online gaming straight out of the box or peer-to-peer gaming between different machines in the vicinity, à la Nokia's Ngage.

As games have grown in complexity, so has their physical size – more and more Playstation 2 games have been driven from the use of CD-ROM to DVD-ROM. The compact footprint of the PSP has forced Sony to rethink storage. Moderate data transfer can be effected by the use of a Memory Stick (or, specifically, a Memory Stick Pro Duo), the staple data-transfer mechanism for Sony devices, but even with the high capacities now offered by these cards, it is not the most viable of delivery methods for games programs.

For game delivery, Sony has produced a new format: the UMD, or Universal Media Disc. With a capacity just shy of 2GB and a footprint size of nearly 65 mm (2½ in) square, UMD discs allow large amounts of rich content (including full motion video) to be delivered to the PSP.

Doubling up

Sony's Nemesis in the gaming world, Nintendo, has enjoyed success for many years with the Game Boy. Not wanting to be eclipsed in the handheld stakes by Sony, the company is now offering the Nintendo DS – and stole several months' march on its rival. "DS" stands for Dual Screen. Featuring – as you would expect – two gaming screens, it allows new levels of interaction in multi-player gaming. You can see, for example, the conventional view from a race car on one screen and an overview (or aerial view) of the race in the other. Or you could play a game on one screen and watch (or send) messages or emails with the other.

Although featuring two identically sized screens, the lower one packs an additional punch: it is touch sensitive. Using a stylus (or your finger) you can use it in the same manner as you would a screen on a PDA, or you can move game characters in unique ways, perhaps changing perspective as you go.

Like the PSP, the DS includes Wireless capabilities that, in this case, can enable gaming between as many as 16 players. Unlike the PSP, the DS features backwards compatibility with the Game Boy Advance, allowing you to play your favourite Game Boy Advance games, albeit in single-player mode. This overcomes many of the objections gamers have concerning hardware upgrades – the need, sometimes, to have to buy new versions of games to play them on the new hardware.

Fig 28 – The PictoChat feature of the Nintendo DS allows owners to send images and hand-written text wirelessly to other DS devices in the vicinity. Even when in sleep mode, the DS can detect other possible devices to communicate with nearby and will spring into life to allow PictoChatting.

Fig 29 – No longer do you have to be disconnected from your digital world. PDAs deliver connectivity and computing power on the move.

PERSONAL DIGITAL ASSISTANTS

It is surprising how much we can come to depend on our computers. They store our music collections, photo albums, correspondence and so on. But, despite the proliferation of the laptop, there are limitations to where we can take all this information. That is where the PDA (personal digital assistant) steps in. Sometimes called simply a "handheld", the PDA is small mobile computer that help you carry your most valued information with you everywhere. And much more.

PDAs were born in the early 1990s when Apple released the Newton. It comprised a screen, on which you could write directly, and some useful applications. A cut-down spreadsheet, calendar and mathematical tools were accompanied by a word processor that added, for its day, extra punch. Special handwriting-recognition technology meant you could write freehand and have your words converted on the fly into printed text. Clever and surprisingly effective.

But the Newton, despite becoming increasingly powerful and comprehensive, was never the hit that Apple expected or needed for its continued development. Some argued that it was the lack of a colour screen, others the size – somewhat larger than a paperback. The project was dropped and never again figured in the Apple line-up.

Those working on the project were convinced of its viability and, shortly after, it was resurrected as the PalmPilot, later known simply as the Palm PDA. With an ultra-compact size – but still boasting a usable screen size – and improved handwriting technology, it proved a modest success. Its loyal following grew in number until that critical mass that had eluded Apple was reached – a sufficient number of users to ensure ongoing development.

Now colour screens are the norm and, more significantly, other entrants – some featuring a cut-down version of the Windows operating system – now market PDAs. It has moved from toy of the gadget lover to the device that organizes the lives of millions on the move and at work every day. Ideal for those who need computing power, but demand something smaller than a computer, most now work seamlessly with computers – desktop or portable – to ensure not only that information is shared, but that it is also synchronized, so that both devices share the latest information.

Choosing a PDA

The question arises: "Do you need a PDA?" Most of us could justify a simple electronic organizer. Something that can take the place of a conventional

Fig 30 – Not to be left behind by the more humble mobile phone, PDAs (here a Sony Clié) can take – and display – pretty good photographs.

diary but add a few alerting features, alarm clock and the like. But would it not be great if we could also browse our email on the go? Or review our picture collection, song collection or read a book?

At one time the PDA was an alternative for a computer for those who found themselves intimidated by the latter; now, the functionality of each is on a par. Indeed, many PDAs offer tools not found on computers. So how do you make your choice?

Price

Price can be a deciding factor. If all you want is a simple calendar and note-taking tool, the cost is comparatively low; go for a well-specified Pocket PC and the price can stretch to that of a basic PC laptop. But saving money can be a false economy. Unless you know that you do not need some of the more advanced features and will not, over the lifetime of the device, then it is better to aim for a mid-priced machine. They may have more functions than you will need now, but they will grow with your PDA skills.

Operating system

The key element of a PDA's functionality is the operating system it runs with. It is a similar choice that faces someone choosing a PC. There you choose between a Windows PC and a Mac. Here, the choice is between Palm OS and Pocket PC.

Pocket PC is a derivative of Windows specifically engineered to run on mobile devices. Like its elder sibling, it is produced by Microsoft, though Microsoft doesn't make any hand-held devices. You will, however, find those stalwarts of the Windows operating system – HP/Compaq and Casio, in particular – also offering handhelds using this operating system. Expect to find these devices offering a broadly familiar screen layout and functionality, but under the control of a pen and sensitive screen rather than a mouse. You will also find these include software tools familiar from Windows, including the Notepad and cut-down versions of Word and Excel. Extensions to the operating system also allow for MP3 music playing (often using an expansion memory card), voice recording and email sending and receiving.

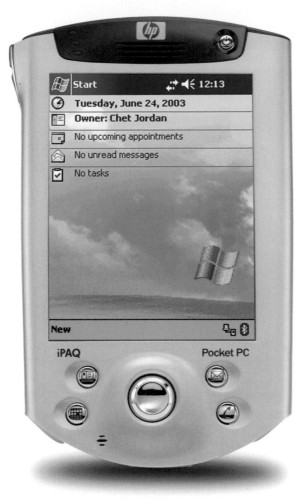

Fig 31 – Pocket PCs runa timmed down version of Windows.

in regard to its licensing of third parties – Palm hived off the software division to a new company called PalmSource. So you can now find the Palm OS on devices produced by other manufacturers, notably Sony in its Clié handhelds. The Palm OS has also been developed for the so-called smartphones, which combine many of the functions of a PDA with those of a mobile phone.

How do you choose between these operating systems? Like the perennial Mac vs PC debate, much comes down to personal choice, familiarity and functionality. And like these two platforms, Pocket PC and Palm OS have their strong devotees.

Devotees of Palm OS will point to it being a lean and mean operating system. It is also easy to use, easy to configure and tends to offer more efficient power consumption. Pocket PC users are accustomed – in most models – to greater power and flexibility in applications. If you want a real trimmed-down PC in your pocket, this is the obvious choice. If you want a no-nonsense digital companion, go for the Palm OS.

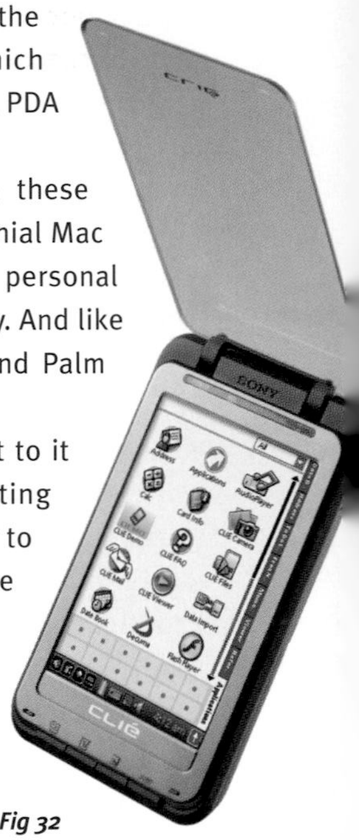

Fig 32 – Palm OS is an alternative operating system designed specifically for PDAs.

The Palm OS is the spiritual successor of the system used on the Newton devices. To help the development of the operating system – particularly

BLACKBERRY

A more specialized PDA, BlackBerry devices pioneered mobile communications, including mobile phone, Internet access and email in a single robust pocketable device. BlackBerry devices tend to be used more in corporate situations where an enterprise-wide solution can be implemented, attaching value-added services specific to the corporation.

Displays and controls

The distinguishing feature of a PDA is its display. Nominally, it is an LCD panel, similar to that of a computer's flat panel, but with the obvious distinction in virtually all cases of being touch sensitive. A fine membrane over the surface – virtually invisible – interprets touch commands. Colour screens are now the norm on most machines, though budget models will still feature

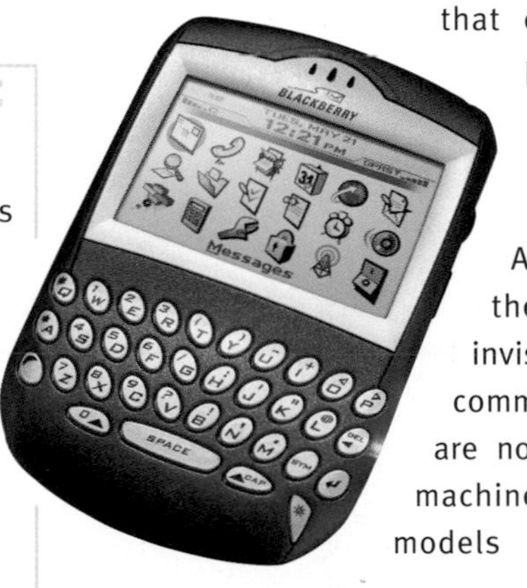

Fig 33 – The BlackBerry is optimized for mobile communications.

greyscale displays. The colour displays obviously tend to consume more power, principally because they need to be backlit at all times to present a clear image. Docking cradles, which recharge the on-board batteries, will ensure that the battery power is always sufficient for a few days' remote working. Greyscale displays don't require permanent lighting and can run for several weeks on disposable batteries.

Other controls generally comprise shortcuts to, say, email, contact lists or frequently used applications. Some more specialized devices may sport compact keyboards – often so compact as to defeat all but the smallest and most delicate of fingers.

Keyboards and text entry

If you find that you do need to enter substantial amounts of text, then you can either learn to be dextrous with these micro keys or invest in one of the accessory keyboards offered for many Palm and Pocket PC devices. Folding away into a package smaller than the handheld, these keyboards are virtually the same size as conventional keyboards and offer the same touch typing feel, with real "clicking" keys.

If you don't expect to enter a great deal of text, perhaps just the odd note, calendar entry or email, then Palm OS handhelds offer Graffiti – a software application that builds on the character-recognition skills of the early Newtons. Using a simplified letter-writing technique, easily learnt, you can achieve virtually 100 per cent successful character recognition at commendable speed.

Size

The term "handheld" tends to suggest that there is little difference in size between types. In fact, some are little larger than a credit card, while the Pocket

Fig 34 – This smartphone from Kyocera offers the convenience of a flip phone with the power of a Palm OS PDA.

PCs are around twice the size of an iPod. As you might expect, functionality expands with size, with the smaller machines offering only limited capacity for data. Larger ones give the prospect of a larger screen, larger batteries (for enhanced performance) and the option of slots for memory cards.

Email

Do you need (rather than want) email on the move? Then make sure your handheld will allow Internet connection. Check compatibility before you buy, as many handhelds will link to the net (to allow web browsing as well as email) using a mobile phone, but some don't. Smartphones, clearly, combine both functions and make remote email and browsing far simpler.

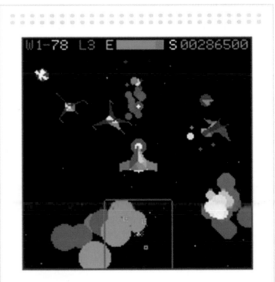

Games on the go

Now that phones offer games on the move, it is hardly surprising to find that PDAs offer a wide range of games that make use of the enhanced screen sizes and memory capacity of the PDA. Games such as 3D Star Fighter Pilot (from the PalmSource website) let you while away many an hour when you should really be checking your email or bank account.

THE USPS OF PDAS

For many of us, there needs to be at least one USP (unique selling proposition) that makes a PDA essential. Gone now are the days when it was the gimmick value or cachet that made it worthwhile to own one. Now, with so many other devices competing for our pocket or purse space, PDAs need to deliver something unique.

Here is a selection of great applications that, for some users, have justified the purchase of a PDA. For many, the ability to stay in touch – with emails as well as by phone – is reason enough, but for others there needs to be something more compelling. And the manufactures of PDAs, along with their software partners, have been quick to deliver.

Pocket-DVD Studio

The high-quality screen of a PDA may not do full justice to the quality offered by DVD movies, but it is still pretty cool to be able to watch a DVD on your PDA, and Pocket-DVD Studio lets you do just that.

Fig 34 – DVDs can be shrunk to fit on your PDA.

The software lets you make a copy of your favourite DVDs in a video format that can be replayed on your PDA's screen. Surprisingly, any movie that lasts up to three hours can be mightily compressed when accommodated on a Palm screen – sufficient to be stored on a 256MB memory card in most cases. Because the movie replays from a memory card, power consumption is modest.

eBook readers

All right, we don't all like playing games or even watching movies on our business or family trips. For those who want something potentially more cerebral, how about eBooks? These are versions of traditional books, along with new works that can be downloaded to your PDA and replayed on screen. You can carry multiple eBooks with you on your PDA, lightening the load in your luggage, and you can enjoy them on your home computer or laptop, too.

There are thousands of titles available covering all the genres that you would expect to find at your favourite bookstore. And they are available through online retailers at the touch of a button. Those with

Fig 37 – Websites such as www.ereader.com provide easy access to an enormous number of eBooks to enrich your PDA-based life.

something to say can even produce their own – you will find software readily available to help you produce your own eBooks for sharing or selling.

Navigation

A particularly fine USP for the PDA has been navigation aids. Aping the in-car navigation devices, but at a nominal cost, these give you clear, concise directions on any journey using the PDA's screen to present virtual views of the road ahead. Dynamic calculations also mean that, should you ignore advice and make a detour (perhaps to avoid traffic jams or roadworks that the system could not have known about) the system will automatically redesign your journey.

To use these you need a receiver to receive and interpret the signals from global positioning satellites (GPS). This can be an add-on box (often car-mounted and communicating with the PDA via Bluetooth) or in-built. An increasing number of top-of-the-range PDAs offer a GPS solution straight out of the box.

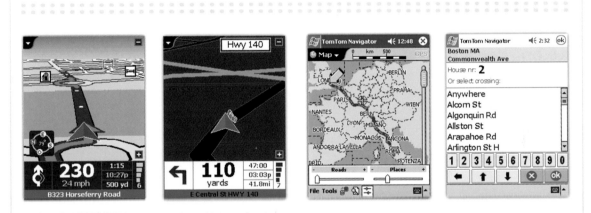

Fig 36 – Navigation displays clearly show road layouts and enable destinations to be selected easily.

PDAs on the move

The TomTom navigation system is available for Pocket PC and Palm OS PDAs and also as a stand-alone device for those not up with PDAs and it offers a comprehensive navigation and informational service that puts many OEM (Original Equipment Manufacturers) automotive systems to shame. In normal use the system uses the PDA screen to display three-dimensional plans of the road ahead. You can configure the system to choose a route for you or enter your own – perhaps taking in places of interest along the way.

If you need to ensure that your route avoids certain areas – for example, one that excludes routes in the London city centre Congestion Charging Zone – you simply hit the "Plan Alternative" button. Similarly, if you want to visit a restaurant or a landmark, you can program these into your route.

The stand-alone version offers the same functionality in a device that is easily moved from vehicle to vehicle.

OUR DIGITAL FUTURE

THE CONNECTED HOME

Technology is nothing new in our homes, but the proliferation of devices is a comparatively recent affair. The digital age, as we have seen throughout this book, has brought together equipment and devices that would otherwise be considered quite separate. Now our homes can truly act as digital hubs. Here, we have shown how devices are deployed in a typical home today.

Let us take a – very – virtual tour and see what today's digitally connected home has to offer us.

CHILDREN'S ROOMS
Games console
Computer with 5.1 audio

BEDROOM
TV/DVD/Audio system

BATHROOM
In-ceiling speakers
LCD TV

CONNECTED HOME
Central control unit for audio, AV and lighting
Central WiFi control

ON THE MOVE
Phone
PDA
Portable games unit
MP3 player

LOUNGE/LIVING ROOM
Home cinema with WiFi
DVD/DivX player
Plasma screen
Surround sound system

STUDY/STUDIO
Main computer, digital TV, digital camera docks, recording kit

KITCHEN
In-ceiling speakers
LCD TV
kitchen computer workstation

Home networking

Wireless and Bluetooth networks underpin the communications. Wireless networks allow the main computer of the home, those in other rooms and other devices to talk to each other and, via broadband Internet connection, the wider world. Some homes also have a centrally located repository for media; a single location where the family's entire collection of CDs and other entertainment media are stored. They could be accessed by control units scattered around the home. The rapid move of media from CD and tape to computer hard discs, made possible by MP3 and its equivalent formats, has rendered this monolithic store case redundant. Music and, increasingly, video collections are now more likely to live on the one or more computers that now comprise the home network.

Fig 1 – Some DVD player/recorders also allow wireless connections with a PC so that media can be replayed through a television.

Study

The study has updated its role, defined in the Victorian age, of being a home to the family's book and ephemera collection by evolving into a creative studio, a place where digital media is downloaded, manipulated and created. This will typically be home to the main computer of the household. Packed to the gunnels with memory and with an enormous hard disc, it is ideal for image editing, movie making, DVD creation and, with a suitable antenna connection, acting as a PVR. PVR recordings can then be downloaded to DVD or, if you are exploring the HDTV world, Blu-ray discs.

Lounge

The lounge, or living room, tends to be multi-purpose. And one of those purposes is as an integrated home cinema. Plasma screens now offer quality akin to traditional televisions but with larger screen sizes at only a fraction of the bulk. Direct recordings

are possible with a hard disc PVR, which might also store your favourite DVDs in the manner of a digital jukebox. If you don't fancy doubling up your PVRs, you could opt for a DVD/hard disc unit with Internet connection that can access the media on the hard drive of your main computer, or any other in the house. KISS Technology is one of the trailblazers in the connected home with its wireless DVD players that can access content from computer hard discs.

Audio shares the same speaker arrangement, but it may use conventional media (such as CD and its variants) or MP3 music streamed from a computer source somewhere within the house. You might even use an MP3 player to deliver the music straight to the hi-fi.

Fig 2 – Wake to the latest Internet feeds.

Bedroom

Modest home cinema kits are now cheaper than basic VCRs used to be just a few years ago. So it is perfectly viable to have a compact home cinema in the bedroom for those late-night movies or if you want to escape from the surround-sound sports presentation in the main lounge. After those late-night movies, you don't want to waste any time in the morning. A device such as the Beyond Home Hub looks like a bedside clock radio, but in addition to offering CD music to wake up to, it also gathers all the essential facts that you need to start your day via the Internet. Weather forecasts, stock market figures, news reports and even important "to dos" are all presented.

Children's rooms

Chances are, the children's rooms will boast a computer, even if it is an older machine that has cascaded down through the family as new machines take pride of place in the home. You will find that these, too, may feature surround-sound speaker systems, ideal for immersive games and watching DVDs. Of course, there may also be a Playstation or an Xbox there, too ...

Fig 3 – This unit from Beyond offers audio and video entertainment along with Internet connectivity, Courtesy Beyond.

Kitchen

We have already seen that the kitchen, since it is used for family gatherings and meals, can have its own media centre computer, along with a television and DVD player. Meanwhile, discrete speakers ensure that the music you enjoy elsewhere in the house can be played there as well. Portable DAB radio can make the kitchen chores less of a, well, chore.

Bathroom

Relaxation time is as important as ever, so the bathroom boasts similar speakers to those in the kitchen. You could even add a flat-panel television to enjoy your favourite shows as you relax.

Control and mood throughout the home

Once, a remote control could only control your television. Then came VCRs, along with another remote. Satellite receivers, DVDs, lighting, audio system, all debuting with their own remotes. Some manufacturers managed to integrate several of their devices into a single unit, or even allow limited cross-brand control.

Today, you need have none of this chaos. Universal remotes – more so than their earlier namesakes – are your gateway to a digital lifestyle. Conventional models sport a large number of buttons, many of which assume different functions according to the device. PDA-like models have a touch screen that morphs according to the device selected to control. These tend to have the ability to connect to the Internet (via a computer) to allow new device controls to be programmed.

Mood? It is lighting that provides the mood throughout the house. Dim, indirect lighting for relaxation, bright task lighting when you need to work. Remote-control lighting has been with us for some time, but for real effect you need to be able to set light scenes, too. Light scenes are light levels applied to multiple lighting sources so that lighting moods can be more effectively set. With one press of a button you can, for example, turn off an overhead light, turn down side and table lamps and activate uplighters for subtle, glare-free illumination.

Fig 4 – Multifunction remote controls let you manage all the technology in your home.

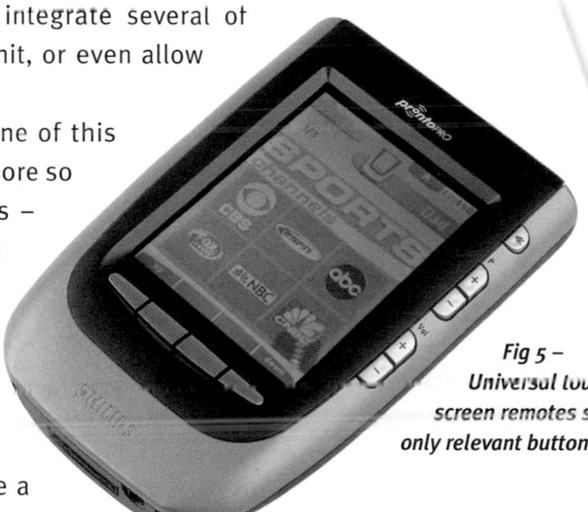

Fig 5 – Universal touch screen remotes show only relevant buttons.

Fig 6 – Lighting control is now simple thanks to infra-red sets.

MONEY NO OBJECT?

If you have to ask the price, so the saying goes, you can't afford it. For those who will make no concessions in their quest for theatrical authenticity, perfection is possible – at a price.

Home cinema has never been so cheap or easy to implement in even the most modestly scaled home. The advent of high-grade speaker systems at affordable prices, and even capable wireless speakers, has meant that many of the obstacles that previously excluded many people from enjoying the audio pleasures already encoded in much of their tape and DVD library have been overcome.

We can now almost all install a discreet audio system in our living room without seriously compromising that room's use. But for some, any compromise is too great a price to pay. For them, nothing short of the full cinematic experience will do. That means not only the best video and audio quality, but also a bespoke environment in which to enjoy these productions. Creating a real movie theatre in your home demands money and space – in

equally abundant quantities – but the results can be breathtaking.

CEDIA is the international organization that represents some of the major home cinema installation companies and hosts annual awards for the best installations. A glance through the entrants shows just what you can get if your pocketbook knows no limits. Here are just a few examples of CEDIA members' work.

Figs 7 & 8 – Connected Technologies in Colorado Springs produced this theatre for one of its clients. No cinema that I have ever visited boasted this luxury, yet the appointments are clearly residential. Courtesy CEDIA/Connected Technologies.

Fig 9 – Not everyone wants their home to rival the golden age of Art Deco movie houses; some people want their cinema fully integrated. For this information hound, one screen was not enough. Four satellite screens keep a watch on additional channels or transmissions; should anything catch the viewer's eye on one of these screens, it can be quickly swapped with whatever is on the main screen. Courtesy CEDIA/All Around Technology.

Fig 10 (left) – The key to getting the best from the installation is the hardware. No simple DVD player here; high-quality components include discrete audio decoders that squeeze every last drop of quality from the sound sources. Courtesy CEDIA/Connected Technologies.

Fig 11 (above, left) – Controlling a mega-system like this is child's play thanks to a comprehensive, but intuitive, touch-control panel, which has been integrated with a PC for additional flexibility. Courtesy CEDIA/All Around Technology.

Fig 12 (above, right) – The downside of an installation on this scale is that it is no longer a DIY job. A quick look around the back of the media cabinet gives you some idea of how complex the installation actually is; once it leaves the cabinet, the cabling is carefully and successfully concealed to make for a very neat look. Courtesy CEDIA/All Around Technology.

NOW YOU SEE IT ...

Some time ago, hi-fi and AV manufacturers discussed the ideal system, a system to which they should all be aspiring. On the one hand consumers seemed to be demanding more features and equipment that offered more switches and flashing lights. On the other hand there was increasing resistance on the part of many users to the intrusive nature of so many components. When you had spent a lot of time designing and building your home environment, it was something of an anathema to compromise that design for the sake of the home-entertainment equipment. For these people, the ideal system would be one that was notionally invisible; delivering content – whether audio or visual – on demand, but in the most unobtrusive way.

Some of us are fortunate enough to devote a room to our hi-fi or AV system. We can ensure that the room is as acoustically perfect as possible and position the furniture and components as the requirements of the system demand. The results will undoubtedly be superb and the performance exceptional. But the rest of us have to make compromises. Our living spaces need to be multi-functional. Fortunately, the compromises we need to make to our home-entertainment systems don't need to be too marked. Many hi-fi systems (or hi-fi components of AV systems) can now adapt to a room

either by you making a manual adjustment of the sound characteristics or, increasingly, by the system mapping the acoustics of the room and automatically compensating for them.

The good news for those who like to hear their music but not look at delivery mechanisms is that discrete audio is now as potent and capable of delivering full sound as those monolithic speakers of just a few years ago.

Fig 13 – Discretion is increasingly the keyword. For those of you wanting music or sound effects that are floor-shaking but not the visual intrusion, there are systems that are subtle. Look hard and you will see the speakers, but they don't conflict with their admittedly minimal surroundings.

How big is your sound?

What is the ideal size for media? That may sound a strange question to ask. Surely it is the content that matters, irrespective of the medium? In fact, the size and type of medium can have quite a bearing, psychologically and practically, on the acceptance and adoption of a standard. The form of the compact cassette is often cited as the optimum. It is big enough to handle and to allow print on the case to be easily read. It is small enough for a large collection of tapes to be stored conveniently. It is also no coincidence that Video 8 (and, subsequently, Hi8) tapes were a similar size.

Media larger and smaller than this form has met with more resistance. A single 8-track tape, for example, occupied the same volume as a whole collection of compact cassettes. DAT tapes, conversely, were considered by many to be too fiddly. Fortunately for that format, acceptance has increased with time, helped no doubt by the similar form-factor miniDV tape.

Similar arguments are now surfacing again as various memory card formats vie for supremacy. In one corner, Compactflash: big and bulky, but robust and easy to handle. In the other, the micro formats lead by the xD Picture card. Tiny, high-capacity and easy to incorporate into the smallest of devices.

Fig 14 – For the true audiophile how about this? The Ulysses, from Sausalito Audio Works, uses the unique acoustic lens to ensure that a sound recorded in a studio perhaps thousands of kilometres away sounds exactly as the artist intended, no matter what the shape of the room. Courtesy Sausalito Audio Works.

TOWARDS OUR DIGITAL FUTURE

Predicting the future is, at best, hazardous and, in most cases, futile. We recounted, at the beginning of this book, those astute (for the time) prophecies made by leading industry pundits that were proven so laughably wrong – and wrong in a shorter timescale than anybody might have imagined.

Let us add another entry to our quote list. It is now barely a century since Charles Duell, Commissioner of the US Patent Office, made an equally sweeping statement. "Everything," he asserted, "that can be invented, has been invented." With scant regard for his own position if this were to be true, his comment came from a position of circumspection; a position that demonstrated with absolute clarity that there was no rationale for any new inventions.

It is easy now to be disparaging of all such predictions, so how do we avoid the same pitfalls and pratfalls as we seek to make meaningful ones regarding our own future?

Looking back just a few years to the mid-1990s, in the business world early adopters were making the first steps into ecommerce. For businesses looking to cut overheads and costs generally, the draw of a merchandising operation that had no need for bricks and mortar retail operations nor for extensive call centres was immense. From these few modest operations came one of the greatest upheavals in business as countless companies – some established, many new – jumped aboard the virtual bandwagon.

By 2000 ecommerce had gone, to use the vernacular, ballistic. Shares in high-tech companies with precious little in the way of track record soared to levels that all industry experts presumed to be unsustainable. But sustained they were, and many continued onwards and upwards fuelled by both hyperbole and the unquestioning faith of investors in this new market segment.

Newcomers – perhaps best characterized by the likes of Amazon and AOL – trounced the more established companies and, in the case of the latter, annexed "traditional" media giant Time Warner. Now, even the most sober of financial market players were having to sit up and take notice.

Fig 15 – Almost an essential in 2004, Robosapien takes computer-controlled robotics to a new level of functionality and popularity. But soon, will we be chuckling over its naive simplicity?

In the UK, even more remarkable was the story of Lastminute.com. A website acting, essentially, as a third-party clearing house for last-minute travel deals and accommodation, and aiming to sell otherwise unsold, short lead-time resources, it was floated on the millennial stock market for £730 million – around US$1.1 billion at the exchange rate at the time. Only months later and the whole dot com marketplace crashed. Many investors, realizing the virtual nature of their investments, cut and ran; even the big names saw their fortunes slashed, although most managed to acclimatize at a new, more modest and sustainable level.

But the migration of our world into a digitally based one was in full swing. Perhaps more surreptitiously, our levels of awareness of all things digital were being raised.

Christmas wishes

Christmas wish lists prove a surprising and interesting barometer of digital trends. Take 2004, for example. For the 8 to 14 age range, gone are the expectations for construction kits, Barbies (and her compatriots) or even board games.

In their place appear MP3 players (and, specifically, an iPod), full-blown computer systems, Xboxes and PlayStation 2s. Kicking dolls, such as Action Men and GI Joes, further into touch is the news that at number 3 in the UK wish list (and with similar positions in other territories) is the NASA-

inspired robot Robosapien. The report, commissioned by TNS Global, showed that the percentages of children wanting the latest digital accessories were somewhat higher than the percentages of parents willing to purchase the same items!

Of course, we could labour long and hard on these statistics (and similar statistics also apply to other celebrations), but the key deduction is how skewed we are to wanting and embracing digital technology. So let us take a circumspect overview of what we might expect to see in the future of digital technologies.

Computers and the Internet

Expect, in the short term, the Internet to become increasingly pervasive in our domestic environment, perhaps more so than in our work. Television and video is already being streamed via broadband in the manner of cable television, but an increasing number of devices beyond the PC will routinely access our residential connection. Toy designers, for example, buoyed by the success of the Robosapien, are predicting that its descendants will include wireless nodes that will allow updates and new functionality to be instantly down-loaded.

Further ahead, the next generation web, the Symantic Web, will transform web use into a truly everyday medium that will be as easy to use and as "comfortable" for everyone – even the most ardent technophobe.

Inevitably, computers will continue to multiply their power and capabilities on a periodic basis, but the point will be reached where gains are so esoteric for all but the most potent of applications that consumers such as you or I will not have need for this excessive processing power. All the applications we will need to run will do so on more modestly supplied machines.

Television and radio

The big news in digital television will be the big turn-off. That is the switching off of analogue transmitters as digital becomes universal. Countries and territories have been guarded on precisely when the switch-off will happen, but by 2012 don't expect

WHAT WE WANT FOR CHRISTMAS		
GIFT	CHILDREN	PARENTS
Film/DVD	32%	51%
GameBoy Advance SP	28%	8%
GameBoy games	27%	11%
Music CDs	26%	42%
iPod	25%	9%
PC	24%	8%
PC Games	24%	24%
Xbox	22%	6%
"New" PS2	22%	7%
Source: TNS Global		

Fig 16 – Pointing the way to television–PC integration. MSN TV, formerly Web TV, acts as a media hub, allowing access on a television screen to all media resources, whether they are stored locally on a computer hard disc or distributed by conventional means. In due course, expect to see more effective integration of personal video recorders to give enhanced off-line services.

to see too many analogue systems surviving.

Keen not to disenfranchise viewers, set-top boxes for existing television sets (many of which, thanks to their unnerving reliability, will still be in use in the 2010s) will become commonplace and economic. Around the world we will see models similar to the UK's Freeview, offering a limited raft of digital channels free of subscription, suitable for serving the second, third or fourth television in the house – not everybody will necessarily want to subscribe to digital packages for all the television sets in the home.

High-definition television is, and will further, become the norm on many channels. These will remain premium channels since some content does not justify the high-definition treatment. More specialized, these non-HD channels tend to attract smaller audiences and lower advertising income.

Digital radio will continue to grow and offer increasing choice. Its unique performance will make it mandatory in cars, while the falling price of the essential chips will ensure DAB appears in most radios within a very few years.

Music, audio and visuals

The traditional demarcation lines between digital photography and digital video have, as we have already seen, become blurred. Although we will continue to see single-function devices (at least at the professional and semi-professional level), the integration of cameras, camcorders, music players and even phones will continue. Quality will improve as flexibility and ease of use become paramount. And all this will be achieved without compromising the use of these devices in any one role.

Conversely, as we have seen with the iPod, there will still be niche products devoted to one genre and excelling in operation within that niche. These will be championed by those with no wish (even if the functionality comes at no extra cost or with no increase in bulk) to adopt parallel technologies.

Mobile communications

Mobile devices – PDAs, phones and, to a lesser degree, laptop computers – will continue to play an important part in our lives. The crossing of technologies we have just described with regard to music player and camera will see PDA and phone integration continue, with a distinct separation between the two. PDAs with phone capability will be favoured by those that demand or need a large screen. Smartphones, compact phones with PDA functionality, will remain in the hands of the dedicated phone user who needs a modest amount of PDA features (elaborate phone books, web searching and the like).

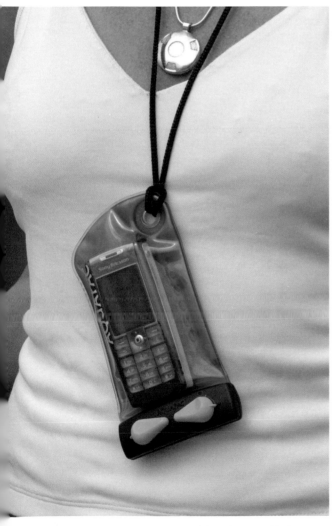

Fig 16 – For some, digital technology needs to go with them everywhere – even when they indulge in extreme sports or face arduous conditions.

The digital divide

Few would argue that the Internet is a strange beast. Essential to many businesses, and equally so to many individuals, it has evolved – rather than been planned – and become a latter-day frontier land where tacit regulation nestles with laissez-faire economics. The result is an ever-more essential resource tinged with an element of anarchy. For many, this is the key to its potency. It is "of the people", an environment where the individual can be heard in equal measure to the corporation.

But there are still many people who do not, through choice, want to use the Internet. Furthermore, neither do they want to embrace digital technology in the same way that many of us have. Their argument is logical: nothing in the digital world offers them anything more than they currently have. Not wanting hundreds of television services, the limited analogue raft suffices; happy with video tapes, DVD is of no interest, and the ability to create or master your own DVD is irrelevant.

Many sociologists are concerned about this, considering it to be a social rather than a technological issue. No one social class boasts a preponderance of these "non-adopters". But with each new technology we risk leaving more and more people behind. A recent survey from telecom company BT suggested in the UK – currently in the first rank of digital adopters – nearly 20 per cent of the population risks being digitally excluded by 2025.

It is against this background that the digital marketplace needs to grow. It is crucial that new technologies present USPs – unique selling propositions – that clearly mark them as "better" than what they intend to replace. They must be simple to use – in an utterly intuitive way. And cost alone should not limit take-up. Only when technology offers these benefits can we truly describe it as inclusive. For now, it is over to the designers ...

GLOSSARY

DIGITAL PHOTOGRAPHY

Automatic exposure: Camera mode in which the camera determines the correct exposure by adjusting the aperture and/or shutter speed.

Backlight: Light coming from behind the subject, towards the camera lens, causing underexposure unless compensation is applied.

Backlight compensation: A setting that increases exposure (by a factor of between two and four times) to prevent underexposure of backlit subjects.

Bayer pattern: Pattern of red, green and blue filters on the CCD (change-coupled device) of a camera sensor designed to allow a CCD (which only responds to light and dark) to respond to subject colours.

Burst mode: Feature of a camera that allows a series of consecutive shots (equivalent to images taken with a motordrive on conventional cameras).

CCD RAW: Data output from the CCD imaging sensor of a camera, prior to any in-camera processing. Often preferred by professional photographers as it is not tainted or biased by that processing.

CCD sensor: The light-sensitive imaging element found in most digital cameras. It comprises a matrix of individual photosensitive photosites (discrete light-sensitive areas) that correspond to the individual pixel elements of the image.

CMOS sensor: Alternative to a CCD, often used because of its lower power consumption.

Colour balance: The relative levels of red, green and blue in an image. In a balanced image, these mimic the colours of the original scene.

CompactFlash: Common form of memory card used in digital cameras.

Compression: The process of compressing an image file so that it takes up less space on a memory card. Compression can be "lossy" (when information is lost in the process) or "lossless".

Depth of field: The distance between the nearest and furthest points in an image that are in sharp focus.

Exposure: The amount of light allowed – determined by the lens aperture and the camera's shutter speed – to reach the image sensor.

f-stop: A ratio (of a lens's focal length to the diameter of the selected aperture) used to describe the amount of light that can enter through a lens.

JPEG: Popular file format on consumer digital cameras. A lossy compression format, JPEG allows a large number of images to be stored on a memory card.

Landscape format: A horizontal photograph.

Megapixel: A concatenation of a million pixels.

Panorama/panoramic mode: Sequence of shots taken (usually) around the horizon and stitched into a single, wide image.

Pixel: Smallest element of a digital image, corresponding to a single photosite on the CCD or CMOS.

Portrait format: A vertical photograph.

Red-eye: Effect caused by camera flash reflecting back from the blood-rich surface at the back of the subject's retinas, producing a bright red appearance in photographs.

Resolution: A measure of the detail in an image; the greater the number of pixels, the greater (all other things being equal) the resolution.

SLR: Single lens reflex. Camera type in which the optical system allows the user to view the scene through the same lens used to take the image.

TIFF: File format used by many digital cameras. A lossless system; files are not as compact as JPEG, and are generally of higher quality.

White balance: Feature of stills and movie digital cameras that (automatically or manually) changes the colour tone of an image to compensate for colour casts in the lighting of a scene.

Zoom lens: Lens with a variable focal length that allows a scene to be magnified or reduced in scale.

DIGITAL VIDEO

8m: Standard-resolution analogue video format devised by Sony and widely adopted. Uses small footprint tape cassettes, identical in size to Hi8 and Digital 8 tapes.

Compression: In digital video, the process of compressing data in each frame to reduce the amount of data required to be written to disc or tape. Compression can be interframe or infraframe. Interframe compression compresses by removing information that is repeated on consecutive frames; infraframe compresses each frame individually. Infraframe compression is typically used with digital video and is the best method for non-linear editing.

Desktop video: Video editing and production using appropriate computer software.

Digital 8: Digital tape format based on 8mm tape cassettes and stores DV-quality video.

Digital video: Generic description of video material recorded and stored digitally. Also the name of the format generally described as DV.

Digital zoom: Technique used in stills and movie digital cameras to produce a zoom effect by expanding the central region of an image to full frame. More acceptable on digital video cameras than stills cameras, but image degradation becomes obvious at zoom ratios of more than 3x.

Digitize: The conversion of analogue source material (such as VHS or 8mm video) to a digital format.

DV: Widely used digital video format offering near-broadcast-quality images and high-quality digital sound. Refinements of the basic format offer enhanced quality and are used for professional and semi-professional recordings.

Electronic image stabilization (EIS): Electronic mechanism that compensates for camera shake when hand-holding a camcorder. Works by recording a smaller area of the imaging chip and varying the recording position according to any perceived movements.

Firewire: Standard connection for linking camcorders to a PC. Also known as iLink (by Sony) and IEEE 1394. Firewire 800 (800Mbps data transfer) operates at twice the speed of standard Firewire.

Generational losses: Loss in quality when an analogue video is copied. Losses are cumulative. Digital formats don't normally suffer degradation when being copied.

HDV: Enhanced version of DV, which uses DV format tapes to record high-quality MPEG-2 video and with support for high-definition recordings.

Hi8: A version of 8mm video that records at higher resolution (420 lines approximately, as opposed to around 250 for 8mm).

MiniMV: An ultra-compact video format devised by Sony to enable the design of very compact camcorders. Quality is slightly inferior to that of DV.

MPEG: Motion Pictures Expert Group. A group given the task of setting standards for video encoding.

Non-linear editing: Video-editing process where scenes or clips are (typically) stored digitally on a computer and can be selected or accessed at will, without the need to wind or rewind a videotape.

Optical image stabilization: An alternative to EIS that uses prisms and gyros to compensate for camera shake. Better than EIS, but often more cumbersome and expensive for manufacturers to implement.

Progressive scanning: Option provided by some camcorders where lines of the video image are recorded consecutively, rather than being interlaced (in other words, when all odd lines are recorded first, then the even lines). Gives a more "film-like" image.

Super VHS, SVHS: Higher-resolution version of VHS, similar to Hi8 in quality terms.

VHS/VHS-C: Standard analogue video format and its small-footprint camcorder format. VHS-C tapes can be replayed in VHS videos using an adaptor cassette.

Video 8: Alternative name for 8mm video.

VIDEO AND DVD RECORDING

AVI: Audio Video Interleave. A file format, like MP3, but one that (unlike most other file formats) supports different codecs. An AVI file can, for example, contain DivX video, WMA audio or even pulse-code modulation audio.

CDi: Compact Disc Interactive. Interactive CDs designed to be played on domestic CD/CDi players. By the addition of a Video Playback module, CDi players could also replay VideoCDs.

CDVideo: Alternative name for LaserDisc format, discs that contain digital audio along with analogue video.

Codec: Coder/decoder. Software that enables a medium (audio and/or video) to be compressed and decompressed. This is often an essential process to place video on a CD or DVD. MPEG-2, MPEG-4 and DivX are all examples of codecs.

Compression: A mathematically based process that makes large files smaller by discarding superfluous data. Lossless compression enables original files to be recreated on decompression without obvious loss. In lossy compression there is some data loss that can compromise image or sound quality.

CSS: Content scrambling system. An encryption system used on DVDs to limit (rather than prevent) copying.

Data rate: In video and DVD applications, the amount of data written or read per second. Bit rates (discrete items of data per second) can be fixed (where a constant amount of data is written every second, irrespective of the content) or variable (where more data is written for "busy" action scenes in a movie).

DivX: A codec based on MPEG-4 video compression. The codec is continually evolving and is usually suffixed by a version number. DivX software is freely available or offered at low cost, compared with commercially priced MPEG-4 software. An open-source freeware version of the codec is known as XviD. DIVX was a failed disc-rental system.

DVD: Digital Versatile Disc. The overall format that describes video discs, audio discs and data discs.

DVD ripping: The copying (generally without CSS) of DVD video and audio content to the hard disc of a computer.

Where the content is changed (say, from MPEG-2 to MPEG-4 or DivX) during the copying, the process is known as DVD conversion.

Encoding: In general usage, synonymous with compressing.

MiniDVD: DVD-format data recorded on a CD, offering MPEG-2-quality video, but for a shorter duration than a standard DVD. As it is an unofficial format, discs will not necessarily replay in all DVD players.

MPEG: Motion Pictures Expert Group. The industry-standards body that defined the codecs that now bear their name.

MPEG-1: Low-grade codec used for VideoCDs (equivalent to VHS video).

MPEG-2: Codec used for DVD, miniDVD and SuperVCDs.

MPEG-4: Low-bandwidth, high-quality video used in some digital camcorders and for DivX codecs.

Subpicture: Part of a DVD that stores extra information, such as subtitles on DVDs, but are supplied as synchronized video).

SuperVCD: Super Video CDs. Video CDs originally specified in China as an alternative to DVD. Records MPEG-2 video on CDs but at a lower bit rate (and, hence, lower quality) than with DVD.

VideoCD: Precursor to DVD video. VideoCD discs contain lower-quality MPEG-1 video on standard CDs. Widely used in the Far East, even after the arrival of DVD.

VOB: Video Object: Files on a video DVD that contains the movie. VOB files typically contain a number of different streams, including video, audio and subpictures.

XviD: See DivX.

DIGITAL TELEVISION AND HOME CINEMA

5.1: A sound system that delivers sound from five different speakers along with low-frequency sound (the ".1") channel.

6.1: An enhanced version of 5.1 that adds an extra rear central speaker for better surround-sound effects.

AV: Abbreviation for audiovisual.

Centre channel speaker: Speaker in a 5.1 or 6.1 system that delivers on-screen dialogue and sound effects.

DBS: Direct Broadcasting by Satellite. Any domestic satellite television (or radio) transmission designed to be received on compact dishes.

Dolby® Digital: Surround-sound audio format used on many DVDs, some digital satellite programming and HDTV broadcasts in the United States.

Dolby® Digital EX: Sound encoding designed to deliver 6.1-channel sound.

DTT: Digital Terrestrial Television. Digital television transmitted over conventional television transmission systems. First used by the now-defunct ONdigital network in the UK in 1998.

DTV: Digital Television. Any television transmission system (terrestrial, satellite or cable) that uses digital encoding.

EQ: Equalization. Automatic or manual technique for adjusting the tone and balance of sound to compensate for the acoustic characteristics of the room in which it is heard.

EPG: Electronic Programme Guide. A software-based application that is broadcast on digital television systems giving access to programme information and allowing programme selection or recording.

HDTV: High-definition television. Television system that delivers more lines of resolution than standard-definition television. Typically 1,080 horizontal lines.

Interactive television: Interactive content included on digital television stations. Ranges from alternate programme feeds (different camera angles), support information or enhanced teletext-like text information.

Letterbox: Widescreen television broadcasting that requires black bars at the top and bottom of the screen.

Widescreen broadcasts appear with a letterbox on conventional televisions.

LFE: Low-frequency effects. Low-frequency sound mostly (but not exclusively) delivered by a special low-frequency speaker (subwoofer). Delivers the deep sounds and rumbles for movies.

Mono: Monophonic. A single-channel sound that cannot deliver spatial information.

PVR: Personal Video Recorder. Video recorder that uses predictive technology to record favourite programmes automatically. Often uses a computer, or computer-like hard disc to save recordings.

RCA connector: Simple coaxial connectors used to connect hi-fi and video components. Mostly used in North America and Asia.

S-Video: Connectors used to pass chrominance and luminance (brightness and colour) signals between video devices and offering better-quality pictures.

SCART: A 21-way connector used for audiovisual connection in Europe. A SCART lead contains all the connections necessary for AV, irrespective of whether the devices will actually use them.

SDTV: Standard-definition television. Conventional television transmitting over a standard number of lines (compare with HDTV).

Soundstage: The virtual stage created when an audio system gives information on the distance and placement of individual voices, instruments or other sound effects.

STB: Set-top box. External box that enables digital television signals to be displayed on a conventional television or one without a respective tuner.

Stereo: Stereophonic. A recording made with two microphones that can provide more detail and positional information on sounds. The term is also applied to recordings where there are more than two microphones and multiple speakers on playback.

Surround sound: Any sound system that gives the illusion that sound is emanating from all directions.

Surround speakers: Specifically, the speakers in a home-cinema system that provide the rear sound effects.

DIGITAL AUDIO

AAC: Advanced Audio Coding. An audio codec that was developed by the Fraunhofer Institute. It achieves better sound quality than MP3 with lower bit rates.

AIFF: Macintosh default sound file format.

Buffer Underrun Proofing: Technology to help with the burning of CDs. Prevents ruined recordings when the data stream is interrupted.

Codec: Contraction of compression/decompression. A process that allows an audio or video file to be compressed for storage or transmission and expanded for replay.

CDDB: Compact Disc DataBase. Online tool to retrieve track/artist information on CDs played on a computer. Gracenote is a common CDDB used with iTunes.

CD-R: CD Recordable. Recordable CDs used for data or music recordings.

CD-RW: CD Rewritable. CDs that can be erased and rewritten. Not compatible with all CD players.

CD graphics: CD that contains graphics (text or illustrative) embedded for replay through a suitable player or computer. Largely superseded.

CD text: CD with text information (track, artist, lyrics) embedded for display on an appropriate player.

DVD-Audio: Variation on the DVD format that uses the enhanced capacity for higher-quality audio recordings than is possible with CDs.

Encoding: Process of converting an original audio file into MP3 or similar.

Jitter: Defect that occurs when an audio track is encoded. Can be corrected using jitter-correction software.

Jukebox: Common term for MP3 music player, derived from the traditional jukebox's ability to play consecutive pieces of music.

MP3: MPEG Layer III. Digital audio-compression format that compresses audio files by a factor of around 10 by removing inaudible data.

MP3 Player: Common term for digital music player, usually portable and not restricted to just playing MP3 files.

Napster: Originally a file-sharing software program and company. Allows music files to be shared between Internet-connected computers. The original concept allowed free sharing of files, breaking copyright laws. The new, legitimate Napster is owned by Roxio.

OGG Vorbis: Encoding system for music that is open source (no royalty payable) and that achieves similar results to MP3.

Peer-to-peer file sharing: File sharing (usually music tracks) between Internet-connected computers without residing on a central filesharer.

Playlist: A list of songs selected from an MP3 collection for burning on to a CD or playing on an MP3 player.

Psychoacoustics: Study of hearing that leads to compression algorithms such as MP3. Studies isolate those components of sound poorly perceived by the human ear and that can safely be discarded to produce compact file sizes.

RA: Real Audio – a file type from Real Networks.

Ripping: The process of taking an uncompressed audio file (typically a CD track) and converting it to MP3 (strictly called "ripping and encoding").

SACD: Super Audio CD. An enhanced CD-quality sound-recording regime introduced by Sony and others.

Server file sharing: The sharing of files (usually music tracks) from a repository on a central filesharer.

VBR: Variable Bit Rate. Encoding process where the amount of data used to record music varies with the type of music. More bits are allocated to complex musical passages and fewer to simpler pieces.

WAV: Wave files. The uncompressed standard for audio files used on Windows PCs.

WMA: Windows Media Audio. A proprietary codec from Microsoft for MP3-equivalent recording.

MOBILE COMMUNICATIONS

1G: First-generation mobile telephony, using analogue technology.

2G: Second-generation mobile telephony using digital technology (including GSM, PDC and CDMA).

2.5G: Advanced second-generation networks that allow high-capacity data transmissions alongside voice and SMS calls.

3G: High-speed, third-generation digital mobile telephony that supports multimedia (video calling and photo transmission).

Airtime: Time spent talking, connected to the Internet or to other resources. Normally characterized by a tariff.

Authentication: A process of verification that confirms that a mobile or wireless device is authorized to use the network to which it is attempting to gain access.

Bandwidth: The capacity of a transmission system (telephone line, radio frequency) to carry signals. A larger bandwidth can accommodate more data.

Base station: The main transmitter and receiver for maintaining cellular communications over a certain geographical area, generally a network "cell".

Bluetooth: Wireless communications system designed for small distances only; typically used to communicate between a mobile phone and a headset (for hands-free operation) or a mobile phone and computer.

CDMA: Code Division Multiple Access. Digital cellular system used in the US, Japan and parts of the Far East.

Cell: A geographical area of a cellular phone system covered by one base station. Cell sizes vary from a hundred metres (or less) in cities to several hundred metres in more open countryside. Phone handsets automatically switch from one cell base station to another as the user passes from one cell to another.

Cell phone: Generic term for mobile phone, more commonly used in North America.

DECT: Digitally Enhanced Cordless Telecommunications. Digital standard for cordless telephones offering high-quality interference-free speech.

Dual band: Mobile phones that can switch between two frequencies. In the UK all new phones tend to be dual band to accommodate the two frequencies used by the key networks.

ESN: Electronic Serial Number. A unique identifying number that is transmitted by a phone to the base station every time a call is initiated.

GRPS: General Packet Radio Service. Data communications upgrade to GSM networks to allow faster (115kbps) data transmissions.

GSM: Global System for Mobile Communications. European digital standard, using one of three frequency bands (900MHz, 1800MHz or 1900MHz).

Hand over: The transfer of a call from one cell to another.

Hands-free: Use of a mobile phone without holding it, typically via a headset or in-car kit. Legal requirement in motor vehicles in the UK and elsewhere.

ISDN: Integrated Services Digital Network. Fixed-line digital telephony used for fast Internet communications (but slower than broadband).

Memory dialling: Speed dialling of telephone numbers using single or multiple keystrokes.

Mobile phone: Generic term for a cell phone in the UK.

PCS1900: Personal Communications System, 1900MHz. Another name for 1900MHz GSM.

Prepay: Pay-in-advance tariff for mobile phones.

Roaming: Using a mobile phone on a network other than that to which you subscribe. Typically used when travelling abroad or (exceptionally) when out of range of your home network.

SIM: Subscriber Identity Module. A Smartcard used in mobile phones for identifying the user and storing numbers and SMS messages.

Smartphone: Phone with additional functionality to handle data and offer PDA-like functions.

SMS: Short Messaging Service. The option to send or receive short text messages (typically up to 160 characters).

Triband: Handset capable of operating over three GSM bands. Essential for those travelling between North America and Europe.

WAP: Wireless Application Protocol. The standard that lets WAP-enabled phones to access selected internet sites.

ARE YOU READY TO EXPLORE THE DIGITAL WORLD FURTHER? OVER THE NEXT FEW PAGES YOU'LL FIND A SELECTION OF SOME OF THE BEST RESOURCES AVAILABLE TO HELP YOU ALONG YOUR JOURNEY OF DISCOVERY. WE'LL SURVEY THE SOFTWARE THAT CAN HELP YOU EDIT MOVIES, PHOTOS AND EVEN CREATE ARTWORK FOR YOUR MOBILE PHONES. WE'LL ALSO TAKE A LOOK AT SOME OF THE BEST WEBSITES TO KEEP YOU ABREAST OF ALL THAT'S NEW IN THE DIGITAL WORLD.

SOFTWARE

Throughout this book specific applications have largely been used, for the sake of clarity and consistency. However, there's a whole range of similar – or more advanced – alternatives to explore. Here's a quick survey of the marketplace. Version numbers are not mentioned – they tend to go out of date very quickly – but the relative capabilities of each tend to remain similar.

DIGITAL PHOTOGRAPHY

Adobe Photoshop Elements (PC and Mac)

The trimmed down version of Adobe's image editing behemoth loses only top-end features but makes image manipulation simple and intuitive. Unless your ambitions are of the highest order, this will be more than sufficient for all your image-editing needs.
www.adobe.com

Adobe Photoshop (PC and Mac)

This is the leading light in professional image editing. If Photoshop can't do it, it's probably not worth doing – and there's enough here to keep even the most avid enthusiast fully occupied. The drawback for most of us is the cost, decisively placing it in the realm of the professional and the serious enthusiast.
www.adobe.com

Ulead PhotoImpact (PC)

PhotoImpact gives the inexperienced – or those not wanting to investigate all that the Photoshop variants have to offer – the chance to create great images fast. Basic and Advanced modes let you see only the commands and features essential to the work in hand.
www.ulead.com

Adobe Photoshop Album (PC) and Apple iPhoto (Mac)

Both these applications provide calendar-based filing of your digital images and will automatically download photos from your camera. Better still, both will synchronize with the iPod photo, letting you download and enjoy your portfolios.
www.adobe.com and www.apple.com

Jasc Paint Shop Pro (PC)

This is a powerful Photoshop wannabe application that delivers powerful image editing techniques fast. Alternatives, such as PhotoImpact, may be more appropriate for the less experienced but Paint Shop Pro allows greater control and more creativity – if you know what you are doing!
www.jasc.com

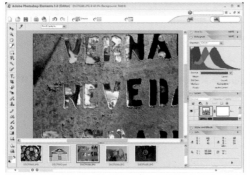

Photoshop Elements

Photoshop Album

DIGITAL VIDEO

Adobe Premiere Elements (PC)

Premiere is Adobe's powerhouse video-editing application, but it doesn't lend itself to simple editing of those ad hoc recordings that you don't necessarily want to compile as mini-blockbusters. Like Photoshop Elements, the key professional tools are gone, but you have all the basic tools – and more – for quickly compiling movies.
www.adobe.com

Adobe Premiere (PC)

Adobe's omnipresence in the media-editing market continues with Premiere. It's the choice of many a professional video editor but that should not preclude it from the keener enthusiast. It's pricey though, so you'll need to ensure that you need all its features and won't be satisfied by anything less.
www.adobe.com

Pinnacle Studio Software (PC)

This is an easy-to-use package that boasts an attractive price too. It includes a major tranche of special effects, titles and music for use in your productions, and also has an instant-touch image enhancement button for giving slightly below par footage a boost.
www.pinnaclesys.com

Canopus Let's EDIT (PC)

A camcorder-to-DVD application that lets you edit your movies and burn direct to DVD. It scores highly

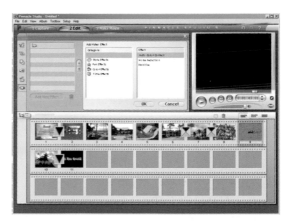

Pinnacle Studio Software

for its speed in applying effects, and not needing time to render (apply) even sophisticated effects.
www.canopus.com

Apple iMovie, Final Cut Express, Final Cut Pro (Mac)

These are Apple's complementary products to the Adobe offerings. You'll get iMovie free with any new Mac, but you'll need Version 05 if you want – or need – to edit high definition video. Final Cut Express and it's Pro sibling equate with Premiere Elements and Premiere respectively.

HOME DVD CREATION

Roxio Easy CD and DVD Creator (PC)

This is a well-established application that can take data of almost any sort and create CDs and DVDs. It is also useful for creating Video CDs and other less common disk formats.
www.roxio.com

Roxio Toast Titanium (Mac)

The Mac version of Easy CD and DVD Creator, this application can create disks in any native format.

Dr DivX (PC)

A simple application for converting any video source (DVD, DV movies or

Premiere Elements   *Premiere Pro*

digitized analogue video) into a DivX file for playing on any DivX compatible DVD player or computer. www.divx.com

DivX Pro (Including DivX Player) (PC/Mac)

This is an advanced DivX encoder that can achieve compressions 30% better than the basic DivX codec. www.divx.com

DivX with DivX Player (PC/Mac)

The basic codec for encoding your video. Not very versatile but has the bonus of being freeware. www.divx.com

DIGITAL COMMUNICATIONS
Ulead Photo Express M-style (PC)

Edit, manipulate and retouch your mobile phone photos and then use them as the basis of eCards to send to friends or family. Go on to create your own image messages and even design your own personal standby screens. www.ulead.com

Ulead VideoStudio M-style (PC)

With this you can take your mobile phone's video capabilities to a new level. This fully-fledged video editor is designed specifically for mobile video editing. Trim and combine video clips, remove or change audio tracks and more. www.ulead.com

VideoStudio M-Style

WEBSITES

Websites provide a useful set of resources including up-to-the-minute news. Here are some of the sites we've found particularly useful. Please note, however, that websites do come and go, change their address and can even change ownership. Google and other search engines can help you find precise and up-to-date information on digital resources.

DIGITAL PHOTOGRAPHY

www.dpreview.com: the number one site for information and impartial advice on all digital cameras and associated equipment.

www.stevesdigicams.com: another great site for digital news and information.

www.ephotozine.com: A UK-based megasite for all things photographic, conventional as well as digital.

www.shortcourses.com: a gateway site for accessing well regarded courses on all aspects of photography.

www.dcviews.com: more tutorials and news at this comprehensive site.

www.photoxels.com: another tutorial site with useful and effective One-Pager™ tutorials.

MP3 PLAYERS AND DIGITAL MUSIC

www.mp3.com: A key resource for digital music, and news and views. Also features reviews and discussions on digital music players.

www.artistdirect.com: MP3, music videos and CDs from artists you won't always find in the more popular sites.

www.ipodlounge.com: all you need to know about the iPod.

www.everythingipod.com: billed as the superstore for the iPod. Users of other digital music players will also find it useful for those hard-to-find or must-have accessories.

www.mpeg.org: All about MP3, video software players and anything vaguely connected to MPEG.

DIGITAL VIDEO EDITING

www.dvmoviemaking.com: Adobe Premiere based tutorials for movie making. No previous experience necessary.

www.computerarts.co.uk: tutorials and info on digital video and other digital arts.

DIGITAL TELEVISION

www.digitaltelevision.com: online version of the foremost magazine for the television business: broadcasting, technology and programming.

www.dtg.org.uk: website of the UK's Digital Television Group. Great resource for news and industry links.

www.digitaltelevision.org.uk: Info site for UK digital television featuring a useful jargon buster.

www.fcc.gov/dtv/: The US version of the above site with a portal for FCC info.

www.digitalspy.co.uk: An entertainment and technology website that is mainly UK focused but also features a strong US presence.

MOBILE CoMMUNICATIONS

www.3g.co.uk: UK-originated website on the world 3g telephony business.

www.smartphonethoughts.com: "Daily News, Views, Rants and Raves", Great for keeping up with the smartphone world.

www.pdastreet.com: promotes itself as the largest PDA information centre.

www.pdabuyersguide.com: Another major site that offers information and advice on PDAs, smartphones and even notebook PCs.

www.pdalive.com: a slightly more eclectic collection of news and info on the PDA world

SUPPLIERS

Apple Computers	www.apple.com
Adobe Software	www.adobe.com
Bang & Olufsen	www.bang-olufsen.com
Belkin	www.belkin.com
Beyond (Home Hub)	www.beyondconnectedhome.com
Blackberry	www.blackberry.com
Bluetooth	www.bluetooth.com, www.bluetooth.org
Blu-ray	www.blu-ray.com
Bose	www.bose.com
Canon Cameras & Printers	www.canon.com
Creative	www.creative.com
DirecTV	www.directv.com
DivX	www.divx.com
Dolby Laboratories	www.dolby.com
Freecom	www.freecom.com
Fujifilm, Fuji	www.fujifilm.com www.fujifilm.co.uk
Griffin	www.griffintechnology.com
Home Automation	www.homeauto.com
HP	www.hp.com
Jamo	www.jamo.com
Jasc Software	www.jasc.com
Konica Minolta	www.konicaminolta.com
Kodak	www.kodak.com
LG	www.lge.com
Macromedia Software	www.macromedia.com
Microsoft	www.microsoft.com
Nikon Cameras	www.nikon.com www.nikon.co.uk
Nokia	www.nokia.com
Olympus Cameras	www.olympus.com
Pace	
Panasonic	www.panasonic.com
Pentax	www.pentax.com
Roku (Soundbridge)	www.roku.com www.soundbridge.co.uk
Roxio Software	www.roxio.com
Sandisk	www.sandisk.com
Sausalito Audio Works	www.sawonline.com
Sony Ericsson	www.sonyericsson.com
Sony	www.sony.com
TiVo	www.tivo.com
Ulead Software	www.ulead.com www.ulead.co.uk
XM Satellite Radio	www.xmradio.com

INDEX

Acknowledgements

The majority of photographs, illustrations and screenshots used in this book come from my own personal archive. However I would like to thank the following sources for their kind permission to reproduce certain pictures in the book:

Apple Computer, Beyond, British Sky Broadcasting, DirecTV, El Gato Systems, Hewlett-Packard, Jamo, KISS, Pace Electronics, Sausalito Audio Works, SES Astra, Microsoft, Nokia, Sony, and SonyErlcsson.

Every effort has been made to acknowledge correctly and contact the source and/or copyright holder of each picture and Carlton Books Limited apologizes for any unintentional errors or omissions, which will be corrected in future editions of this book.